WARRING SOVEREIGNTIES

WARRING SOVEREIGNTIES
Church Control and State Pressure at the University of Ottawa

adam p. strömbergsson-denora

University of Ottawa Press
2020

University of Ottawa **Press**
Les **Presses** de l'Université d'Ottawa

The University of Ottawa Press (UOP) is proud to be the oldest of the francophone university presses in Canada as well as the oldest bilingual university publisher in North America. Since 1936, UOP has been enriching intellectual and cultural discourse by producing peer-reviewed and award-winning books in the humanities and social sciences, in French and in English.
www.press.uOttawa.ca

Library and Archives Canada Cataloguing in Publication
Title: Warring sovereignties : church control and state pressure at the University of Ottawa / Adam P. Strömbergsson-DeNora.
Names: Strömbergsson-DeNora, Adam, 1992- author.
Description: Series statement: Regional studies
Identifiers: Canadiana (print) 20200227483 | Canadiana (ebook) 20200227815 |
 ISBN 9780776629148 (hardcover) |
 ISBN 9780776629100 (softcover) |
 ISBN 9780776629117 (PDF) |
 ISBN 9780776629124 (EPUB) |
 ISBN 9780776629131 (Kindle)
Subjects: LCSH: University of Ottawa. | LCSH: Church and college—Ontario—Ottawa. | LCSH: Secularization—Ontario—Ottawa
Classification: LCC LC383 .S77 2020 | DDC 371.071–dc23

Legal Deposit: Fourth Quarter 2020
Library and Archives Canada

© University of Ottawa Press 2020

All rights reserved.

Production Team

Copy editing	Michael Waldin
Proofreading	Robbie McCaw
Typesetting	Édiscript enr.
Cover design	Steve Kress

No part of this publication may be reproduced or transmitted in any form or by any means, or stored in a database and retrieval system, without the prior permission.

In the case of photocopying or any other reprographic copying, please secure licenses from:

Access Copyright
www.accesscopyright.ca
1-800-893-5777

Cover image

Photo of Tabaret Hall with many individuals standing and sitting on the steps – 1905 University of Ottawa Records and Archives Management PHO–NB–6–31. Photograph: unknown.

For foreign rights and permissions:
www.iprlicense.com

The author has made every effort to contact rights holders to request permission to use their images, but in case of omission, the publisher will gladly make amendments and updates to the publication at the earliest possible opportunity.

The University of Ottawa Press gratefully acknowledges the support extended to its publishing list by the Government of Canada, the Canada Council for the Arts, the Ontario Arts Council, the Social Sciences and Humanities Research Council and the Canadian Federation for the Humanities and Social Sciences through the Awards to Scholarly Publications Program, and by the University of Ottawa.

Abstract

This documentary history of the University of Ottawa describes the lead up to and the aftermath of its 1965 reformation under government pressure. It traces a clash of cultures during the secularization of Ontario higher education: the University of Ottawa was the last major university to cede religious control in favour of a nondenominational Board of Governors. The Oblate Missionaries of Mary Immaculate held out longer than their finances allowed; the government pressured the religious order to cede their university, thus relegating the Oblates to a small Catholic university. This pressure, however, spurred further Oblate resistance after reform. The government's response highlights the University of Ottawa's dependence on government. A running analysis of this dependence is woven into the text by examining the office of university visitor. This office, long forgotten, granted a right of supervision to a university's founder. The Oblates always had a version of this right; the Catholic Bishop of Ottawa possessed a similar jurisdiction; the Pope, in 1889, claimed yet another right; and the Government of Ontario also laid a claim. These competing powers come to define the government's actions in 1965 and in ensuing years. Though this work does not speculate much on the effects of this struggle, one striking issue is the level of government interference, and the quick acquiescence of University administrators. He who pays the piper calls the tune: Can universities with histories such as Ottawa's truly be independent?

Table of Contents

Abstract v

Preface xi

Introduction 1

CHAPTER 1
Overview of the University Charter (1849–1965) 21

CHAPTER 2
The Road to Reform: 1959–1964 53

CHAPTER 3
Reforming the University Government: 1964–1965 99

CHAPTER 4
Contract with Saint Paul: Meshing the Old and New 135

Epilogue: Settling the Religious Character 181

Appendix A: The Charters, including the Oblate Charter 199

Notes 255

Bibliography 281

[…] Nor was it least
Of many debts which afterwards I owed
To Cambridge and an academic life,
That something there was holden up to view
Of a Republic, where all stood thus far
Upon equal ground, that they were brothers all
In honour, as in one community,
Scholars and Gentlemen, where, furthermore,
Distinction lay open to all that came,
And wealth and titles were in less esteem
Than talents and successful industry.
— William Wordsworth, *The Prelude*

Ainsi se conjugueront les deux magistères, ecclésiastiques et profane, l'un reposant sur la pensée divine et l'autre sur la pensée humaine, l'un dérivant de la foi et l'autre de la raison. Leur dialogue est parfois hésitant, malaisé, du moins au début, comme entre des étrangers parlant des langages différents. Mais lorsqu'il se poursuit avec sincérité dans un climat de respect et de sérénité, il est toujours enrichissant.
— "Discours de la collation des grades,"
Roger Guindon, speaking at the Old
University's final convocation, May 30, 1965

Preface

This book took shape because the University of Ottawa's Senate was (and, perhaps, is) too tame a body. Its meetings are quiet, dignified affairs punctuated by the odd student protest. Yet academe writ large seemed, in 2014, to be increasingly siloed; professors viewed themselves as employees rather than office holders. These observations are self-evident to a university crowd. Canadian provincial governments manage universities through the power of the purse—golden chains, as one commentator puts it in this book. Those chains are becoming increasingly apparent. The managerial state demands universities achieve performance targets and, in some provinces, that they differentiate themselves from each other.

Senates should, in this author's opinion, raucously resist such measures, even if such resistance causes them to peter out. The Oblates of Mary Immaculate (OMI) are paragons of such fruitless resistance. Their example has at once conditioned the University of Ottawa Senate and suggested its way forward.

Put simply, performance targets impose education as a socio-economic boon. That it is, yet an older view of education aims in religious wise at the spirit. Education, to frame it in terms similar to Marsilio Ficino's Neoplatonism, stokes God's flame within each spirit. Once properly lighted, that flame may open onto the City of God—in whatever relative form that City now takes. Jean-Jacques Rousseau relied on the maxim *ab assuetis non fit passio*: habit does not make passion. Performance targets make education routine, yet standing in a classroom is an opportunity to experience the mystical quality of self-transcendence; learning in a classroom sees a professor at their most vulnerable. Passion is all in this exchange.

Passionate professors have informed this book from the start. There were many that helped, yet three deserve special mention: David Staines, who patiently read over my funding proposals for this project and who provided valuable advice in this regard; Christian Detellier approved funding for this project, without which I could not have accomplished anything; and Frans de Bruyn, who supervised this research. Without these men and their counsel, this project would not have gotten off the ground.

I am further indebted to Andrew Taylor, once a vice-dean of the Faculty of Arts and a member of Senate. He gave me a first taste of archival research just before beginning this work. I've caught the bug.

Nicholas von Maltzahn, my MA thesis supervisor, also deserves thanks: he taught me how to write. My errors in this text are my own; Nick's influence has inspired the better elements.

The archival staff at the University of Ottawa, especially Théo Charles Martin, helped me navigate through the University of Ottawa's archives in the early stages of research. Jacinthe Duval took over during the second stage of research, and she was very patient with my many requests, as was Lucie Joubert. Michel Prévost, now the book's editor, then the University archivist, was good enough to read over my draft manuscript, and his expertise remains invaluable. The University of Ottawa's archives staff more generally was wonderful. They operate on a shoestring but have made the best of their situation. They are a shining example of dedication and stewardship.

Daniel Hurtubise, of Saint Paul University's archives, was so obliging: his was the perfect encouragement for a budding project. Liz Hayden, temporary chief librarian at University Saint Paul was very helpful treating my requests for information and sources. Professors Paul Axlerod and Tim Stanley read through my draft introduction, proposing useful changes and supplying further secondary sources that helped frame the project. Professor Pierre Hurtubise, OMI, read the whole work and was encouraging, supplying confirmation of the fact pattern as I have set it down.

Finally, my friends and family served as a sounding board for my writing and my worries throughout the project, notably my friend Nicole Taylor, and my one-time roommate turned reader, Joël Rocque.

My partner, Sandra, has for years listened to me babble about visitors and their importance. Her forbearance will, I hope, bear fruit in the present work. Their patience is greatly appreciated.

adam strömbergsson-denora
February 2020

Introduction

> Howbeit we speak wisdom among them that are perfect: yet not the wisdom of this world, nor of the princes of this world, that come to nought:
> But we speak the wisdom of God in a mystery, even the hidden wisdom, which God ordained before the world unto our glory:
> Which none of the princes of this world knew: for had they known it, they would not have crucified the Lord of glory.
> — 1 Corinthians 2:6–8

The history of the University of Ottawa in the decade of the 1960s is a struggle between princes, one claiming divine power, the other temporal. It is an allegory for the increasing ills Canadian (and, dare I say, Western?) universities face. Waning religious instruction, though able to meet the needs of a multicultural and individualist society, destabilized the historic pattern of universities and university colleges erected *ad studentum et orandum*—for study and prayer.[1] The University is not alone in this regard, for other Ontario institutions underwent similar fates, where a religious order facing financial crisis was edged out by a civil government capable of filling the financial vacuum. This is the basic narrative[2] underpinning the Oblates of Mary Immaculate's (OMI) ceding control of most university assets to the non-denominational structure that we see today.

Such a narrative, however, is far too easy an explanation for the personalities and tensions that brought change. The University of Ottawa was the last major Ontario university in the decade to relinquish its religious character in exchange for government support. It was also the oldest university in Canada to have a pontifical designation, which perhaps influenced the pride Oblates felt for their work and its place in Canadian society. That pontifical designation played into the Oblates' missionary purpose in Canada and, increasingly, in the world at large.

The University's financial crisis was very real—there is no doubt that the Oblates could not continue to operate their university for much longer than they did. The University doubled, if not tripled, in size between 1945 and 1965. Such a rapid increase disrupted collegial governance and led to burgeoning costs. Even so, however, Oblate resistance to government intrusion was pronounced, cantankerous, and principled. They embodied an ancient tradition of almost feudal service to their lords, which, most annoyingly for Ontario premiers Leslie Frost (1949–1961) and John Robarts (1961–1971), meant that the civil power possessed little control over what the Oblates thought and taught. The push and pull between government and church took on existential significance. Lack of state control flew in the face of Ontario's burgeoning welfare state even as secularism was taking root in the lay population.[3] The Oblates saw their University as the jewel in their crown, one which brought status within the Church and accomplished the Oblates' salvific mission in Mary's name.

Hence two princes coming into play. The University's transition was the ground on which the state finally asserted sovereignty over a Catholic work as society shifted from one that depended on religious charity for some social services to one in which the state assumed control over those same services. This movement led to an "academic revolution in higher education": colleges, where each academic member had a deliberative voice, were replaced by universities too large for such personality. Denominational institutions (especially minority Catholic ones) were most affected by this turn toward bigger, diverse universities.[4] The *universitas* at one time inhering in collegial governance gave way to siloed academics in faculties increasingly specialized to serve economic aims. The Catholic university instead deployed its faith as a web between disciplines. The four ecclesiastical faculties, theology, philosophy, canon law, and arts, oriented other disciplines toward God, thus imbuing disciplines that tended to be secular with Catholic purpose. The Oblates represented that older view in their university; the Ontario provincial government under John Robarts was an aggressive force for change.

These exchanges were a symbolic fight for sovereignty. As Roberto Perin suggests in his book, the Vatican ranked third in Canada's colonial powers.[5] It was a tenacious international rival for the hearts and minds of subject citizens in a country and time that very consciously owed its intellectual inheritance to France and England. Bishops deployed unique logic and political reasoning that influenced Upper Canadian subjects who were willing to listen. Indeed, these collective efforts were (and notionally remain) enshrined in statute law.[6] This influence was not always welcome over the University's history. The post-war welfare state, a boom economy already requiring devoted subjects, further required universities that were increasingly utilitarian. This utilitarianism opposed the Oblate's missionary care for souls; it emphasized the state's legal regime in order to manage the Catholic order and its expectations.[7] It also laid the ground for the evolution of increasingly neo-liberal power structures that ostensibly made academics more accountable for public funds while also forcing them to focus on quantity over quality—the difference of being "calculable rather than memorable."[8]

This book details the loss of some institutional memory wrapped up in the Oblates' decline and fall at the University of Ottawa. The intellectual backdrop that frames brave Oblate resistance to an insistent provincial government has not been explored. Canada is still young—we only won complete self-government in 1982, even with allowance made for the *Statute of Westminister, 1931*.[9] Such short separation from our colonial masters stunts historical theorization; my text is, perhaps, no better in its reliance on English, French, and Catholic thought to illuminate the University's history. These were, however, the conditions for Oblate and Ontarian decision makers who found themselves at odds in the 1960s. Ottawa's situation on the periphery leaves it out of the provincial historical narrative; its place further away from the Anglo-Protestant mainstream leaves its memory in the hands of very capable French Canadian scholars. Some have contributed in manuscript accounts of the University of Ottawa's history.[10]

Rather than touch on this linguistic divide, I emphasize the intellectual strains of Oblate resistance as they managed an emotional transition.

This narrative also extends Brian McKillop's story about Ontarian universities and colleges. His account leaves off around 1950, which keeps the field open to scholars like Paul Axelrod to fill the void by showing that universities between 1950 and 1970 increasingly depended upon corporate and government aid to survive.[11] Axelrod's focus on twentieth-century economic history explains the changes at the University of Ottawa as part of the utilitarian trend that McKillop identifies. Just like the University of Toronto, the University of Ottawa was "modernized to become more business-like."[12] Though scholars generally agree that Ontarian universities (still legally distinct from the government) benefit from a strong degree of academic independence, their interaction with Ontarian society is so conditioned on the need for funds that Axelrod's analysis becomes portentous.[13] Such an explanation only scratches the surface of the fight as it played out in Ottawa, along with its own portents. While those economic forces give us a simple explanation for how and why the University of Ottawa ultimately shifted from Oblate to non-denominational control, a more nuanced intellectual history shines further light on Oblate preoccupations.

The transition at the heart of this book defines the manner in which we forget. The sovereignties at war in these pages are the sides of a university's coin: the government wanted to see more study—and especially graduate study producing new knowledge; the Oblates sought to recreate the sublime mystery of faith that so informed their lives. They did so with a focus on the older English tradition of undergraduate humanist education and collegial governance. The government's focus instead followed nineteenth-century developments at German universities. The German focus on graduate research was imported to North America by American university administrators in the early twentieth century.[14] The Oblates would take this focus up after the Second World War but did so at their peril: graduate studies in science-required scientific installations, which caused the University to become heavily indebted by 1965.

Such focus on market forces undermined Catholic higher education, which at times fell into a defensive rut. The foremost example is ultramontanism, a movement that began in France in the eighteenth century as a conservative reaction to the Enlightenment principles that drove the French Revolution. Ultramontanists emphasized papal infallibility, which justified resistance toward intellectuals beyond the Church. Eugène de Mazenod (1782–1861), the Bishop of Marseilles, founded the Order in response to the French Revolution (1789–1795), and the movement reached its apogee under Pope Pius IX (r. 1846–1878) at the First Vatican Council (1870). This period of development coincides with the University's foundation in 1848 and its growth as a college.[15] The University's and Canadian Oblates' foundation, moreover, grew up under an ultramontane influence. From its earliest moments in 1816, the Oblates of Mary Immaculate were designed to work in the ultramontane vein. De Mazenod was himself of aristocratic lineage and sought to return France's aristocracy to its pre-revolutionary prominence. His reactionary view reasserted Catholicism among the French poor of Aix (and France generally) in order to pave the way for a resurgent crown that could bring with it his peers.

The oracular logic of papal supremacy enhanced Oblate prestige with Pope Pius IX's 1854 dogmatization of the Immaculate Conception in *Ineffabilis Deus*. The Oblates' work increasingly took on papal authority and privilege through the nineteenth century as worship for Mary was endorsed by papal rescript.[16] This view would persist. Service in devotion of Mary Immaculate would, some Oblates in the 1950s thought, strive toward "the restoration of the Church."[17]

The starting Oblate philosophy was thus arch-conservative. It took an Augustinian approach that emphasized "suffering, fatalism and original sin, that is dominated by a vengeful God and which, in its extreme, viewed human free will as hopelessly destroyed and dependent on grace alone for its salvation."[18] This stark view of religiosity promoted an us-versus-them mentality that would be confirmed across the Church at the First Vatican Council.

The Oblates exploded with ultramontane fervour in Canada such that, by 1871, when the University of Ottawa was taking firm root armed with its 1866 charter granting university powers, the Oblates dominated the French Catholic preaching scene. From its formal approval by Rome on February 17, 1826, the Order expanded so aggressively that, when de Mazenod died in 1830, foundations had been set up in Switzerland, England, Ireland, Scotland, Ceylon, Algeria, Natal, and Canada. Oblate expansion in Canada moved quickly after 1840 (when the Canadian Church increasingly identified with French nationalism). Oblate priests took up vocations in local churches, thus giving them platforms from which to achieve clerical dominance. By 1871, three Canadian bishops were Oblate: Ottawa,

St. Boniface, and St. Albert. The priests underneath these bishops were also disproportionately Oblate.[19]

Oblate success inculcated their ultramontane beliefs, which came to characterize French Canadian Catholicism more generally. The pressure between church and state influenced the theology of bishops like Cardinal Louis-Edouard-Désiré Pie, the Bishop of Poitiers, who viewed Church and state as central authorities vying for ultimate control of hearts and minds.[20] Oblates considered themselves a civilization *tout court* indissoluble from Roman Catholicism.[21] This zeal may explain the darker side of Oblate history that is only now coming to the public's attention with the Truth and Reconciliation Commission's findings and efforts at justice inside and outside courtrooms.[22] The Oblates applied their divine mandate as they migrated out from Quebec. Ottawa and its university were staging points in this movement that allowed the Oblates pause to do good work for Catholics in northern Ontario and to train clergy for service in western Canada.

Despite their zeal and its apparent hierarchical structure, the Order and the Church were, in their pre-Vatican II context, a loose hierarchy that relied on theocratic politics. Local provincials and bishops were the true princes in local organizations. Their power stemmed from the divine papal monarchy that on its face resembled the frontispiece to Thomas Hobbes's *Leviathan*.

Catholic bodies were, between 1870 and 1965, part of the infallible papal body, even if wide swaths of Catholic faithful dissented from this doctrine proper. The language of ultramontanism appropriated these bodies to support itself in antiquated terms that Hobbes reserved for civil government:

> men that are once possessed of an opinion that their obedience to the Sovereaign Power will be more hurtful to them than their disobedience will disobey the laws and thereby overthrow the Commonwealth, and introduce confusion, and Civill war; for the avoiding whereof, all Civill Government was ordained.[23]

Papal sovereignty claimed subjects through the operation of canon law. The people of God served God through mediating canonical rules. The sovereignty of such a legal system vied against Canadian and, after Confederation, Ontarian laws, yet Canadian Catholics, particularly those in English Canada, consistently served the civil power.[24] The Catholic ghettoization promoted by ultramontane thought increasingly fell out of step with Canadian Catholics.

The historic arc of civil government displayed a complementary trajectory culminating in individual rights. First the Province of Canada, then the Ontario government grew by degrees away from any notion of state power that took a crown (let alone the Crown) as a corporate expression of the community. Nineteenth-century legal discourse about rights focused on communal and legislative power—powers appropriate in a constitutional monarchy equipped with parliamentary supremacy.[25] The development of individual rights, however, led to a reduction in collective religious power—a reduction that reached its peak in the 1950s and 1960s, when Canadian human rights legislation was enacted.[26] Subjects acquired rights that could be set up against the Crown under a guise of minority protection. These rights were confirmed in 1848 with the advent of responsible government, which made the electoral franchise effective. The colonists inherited an albeit imperfect separation of church and state (Canada had no recognized church) that was applied in 1960 as the leading justification for denying the Oblates grants that would have allowed the University to continue operating. Such a justification only differed a hair from what the Oblates had in view, but it is that hair that ultimately determined the issue and that created such animosity between negotiators who could not understand each others' position.

The stakes in this game were for souls in a rapidly changing context. On one hand, the Oblates represented the traditional Catholic interest in saving souls, and saving them its way. Marcel Bélanger, a senior Oblate administrator during the transition, qualified Oblate practice as a means of confronting the Church's lessening influence:

> Ce sens du pauvre, qui est un engagement dans le social par l'âme avant de l'être par l'action extérieure, se définit au mieux par la compassion miséricordieuse du Sauveau réincarnée dans l'O.M.I. et l'imprégnant à fond. Même les occupations en apparence les plus intemporelles, tels la contemplation affective, l'étude et l'enseignement à tous les degrés, se poursuivent sous le signe ou dans le climat de la Miséricorde divine œuvrant au cœur de la détresse humaine et tenant partout le langage de l'espérance et de la charité théologales. Si la misère logée par permission divine dans l'univers met nos esprits à l'épreuve, elle n'en demeure pas moins un fait que l'on doit s'efforcer, non seulement d'accepter,

mais de voir comme Dieu le voit, par conséquent, insérer dans un plan de sagesse et de bonté infinies, donc exigeant que l'on aborde le miséreux avec une confiance communicative.[27]

The Oblates communicate a mystery founded upon God's mercy for each subject.[28] Such mercy could be taught through the Order exemplified by the Virgin Mary who, by 1959, was further dignified by Pius XII's *Munificentissimus Deus* (1950). Mary was now of immaculate birth and free from worldly death. She ordered Catholic practice by inspiring a maternal love for the object of belief, Christ. In so doing, Mary's image became a chief aspiration for the Church and for Oblates against "the illusory teachings of materialism and the corruption of morals that follows from these teachings."[29] Breaking from these teachings was, in Bélanger's estimation, generative of hope and aspiration capable of rising above life's destructive and lapsed routine: "Frankly our vocation is the same as that of the Immaculate Mother: to give birth to the Redeemer, to christianize in the full meaning of the word that which routine has emptied of all its beauty."[30]

This mission translated well to the university setting in the 1950s. Liberal arts now tended toward a humanist education, but one not fully Catholic or Christian. These arts had been touched by pervasive materialism. Oblates instead framed their Catholic education along theological lines:

> [L']humanisme sur lequel elle doit élever la vie universitaire est un humanisme intégral et chrétien. Or, cet humanisme chrétien les Arts libéraux seuls ne peuvent le fournir. La véritable pierre d'angle, c'est le savoir chrétien proprement dit et dispensé pour lui-même, la philosophie chrétienne et surtout la théologie, telles qu'on les enseigne dans les facultés ecclésiastiques.[31]

The Oblates thus applied Marian theology as administrators of a pontifical university. Their teaching required this status because the underlying theology that imbued their work emanated from three academic centres: the faculties of theology, philosophy, and canon law. Each of these theoretically informed the work of other faculties teaching adjacent disciplines. Part of the Oblates' crisis involved the renunciation by secular scholars of the ecclesiastical faculties' influence.

The influence of the University's pontifical charter within Catholic circles must not be underappreciated. Not just an ecclesiastical corporation founded by Bishop Joseph Eugène Guigues in 1848, the Pope's charter in 1889 elevated the College of Ottawa (as it was then known) to an international dignity. The College existed apart from other Catholic institutions in Ontario. It could only be compared to the University of Saint Michael's College's Pontifical Institute of Medieval Studies, but even such a comparison pales. Saint Michael's only received limited papal recognition for a course of study, and this granted fifty years after Ottawa's more general recognition. Regis College stands in similar wise. It was created a pontifical theological university in 1956 by the Sacred Congregation of Seminaries and Universities[32] — a far cry from Ottawa's much older (and more general) inheritance.

The other hand saw a government intent on promoting a quasi-nationalized system of universities that could provide instruction through the Atomic era. The cleavage was one that government was destined to win, for it is one precursor to a "quasi-neoliberal" program that fully takes root in Ontario under the Harris government (1995–2002).[33] A generous reading of the government's move shows Ontario claiming provincial control over universities that otherwise were influenced by sometimes international and sometimes intensely local organizations.

A more skeptical view, however, explains the current managerial state of higher education in this province as the result of competing fields of power. These were evidenced within and without the University of Ottawa as it moved toward non-denominational status. This dour perspective pits nominally papal and Ontarian sovereignties against each other in a battle that was being simultaneously fought across Canada and across the Western world for a more distinct separation of church and state. Asserting state sovereignty over higher education created a vacuum where the Vatican and its legal apparatus once stood. The state filled this vacuum by insisting that representatives from the community, which is to say captains of industry and other leading lights, be appointed to non-denominational boards of governors. One leading class was exchanged for another; a veil of independence still clothed universities as academic freedom became an increasing watchword. The Government of Ontario claimed indirect but more immediate control over the University of Ottawa and its fellow institutions. It might be more appropriate, however, to hand the baton to industrial actors whose influence would help play spiritual and moral development down in favour of market forces like efficiency and productivity.

These forces are most effectively seen with reference to the University's visitor role, a forgotten office but one that remains defined in Quebec regulation of religious institutions as exercising "the powers conferred upon any general or special meeting of the members by the Companies Act."[34] In other words, a visitor's power extends over all matters pertaining to the corporation, which allows the visitor to overrule corporate assemblies on any matter relating to the corporation. This sweeping power translates into other Canadian jurisdictions with specific reference to universities. The heart of this jurisdiction is the right of a charity's founder to supervise their foundation. Visitors are born in the disposition of property to a charitable purpose.

The power of this office remains little explored; a brief digression illustrates the stakes. The Alberta Court of Appeal's recent scanting reference to visitors helped the Court find that the *Canadian Charter of Rights and Freedoms* applied to the University of Alberta to protect anti-abortion speech on the University's campus. The Court said:

> The University is an institution of higher learning which was first legally established in the first legislative session of the new Province, with Premier Alexander Rutherford as a principal supporter: *An Act to establish and incorporate a University for the Province of Alberta*, SA 1906 c 42. Section 4 of the *Act* designated *the Lieutenant Governor* as the "Visitor" of the University.
>
> The Visitor role calls to memory *Philips v Bury* (1694), 1 ER 24 at p 26, where the Bishop of Exeter was designed a Visitor and was charged *inter alia* to ensure "Virtue and Learning be nourished." The case also noted that a College "is to Educate them in Learning." In other words, the historic role of the Visitor has been for centuries very much that of an ombudsman, and inquirer and a judge of performance of university affairs by its operational masters. From its starting point, then, the University and its purposes were a subject of great significance to *the crown* when it enacted the University into existence. [Emphasis in original][35]

The Court of Appeal used the historic existence of a visitor to help justify the extension of constitutional rights applied only to government. Universities have traditionally not been captured under the government's formal sovereignty; they have just benefitted from government's charity.[36] The Ontario Divisional Court confirmed the legal assumption that universities are autonomous corporations in the recent dispute between the government of Ontario and the Canadian Federation of Students. The Ford government's 2019 directive mandating the end of university collection of student association fees was declared illegal because it was "inconsistent with the universities' autonomous governance."[37] Ontario's treatment of the University of Ottawa between 1965 and 1969 puts paid to this notion of autonomous governance. Ontario began to exercise de facto visitor's powers at the University of Ottawa after 1965, though it never formally claimed such a role.

The existence of a visitor and the use of visitatorial powers defines the University's dominant sovereignty as a property right. The office is a legal-historical means of framing the institutional analysis based on financial and political measures. Though these means are more obvious—and receive the lion's share of attention—the visitor grounds them in a formal power to intervene in the university's affairs. The Oblates, as shall be seen, liberally exercised their rights, which have always received definition in canon law. The Ontario government was less adroit, though its power of the purse effectively gave it a right that was enhanced by changes to the University's legislated charter.

The market forces championed by government were anathema to the University of Ottawa's historic pontifical mission. The ecclesiastical charter of 1889 finalized incorporation of the University of Ottawa at canon law. It accomplished the same process as the University's early civil charters of 1849 and 1866 in a different field. The Pope claimed a supervisory jurisdiction that twinned with the Bishop of Ottawa's traditional right to supervise and the Oblates' supervision of its members, who were the College's chief administrators. This grant set the University apart from its cousins, founded around the same time, in Windsor (1857, Basilian), Saint Jerome's College (1865, Jesuits and Resurrectionist Fathers), and Sudbury (1959, Jesuit). Though these other institutions were Catholic, they were local training centres for clerics and laypersons supervised by their diocesan bishops and founding orders. Ottawa's new dignity in 1889 meant it educated for the faith, much like its Oblate masters, its academic degrees were recognized across the Church, and its program was consequently submitted to the Holy See for approval.

The elevation also focused Catholic support on the University of Ottawa, which in part explains Leo XIII's decision to grant the papal charter. The Oblates were the most successful nineteenth-century

Catholic order in Canada.[38] Unlike its cousins, the University's placement was geographically convenient in Ontario and in Canada. The University, in the newly formed Dominion's capital, became a centre for Catholic teaching. Bishops the province over would send clerics to Ottawa to receive the University's ecclesiastical training. This centre was at once close to the Canadian seat of power (a position to which the Catholic Church had grown accustomed since the Conquest in 1760) and removed from Protestant and English-Catholic centres in southern Ontario.[39] Extended lines of communication allowed the French Oblates to develop their institution far from political distractions while permitting the Church (which existed in Canada without a nunciate until the 1960s) an official footprint beside Parliament. Pope Leo XIII, who was interested in Canada's Catholic population, no doubt appreciated the University's situation.[40]

It is this historic footprint that, in the decade of the 1960s, began to wane as Catholic religious belief became more diffuse. The Quiet Revolution in Quebec and Vatican II shifted the Church's institutional priorities in the face of an increasingly secularized population.[41] Rigid adherence to canon law and devotional ritual gave way to an openness newly focused on the spirit rather than the act.[42] This movement mirrors the crisis of belief that rocked Canadian Protestantism in the late nineteenth century. The development and result of that crisis has been tracked by Ramsay Cook: "The orthodox Christian preoccupation with man's salvation was gradually replaced by a concern with social salvation; the traditional Christian emphasis on man's relationship with God shifted to a focus on man's relationship with man."[43] Vatican II maintained a relationship with God. The Catholic emphasis in the 1960s, however, shifted in quality from (at its worst) rote worship to worship that sought life among the wider community. Father Terence Fay attests to this reality when he speaks of "sacredization," the Catholic response to increasing secular sentiment. Ecclesiastics and laypeople were encouraged to come together to articulate common culture.[44]

The Catholic response to changing social realities came much later than the Ontarian Protestant majority's, but a comparison of the two illustrates the existential pressure that Oblate university administrators faced. The rapid growth of Canadian industry in the nineteenth century brought science to the fore, while shaking the fundaments on which Protestant theology rested. Belief in a sublime creator, one who granted mankind the promise of redemption through individual virtues, lost ground to a consumer society.⁴⁵ That emerging society was underpinned by Darwin's scientific appreciation of Nature and an emphasis on John Locke's separation of church and state.⁴⁶

The Protestant movement toward firmer separation of church and state was seen as early as 1868. The newly independent province of Ontario faced backlash for its handling of the "university question": John Sandfield Macdonald's government—the last led by a Catholic until Dalton McGuinty's ministry—announced the end of college and university subsidies in a speech from the throne on December 27, 1867. This announcement sparked such debate that the government held its proposal over to the following year, but then stood firm despite still vigorous debate in the House of Assembly.⁴⁷ Denominational colleges and universities would never again receive general financial aid from the province. Increasing emphasis was placed on federation with the non-denominational (and provincially controlled) University of Toronto. Only special grants would be provided.⁴⁸

These grants were predicated upon the slow creep of a liberal and utilitarian mindset. A. B. McKillop traces this evolution into the post-war period. The University of Ottawa does not feature much in this narrative because of its situation at the periphery of Ontario life—a situation created both by its location and its denominational history. Even so, the rise of utilitarianism coincides with the increasing division of arts and science. McKillip's history breaks into three phases: pre-Great War (1880–1914), interwar years (1919–1939), and post-Second War (1945–1950). In Ontario's nineteenth-century industrial revolution leading up to the Great War, university curricula created a wedge between humanities and sciences. Such fragmentation was due in part to rising industrial needs for graduates, but it was also simply a response to an information explosion brought on by post-Darwinian advances in science. Religious understanding of Ontarian society was shifting in Protestant circles, and the universities responded in kind.⁴⁹

The interwar years enshrined Ontarian universities as "powerhouses" for advanced economic activity, which brought a utilitarian logic more fully into view—one that was felt even at the College of Ottawa, as the University was known up until 1933, when a new civil charter expanded its powers by allowing it to create faculties. The trend was best represented in expanding professional programs, though the University of Ottawa would only truly partake in these after the Second World War. McKillop places two phenomena in conjunction in this first period. Business and society needed graduates for its increasingly technical ventures; universities needed students and were thus willing to tailor their offerings. They increasingly became participants in social change rather than working simply as "finishing schools" for elites.[50]

The post-Second World War baby boom brought more students into universities than had ever been seen before. At the same time, industry required increasing numbers of highly trained professionals in technical fields. The Atomic Age brought greater industrial and technical growth that necessitated a new flock of managers and professionals. The baby boom created huge social pressure on schools and universities to accommodate a large cohort interested in and qualified for higher education. These expectations of universities created an "educative society," with universities eminent as social and economic tools. These needs drove a wedge between the humanities and the sciences. Religion's influence steadily decreased in this educative society.

The Oblates' eroding influence in their University and in the wider community hit hard. An influx of lay professors watered down the University's traditionally Catholic staff. These new additions sundered the University's tenuous unity of purpose, which had before only been divided between English Catholics and French Catholics. More to the point, however, the Oblates were faced with changing social expectations of the Church's role in society that did not line up with Catholic doctrine. As previous Ontarian debates in the early twentieth century about education reveal, Catholic instruction (when it was not internecine) was an essential element of spreading Catholicism.[51] The proselyte mission was complicated by the ethnic differences within the Church. French and Irish proselytes each viewed themselves and their language as the manifestation of a "divine mandate" that commanded them to spread the faith throughout North America.[52]

Universities generally and Ottawa in particular were prime ground on which to take a stand against the erosion of faith. Secularism was as much a belief system as Catholicism.[53] Universities propagated both world views. They created institutional structures that mediated between the *vita activa* and the *vita contemplativa*. Aquinas, a mainstay of Catholic thought, evokes these lives in relation to the active and the passive intellects.[54] The active intellect takes information in and instinctively responds. The passive intellect relies upon memory to systematically work through problems. The more modern Pierre Bourdieu relies upon this distinction to import social events and assumptions into an academic setting. While Bourdieu speaks principally of disciplining students, his view of academia writ large speaks to universities' power structures and the way in which they alter perception. Academic minds exist within institutions designed to classify reality into blocks that may be studied. In so doing, they import from the active life, but they "misconstrue" these classifications to naturalize them to contemplative life.[55]

Such misconstruction works through power structures that, in a similar way, create legal bridges between academics (and the contemplative life) and their societies (which form the active life). This bridge must be imperfect, and historically amenable to influence from religious and secular quarters.[56] It ignores the classification of academics as people beyond their disciplines and minds. Bourdieu accounts for such imperfection in religious terms:

> The agents entrusted with the operations of classification can fulfill their function of social classification only because this is performed in the guise of an operation of academic classification, that is, through a specifically academic taxonomy. They successfully perform what they (objectively) have to do only because they believe that they are doing something different from what they are actually doing; because they are actually doing something different from what they believe they are doing; and because they believe in what they believe they are doing. As mystified mystifiers, they are the first victims of the operations which they perform.[57]

Academic systems warp language into a series of filtering beliefs on personal and systemic levels. These beliefs require buy-in from their adherents in much the same way as religion. Religion, however, mediates all forms of social experience in a way that Bourdieu's individualist view of the *vita contemplativa* does not encourage. Individualist academics aim to euphemistically remove themselves from the active life in only certain areas of their practice: a dissonant goal compared to the fundamental collegiate purpose of academies *ad studentum et orandum*. Academics must rely upon the active life to some extent; abstracting oneself into a purely contemplative existence invites a mysticism that, if not conscientiously pursued, dashes the psyche upon rocks of anxiety and dishonesty. This was the experience that the Oblates, whose faith even in the academy was religious, exuded.

That mystery of faith assigns meaning to facts, objects, and subjects based upon individual interpretations of the relationship between subject and object. This sentence seems a platitude, but it affects the way in which academics discover and reproduce knowledge. Such discovery is a legislative process of difference and recognition that, if done correctly, brings the individual academic closer to the single event with which they are confronted in the active life, as opposed to more general philosophical concepts that are better said to inform the contemplative life.[58] Recognition in these terms unveils a "spirit" in everyday facts[59]—a spirit that Rector Jean-Charles Laframboise recognized at the University of Ottawa in 1950 when he noted that professors were systematically encouraging students to work outside of purely academic relationships.[60] Two spirits emerge from Laframboise's observation. The academic spirit and the active spirit. Combining the two is an apostolic exercise that, for the Oblates, relied on their faith in a Supreme spirit.

Academics too often theorize on facts by projecting their perception of meaning onto the subject of study. This purely academic spirit may be said to be selfish, for it speaks only to a few without engaging the rest of the world. The challenge is always to step out of that contemplative mould to capture the vivacity and beauty of an active life. The act of theorizing imbues reality with a spirit, and one closely associated with the theorist. Put differently, academics create meaning by applying concepts only when they are filtered through the academic's mind. This filtering is its own mystery. It calls for faith in oneself, but also in others as academics engage in and with their society. Academic institutions condition their members by creating standards for reposing faith in others. At present, those standards are rightly stringent. They also, however, isolate academics by emphasizing personal responsibility for publishing and career advancement, while fostering a corporate culture that encourages a "logic of profit-making" over more patient forms of critical engagement and "public morality."[61] The mystery of faith required to string together ideas is de-emphasized in this regime to instead promote a utilitarian need to accrue plaudits in order to remain relevant to a wider academic community.

Such a utilitarian focus leads to changing perceptions of universities as more readily commodified parts of industry. A recent judicial opinion has framed universities as "gatekeepers" to professions and jobs that merits increased judicial regulation rather than the internal regulation to which courts typically defer.⁶² Justice Paperny in this case ignores the deeper, religious roots in the university that require faith between master and student to give and receive knowledge.⁶³

Ontario's government seemingly agrees with this assessment, as does the University of Ottawa. The second round of strategic mandate agreements now coming into effect exchanges government funding for measurable performance outcomes.⁶⁴ While this might not seem alarming to most (government cash should be accounted for), measuring education and research production is a tricky business that places enormous pressure on academics of all stripes to perform, not just as researchers but as teachers and administrators. This pressure may detract from local and wider academic exchange, which is the root of healthy academics.⁶⁵

Such was the view of the Oblate owners of the University of Ottawa at its coming of age. Healthy academics required the time and ability to uncover and appreciate the spirit. The 1950s and 1960s were a period of unprecedented expansion in higher education across Canada. The Oblates experienced those growing pains as a respectable Catholic outpost with a single civil faculty teaching both arts and science, three professional schools, and a school of political science. This nucleus grew into an institution with six civil faculties between 1945 and 1965.⁶⁶ That holy mission was described at the beginning of this period by Rector Jean-Charles Laframboise on December 31, 1946:

> D'aucuns croiront peut-être que leurs efforts pourraient être consacrés à des œuvres plus apostoliques, plus directement en relation avec la conversion et la sanctification des âmes. Nous ne le croyons pas. Tout d'abord il ne faut pas oublier que l'éducateur véritable est nécessairement un apôtre. C'est son devoir en effet de transmettre aux âmes qui viennent à lui pour être instruites tout le message du Christ, de leur donner des convictions chrétiennes profondes et durables.⁶⁷

Education remained at this Catholic university an exchange between souls. The apostolic mission was a sublime exchange of knowledge and, perhaps, of conviction. With this knowledge came an organizing force that valued the supernatural.

This theme would play out even after reform. Rector Roger Guindon's 1971 retrospective on the six years following the transition described the University's mission in muted, yet still spiritual terms:

> L'université visible et invisible—et l'homme qui l'habite et qui en est le maître—sont trop complexes pour qu'un individu—ou un groupe—si savant soit-it, puisse prétendre posséder en exclusivité l'ultime explication.
>
> C'est pour cela que les universités ne peuvent limiter leur recrutement de professeurs et d'étudiants aux frontières de leur province, de leur pays ou même de leur hémisphère. L'Université doit être une *cité de l'univers*.[68]

That city might, to a Catholic's ear, be close to God's; for others, it may reflect the new official Catholic openness following Vatican II. In either case, the role of education as a moulder of souls remained. The explication of visible and invisible worlds in a pun on universities replicates the Christian and Catholic concern with the supernatural.

No single faith could claim a monopoly on such explication, but the Oblates in 1965 humourlessly observed the University's transfer to a non-denominational corporation alongside their dwindling fortunes in Canada. Their spiritual redemption required continuously spreading their faith, and a reduced stake in such a project diminished that aim.

On the other hand, a drastic decrease in Oblate membership decimated Oblate finances in the 1960s, which had a knock-on effect at the University. By 1958, when Rector Henri Légaré was settling into office, the University had expanded so much that, out of 266 professors, only 71 were Oblates. This was a ratio of roughly four lay professors to every Oblate. Another 275 sessional instructors were on staff.[69] Three years later, in 1961, the number of Oblates had been reduced to 68 professors out of 342—a ratio of 5:1—with another 400 part-time professors.[70] Between 1965 and 1973, the Order's international membership decreased by 14.6 percent, or 1,081 fathers and brothers. The population was, furthermore, generally ageing, for few young recruits were entering the Order.[71] Vatican II spurred this decrease on as age and disillusionment with the Order took their respective tolls. This decrease in influence at the University and on a wider stage translated to a decrease in revenue as productive members dropped off. At the University, with material and personnel costs rapidly mounting, the Order could not sustain its investment. By 1965, the crisis reached fever pitch and the Oblates swiftly backed away from their long association.

The present work gives some evidence of the seriousness of Oblate concerns. I work through the University's structure to focus on the main decision makers for which documents survive. These documents were low-hanging fruit in a largely unexamined trove. My method (if method it was) connected actors as much as possible through their own association. At times, however, it was necessary to link them by physical or intellectual proximity rather than a better documented personal connection. Such moves are more familiar to the literary critic than the historian. At heart, this work argues that cultures clashed at the University of Ottawa, which brings my analysis into the hazy atmosphere between literature and history. This is where I am most comfortable, and it seems appropriate to discuss Oblate difficulties in such a haze. While both literary criticism and history must examine their subjects from a contemplative remove, it feels more permissible for the literary scholar to take leaps that bring characters having no close association together because their ideas or their expressions twin so nicely.

While this analysis is primarily a history, it thus also takes some leaps of faith. I have restrained my leaps. Where subjects' rhetoric throughout this book seem similar, such similarities are noted. My faith is in the cultural similarities between Oblates on one hand and government actors on the other. Each share in a field of language that conditioned their rhetoric. These fields underpinned claims to sovereignty that proved incompatible as economic forces were prioritized over a religious view of education.

The four chapters before you work through the University's history. Chapter one details the University's history and structure leading up to the 1960s. It demonstrates Catholic influence in the University, and the legal discourse used by Oblates and Catholics to describe that interest in founding documents. Chapter two properly delves into the exchanges between Oblates in the 1960s. It shows increasing government financial pressure to reform, and theorizes why that pressure might have been instrumentalized against the Oblates. The Oblates break in chapter three, and the University reforms. I suggest, however, that Catholic discourse and sovereignty inform the Oblate capitulation. The Oblates try to persevere in the spirit of Vatican II. In so doing, they overstay their welcome, which is the subject of chapter four. Here, Oblate claims to control and historic dominance fail in the face of the government's power politics. Even a Catholic board of governors does not avail the Oblates. The epilogue details the immediate aftermath of the government's assertion of control: the Oblates continued to promote a Christian worldview as the 1970s approached, but their waning numbers and the provincial government's waxing control lessened the impacts of their message.

CHAPTER 1

Overview of the University Charter (1849–1965)

> And God is able to make all grace abound toward you; that ye, always having all sufficiency in all things, may abound to every good work:
>
> (As it is written, He hath dispersed abroad; he hath given to the poor: his righteousness remaineth for ever.
>
> Now he that ministereth seed to the sower both minister bread for your food, and multiply your seed sown, and increase the fruits of your righteousness)
>
> — 2 Corinthians 9:8–10

The Oblates themselves give a noble account of the University's[1] early days. The thrust of their histories cast the University as a beacon shining in Ottawa's night, one shining with the grace described in 2 Corinthians. In 1960 Gaston Carrière, the most prominent of the Oblates, published his account of the College's critical first thirteen years.[2] George Simard, well known for his theology, touches on the University's early history in the 1930s through to the 1950s in a series of published works about Catholic universities more generally.[3] Both are Oblate priests, and both demonstrate the Oblates' long twilight at the University as they deploy Catholic history to legitimize the University's place in Ottawa. In so doing, they hoped to legitimize the University's government by their Order.

The 1965 shift to non-denominational status is formal: a new University of Ottawa is created that buys most of the old Bytown College's property. This purchase depends upon and is the culmination of a legislative history that blends Canadian, Catholic, and Oblate norms to create a unique institutional law and culture. This culture relied upon custom. There is no doubt that the Catholic Church occupied a privileged position at the University between 1848 and 1965. That privilege, however, was subject to the strictures of a civil government increasingly intent throughout the nineteenth century to restrict the proliferation of independent centres of study.

This chapter extends these seminal texts by tracing the legal evolution of the university corporation. The role of the visitor takes centre stage, for this office becomes complicated by nineteenth-century assertions of sovereignty that seem a matter of course until their legal implications are teased out. The analysis is, of necessity, less graceful than the Oblates might have liked. Decoding the prevalent power structures at the University is a technical exercise made fraught by similar, but not wholly identical, legal institutions. The twin sovereignties at work each claimed rights of visitation. The civil power's creation of an eleemosynary corporation created a common law right to visitation. The right to visit was an enforceable legal power that allowed the founder to ensure that her or his assets were being properly used. The nineteenth century recognized this right as conferring the power to correct institutional defects up to and including disallowance of bylaws or local statutes.[4] That right eventually vested in the Crown; it initially lay with Bishop Guigues. The existence of Catholic authorities in and at the College complicated the visitor's jurisdiction. In the University of Ottawa's case, the visitor's power was shared among three or four heads of power. The Oblate Order had a supervisory jurisdiction over its property and members; the Catholic Diocese of Bytown held a first right to visit; the Crown legislated its right as visitor (as was often the case);[5] and the Vatican assumed supervision of the College's curriculum and statutes. While such power sharing did not inherently divest the Crown of its civil authority, it confused lines of reasoning that in the institutional theory of eleemosynary corporations could never be confused: there was one visitor or, at the very least, one set of visitors emanating from the same class.[6] While basic Oblate conclusions about the University are maintained throughout this analysis, the added structural nuance highlights the potential disharmony between ecclesial and civil powers during the University's long adolescence.

The analysis of the University of Ottawa's constitutional history demonstrates continuous institutional growth from its foundation in 1849 until Rector Henri Légaré took office in 1959. The University was formally created and expanded by private acts of Parliament.[7] Its founding document, An Act to incorporate the College of Bytown, Canada, created a skeletal frame on which Bishop Joseph Eugène Guigues hung those first collegial hopes. The College changed its name from "The College of Bytown" to "College of Ottawa" in 1861 to reflect the city's name change. Bishop Guigues was at this time formally removed from the Canadian corporation. He had sold the college from his parish's control to the Oblate Congregation in 1856. Only five years later, on the eve of Canadian Confederation, the Oblates correctly surmised that francophone rights would have a restricted place in the Province of Ontario. They petitioned and won university powers for the College while the Province of Canada's last Legislature sat in Ottawa. These powers were only slightly disturbed in 1885 and 1891, when minor amendments were made to the College's constitution. It would not be until 1933, when the provincial parliament passed An Act respecting the College of Ottawa, that the College's structure began to look like that which we see in today's University of Ottawa. Indeed, that charter lived on even after 1965 as Saint Paul University's constitution, one since amended in its own right.

The Catholic Church was a presence throughout this period, but the Church was far from unified. Bytown College existed in three Catholic spheres of influence. The constituent elements of the Church and Oblate Order in Ottawa influenced the College's development in respective ways. The Bishop of Ottawa was responsible for the overall education of his parishioners and for sustaining the clergy by training priests. The Oblates, once they entered the picture, also trained priests for missionary activity elsewhere in Canada. They also used the College to bring their proselytizing activity to the Ottawa Valley. The Vatican, last but not least, operated at a remove. It came principally into play with the grant of a papal charter in 1889, but its regulatory influence could also be felt, although its power was not terribly strong in this period. The Pope had not yet fully assumed control of seminaries and universities. That control began at the turn of the century, when Pope Pius IX adopted *Sapienti Consilio* (1908), which expanded the scope of the Sacred Congregation of Seminaries and Universities.[8]

These Catholic bodies remained at arm's length from the University corporation proper. The Oblates, once they had taken over the enterprise, controlled the nomination of the College Superior and of the Superior's immediate advisors. It was expedient for the Oblate Congregation to keep out of the College's internal affairs and, until papal reforms in the 1900s and 1910s came in, nineteenth-century Catholic culture supported a view of colleges and universities as proselytizing institutions—a view in vogue in the nineteenth century—but also as autonomous bodies left largely to their own devices. The autonomy thus accorded did not admit the medieval view of professors as the lowest rung of *cathedra magistralis*,[9] but rather as a shield with which the faithful ensured preservation of a unique culture responding to unique institutional challenges.

Those challenges are best fleshed out with emphasis on the University's constitutional history. This chapter considers that history by using the University's civil charters as waypoints. It details the period 1849–1959, years that witnessed progressive industrialization and secularization of Ontarian and Canadian society. The changes to the University's constitution through this period reflect its growth and its responses to pressure from civil and ecclesiastical government. These pressures forced constant growth, and that growth was informed by competing jurisdictions pushing and pulling at the edges of the University's constitution.

I

The College of Bytown began life under the three jurisdictions I have mentioned: civil, Catholic, and Oblate. Even before the College's founder, Bishop Joseph-Bruno Guigues (ordained 1828–d. 1874), arrived in Ottawa, the prospect of a Catholic college was studied by Catholic priests. Patrick Phelan, Bytown's parish priest before Guigues arrived, obtained a parcel of land from Louis-Théodore Besserer, a successful notary who owned much of Sandy Hill.[10] His success in this regard was promoted by Montréal's Bishop Ignace Bourget, who had supported Phelan's efforts since 1843.[11] The parcel became the basis for the College, which was announced soon after Guigues was installed in the newly created Diocese of Bytown.[12] The College taught from the Roman Catholic Church property fronting onto Sussex Drive and was dedicated at its opening in 1848 to Saint Joseph.[13] The College subsequently received incorporation on Guigues' petition to the Legislature in 1849.[14]

Guigues' leading role at the College brings his personal history as an Oblate in Canada to bear. Oblate and Catholic interest in the College twinned from the outset in connection with Guigues' biography. A conscientious bishop, Guigues was aware of his power and the powers of the Congregation, although these were not well distinguished in practice. Before being appointed bishop on July 9, 1847, Guigues was one of the first priests to enter the Oblate Congregation.[15] He showed academic and administrative promise early in his career by being appointed a professor of philosophy and the bursar of the seminary of Marseilles at twenty-two, in 1827.[16] He served as the Oblate extraordinary visitor of the Province of Canada in 1844—just three years after the Oblates arrived in the country. He effectively organized the congregation's Canadian presence until 1851, when Father Jacques Santoni took the one role.[17] Visitation was used in religious orders to correct errors in a specific territory. The sweeping powers were routinely delegated, for the Superior-General himself could not leave his administration of the entire Congregation in France for the time it took to travel and see the province being visited.[18] The Superior-General's powers were delegated to a visitor; Guigues' appointment in this regard effectively made him the leader of the Oblates in Canada. His appointment continued, though not without chagrin, into his tenure as Bishop of Bytown after his consecration on July 20, 1848.[19]

That interest took on fuller expression through Guigues in the wake of Lord Durham's report. Lord Durham suggested that the lack of education in Lower Canada contributed to the 1838 rebellion:

> Passions inflamed during so long a period cannot speedily be calmed. The state of education which I have previously described as placing the peasantry entirely at the mercy of agitators, the total absence of any class of persons, or any organization of authority that could counteract this mischievous influence, and the serious decline in the district of Montreal of the influence of the clergy, concur in rendering it absolutely impossible for the Government to produce any better state of feeling among the French population.[20]

The Church was a central pillar of ordered society. Lord Durham assigned it importance alongside training an elite for government. The interests of church and state aligned in the Ottawan outpost: the Montréal clergy extended their reach even as the new Diocese of Ottawa was erected to ensure that French and English alike had access to education. Such access tempered radical political views, thus potentially ensuring a happier state among French and English, or Catholic and Protestant, settlers. Indeed, upon learning of his selection as bishop for the new parish, Guigues went out of his way to ensure harmony between English and French populations in his diocese. He was aware at the outset that his parishioners would be a bilingual crowd and spent months in an English village in Quebec to learn English.[21] Bilingualism was a budding issue within the Canadian Oblate Congregation, a need that Guigues addressed by pushing the Oblate Superior-General, Eugène de Mazenod, to send more Irish-Catholic congregants to Canada to bridge the linguistic divide.[22]

Guigues' enthusiastic disposition to his future parishioners was in some measure reflected in the Diocese of Kingston just before the Legislature received Guigues' petition to incorporate Bytown College. The Catholic college, Regiopolis, had been founded just before Lord Durham's arrival. Regiopolis was incorporated as a trust in 1837, run directly by the Bishop of Kingston. The College quickly became an encumbrance upon diocesan finances so that, just before the College of Bytown was founded, Patrick Phelan requested government support from the Jesuit's confiscated estates in an 1847 open letter.[23] Regiopolis was granted £500 that year and, by 1858, it was receiving $3,000 (currencies had changed in the interim).[24]

Two years later, College supporters went further. On January 22, 1849, Kingston-based Catholic clergymen petitioned parliament to increase the College's funding. The petitioners reminded the House of Assembly of the troubles that had led to its composition. One-fourth of the population of Upper Canada was Catholic and, in the clergy's opinion, it was important

> for the general prosperity of the Country at large, that no feelings of mistrust should be allowed to take root in the minds of Roman Catholics of this Country, as to any want of solicitude on the part of Government to afford them, in common with any other Religious Denomination, a proportionate share of its patronage, as well as support, out of the public revenues, in aid of education.[25]

The clergy's plea for tolerance was meant to prevent ethnic tension between the solitudes. The pushed their point with allusion to the provincial university, the University of Toronto, which was established as King's College in 1827, but which was redesigned in 1849 to become a fully fledged university, based on the University of London model wherein a university examined for and granted degrees and colleges provided education.[26] The University of Toronto would, Kingston clergy feared, be a bastion of Protestant teaching that would disrupt Catholic beliefs.[27] The Protestant majority would possess a better trained elite able to suppress the Catholic minority—only education, as Lord Durham pointed out, could supply some sort of equal playing field. Government funds would continue to Regiopolis while the Province of Canada survived.[28] Even for this success, however, Regiopolis was by 1869 closed for want of funds.

Guigues faced similar pressures, but his college was far more distant from Toronto and benefitted from a less mobile catchment. The new college required public aid for capital expenses and land use authorization. This aid was not forthcoming. Rather, the administrators of the local military ordnance refused to grant Guigues' requests for land use authorization.[29] Guigues even went to the ordnance's colonial masters in London, but to no avail.[30] Similarly, the Province of Canada's governor and his council granted only a small sum to the fledgling Catholic college, and this money would disappear as the University of Toronto was restructured and got off to a fresh start between 1852 and 1854.[31] Lack of government aid irked Guigues, whose mission was quite personal. He declared his irritation in a circular letter to parish priests on April 25, 1854:

> Peut-être bien qu'un jour le gouvernement, touché de Nos efforts comprendra qu'en Nous accordant quelque part aux sommes énormes dépensées à Toronto pour quelques élèves privilégiés, il travaillera efficacement à l'intérêt de l'éducation et Nous serons alors heureux de faire plus encore que ce que Nous Nous proposons de faire aujourd'hui.[32]

Government patronage of the provincial university, a symbol of English elitism, ignored growing communities outside of Toronto. Guigues' efforts were destined for talented students across the Ottawa Valley: government investment in a single university close to the seat of power ignored regional needs.

Bytown's isolation is attested by Superior-General de Mazenod's correspondence with Patrick Phelan before the creation of Guigues' diocese. Bytown first existed in the Diocese of Kingston. Phelan, as coadjutor to an ailing bishop, welcomed Oblate priests into the diocese in 1844 with the promise of livings in parish churches. De Mazenod's enthusiasm was hyperbolic and ultramontane to a fault, though he understandably appreciated the loyalty a bishop requires from his priests:

> Les Oblats de Marie Immaculée sont éminemment les hommes des Évêques; ils n'ont été institués que pour être entre leurs mains comme les instruments de leur propre ministère pour la sanctification de leurs ouailles; les Évêques n'ont de prêtres plus soumis, plus dévoués qu'eux.[33]

The unflinching loyalty of Oblate priests seems rich coming from de Mazenod's vantage. The Superior-General was not fully able to appreciate events on the ground. This was a problem that would recur for de Mazenod under Guigues' leadership. The Oblates' founder complained that local Superiors and that Guigues himself did not report sufficient detail at useful intervals (three months seems the norm).[34] Regardless of these difficulties, de Mazenod was sufficiently apprised to know that an Irish Oblate, Father Michael Molloy, was nearly killed in the passage from Montréal to Ottawa as the Oblate Congregation there expanded in 1846 to account for Bytown's bilingual population.[35] These priests relieved the Diocese of Kingston, for Regiopolis was not producing a sufficient number of clergymen for the task.

The Oblates' missionary goal suffused the College's existence from the start because Guigues was bishop and Oblate leader. His dual function was a point of controversy among his priest and with de Mazenod. The clergy were difficult to govern and allowed their opposition to his appointment to spill into the public realm; the Superior-General wished only to continue the Order's stable government, hitherto preserved through Guigues' leadership.[36] De Mazenod's concern shone through in his letter of December 27, 1846, when he cautioned Guigues against accepting nomination to become bishop:

> Il y a donc obligation pour vous et pour moi de maintenir le bien qui s'est opéré et de ne pas nous exposer à voir l'édifice s'écrouler après toutes les peines qu'il vous a coûté [es] pour les relever...

> Je ne vois que trop quelle espèce d'hommes sont les Canadiens qui ont été admis dans la Congrégation; et ceux qui vous sont venus de France ne sont guère plus faciles à gouverner. Je n'ai que vous pour dominer les uns et les autres par l'ascendant que vous avez sur eux.[37]

It is perhaps this strength of character that led Guigues to take both roles under such pressure to perform in capacities that were not perfectly aligned. The cracks began to show early in Guigues' tenure when, on September 26, 1848, in defiance of his own view of episcopal propriety,[38] de Mazenod ordered Guigues to live in the Oblate congregation's, Bytown house.[39] The Superior-General's judgment was expanded two months later when he wrote to Guigues' Provincial Council on November 1, 1848:

> Je crois préférable et même indispensable que l'Évêque vive en communauté avec les Pères. Je regarderais comme une sorte de scandale qu'il en fût autrement. Pour le temporel, il vaut donc mieux qu'il y ait fusion que séparation entre le diocèse et la Congrégation; le diocèse étant en quelque sorte identifié avec la Congrégation, son Évêque et les prêtres appartenant à la même Congrégation. Dès lors, l'Évêque perçoit tous les revenus de l'Église de Bytown, et de ces fonds il pourvoit aux besoins du diocèse de Bytown et à ceux de la Congrégation.[40]

De Mazenod respected the formal distinction between diocese and Oblate Order. In practice, however, he elided the two for ostensibly mutual benefit. The Oblates were still so new to Canada that their dominance in Bytown seemingly over the Bishop benefitted them far more than the new diocese could hope to be served in return. The College was born in this political landscape so that, even if Bishop Guigues was its formal founder and owner, the Oblates already had some stake in the College's business.

Establishing the College in Bytown served the growing regional need for higher education of both francophone and anglophone populations along the lines laid down by Lord Durham. Bytown's Bishop, if not the wider clergy, recognized the need to fold both communities together. Guigues was clear on this point in his failed appeal to the controllers of the ordnance. The newly ordained Bishop of Ottawa argued that the College could contribute

> puissamment à cimenter les liens les plus durables de tous ceux de la jeunesse entre les hommes d'origine et de religion différentes et [il] effacera les antipathies naturelles et toujours déplorables parmi les citoyens de la même patrie.[41]

Even after this failed attempt to bridge the linguistic divide, Guigues' petition to the Legislature won him incorporation on May 30, 1849, which first included the "Professors of Philosophy and Belles-Lettres," alongside the Bishop himself (who was also the president), and the bursar. No senate was provided, for none was necessary. The College did not confer degrees; it educated purely *ad studentum et orandum*:

> Provided always, and be it enacted, That the rents, revenues, issues and profits of all property, real or personal, held by the said Corporation, shall be appropriated and applied solely to the maintenance of the Members of the Corporation, the construction and repair of the buildings requisite for the purposes of the said Corporation, and to the advancement of education by the instruction of youth, and the payment of the expenses to be incurred for objects legitimately connected with or depending on the purposes aforesaid.

The Act gave simple "corporate powers" to the College and restricted its mission.[42] Revenue could only be expended on the College's members, whether students or professors. The College's charity was to maintain a group of fellows devoted to education instead of religion (although few would have made such a distinction at the time). The charity received the backing of Bytown locals. A petition from "Robert Conroy and others" was enrolled in the House of Assembly's journals just after Guigues' petition for the College's incorporation. Bishop and parishioners requested government funds in aid of the College.[43]

Guigues' other responsibility, the Oblates, were incorporated in Canadian law on the same day as his College by act of the Legislature. This was no small act. Guigues no doubt took the opportunity to address multiple requests in different capacities to the Parliament of the Province of Canada at the same time. Those requests symbolically joined the College's prospects with the Oblates'. This symbolism was expressed again in de Mazenod's ruling that Guigues share the Oblate house with his Bytown brothers. The denial of episcopal dignity fit with Oblate rules; it also illustrated just how intertwined the new diocese and the Oblates would become. Indeed, the University of Ottawa would become the jewel in the Oblate crown for a time in the twentieth century such that successive provincial Superiors would first serve as rector of the University before being elevated in the Oblate ranks.

The Oblates' articles of incorporation established an independent charity for these apostles that mirrored the College's structure. Both acts were minimalist because each only created bodies corporate. Each, however, was a corporation of a particular kind. College and Oblate were eleemosynary corporations: charities founded to distribute the founder's charity.[44] The College received subscriptions from students and received regular assistance from Guigues' diocese. Those funds were redistributed to fund less well-off students through scholarships and bursaries; they also maintained the professors hired to teach. The Oblate Congregation, similarly, received assistance from its French base controlled by the Order's founder. The Congregation also received funds in the traditional manner from parish churches under its control. These funds were amassed in the new Oblate corporation and distributed to support the Canadian priests.

The quality and means of distribution within the Oblate corporation were scantily laid out in An Act to incorporate Les Révérends Pères Oblats de l'Immaculée Conception de Marie, in the Province of Canada. The Oblate mission was charitable: for "the establishing of missions, procuring Instruction and Education, erecting and conducting Hospitals for indigent sick persons."[45] All of these things were objects of eleemosynary corporations[46] laid down in the 1601 English Statute of Uses.[47] The corporation was composed of the

> Reverend Fathers Joseph Eugène, Bishop of Bytown, the said Jean Claude Léonard, Damase Dandurand, John Ryan, M. Molloy, and such other persons being natural born or naturalized subjects of Her Majesty as may now or may hereafter become under the provisions of this Act, Members of the said Institution.

"Members of the said Institution" refers to the totality of members, not to the restricted membership of named persons. This language creates a charity of peers, all of whom were affected equally by the corporation's decisions—fellows all devoted to a single charitable end. The revenues of the corporation were explicitly diverted to these members:

> And be it enacted, That the rents, revenues, issues and profits of all property, real or personal, moveable or immoveable, held by the said Corporation, shall be appropriated and applied solely to the maintenance of the Members of the said Corporation, the construction and repair of the buildings requisite for the purposes of the said Corporation, and the payment of the expenses incurred for objects legitimately connected with or depending on the purposes aforesaid.

The diversion of all the corporation's assets to a single purpose is a definitive eleemosynary mark, one repeated in the Act creating the College. Granting the fellows a corporate personality did not modify their obligation to charity; it enshrined that purpose in Canadian law, and derogations from the object of the corporation as it was set out in the act could be reviewed by the law courts, or the Crown *parens patriae*.[48] The Oblate constitution was received in Canada by this Act and enshrined as bylaws of what William Blackstone might call a "little republic," though his phrase is better modified to read "little kingdom."[49] The Act confirmed that Oblates living in Canada governed themselves and submitted to their own Superior-General in France and the bylaws flowing from him.

II

The curious conundrum of the College's early history is that Guigues was at once Bishop and Oblate Provincial. He filled two visitors' roles through separate offices. The roles were, however, restricted in Canadian law for the duration of Guigues' term as a member of the College corporation. This rule was acknowledged in *Wilson*'s case, where a Nova Scotian professor in Halifax was fired by the Board of Governors at King's College.[50] The visitor there was the Anglican Bishop of Nova Scotia, who was also a member of the Board. Justice Thompson (who later became Prime Minister) ruled that a visitor could not visit themselves, so the court was temporarily the visitor until the Bishop left the college. A similar principle applied in Bytown: until Guigues left the College, any visit he performed would not be recognized in Canadian law. The civil power thus had the upper hand in the College's early years, although the government's passive relationship to higher education beyond the University of Toronto meant that little came of its power. The

Oblates instead consolidated their hold in Bytown by becoming the College's owners.

Oblate self-government and its creation in the same legislative moment as Bytown College demonstrates the College's early allegiance. At the outset, with the College's incorporation as a simple offshoot of the diocesan administrative apparatus, Bishop Guigues held all of the rights of the founder. These rights, however, existed in abeyance so long as he was in direct control of the college's administration. These rights sprang from common and canon law. The Bishop was founder and thus had the right; he was also mandated to correct errors within his diocese and did so with the same zeal that he deployed visiting the Oblate missions across Canada before his elevation.

Guigues' zeal placed him in hot water as he attempted to negotiate a path between his dual corporate functions. His role as bishop and as the ranking Canadian Oblate forced him to equivocate on ceding control of the College. By January 10, 1851, de Mazenod was writing to Guigues to push him toward building the College building for eventual transfer to the Oblates.[51] Guigues' impulse to maintain the College in his diocese ran counter to de Mazenod's view that Guigues should promote the Oblates' interests as the very thing that the diocese needed. The founder descried Guigues' change of heart on the eve of the usurpation of his power as provincial superior with the arrival of de Mazenod's new visitor, Father Henry Tempier:

> Notre bon père Allard a donc pris la tournure convenable d'un religieux affectionné à son Ordre, qui ne nous fera jamais regretter de l'avoir choisi. Je voudrais pouvoir en dire autant de l'autre qui marche dans une toute autre voie. Qui aurait pu croire à un oubli si complet de toutes les conditions de mon consentement à son élévation ? Vous aurez donc à être ferme, quoiqu'il puisse dire, dans la séparation de ses intérêts pécuniaires de ceux de la Congrégation.[52]

The Superior-General's tone is one of severe disappointment, for de Mazenod expected his 1848 edict to hold just three years later, when College staff had experienced cohorts of students.[53] Guigues' hesitation in this regard seems to have lost him his twin functions, which is perhaps the genesis of Canadian and Oblate whispers that he was not always faithful to Oblate priorities.[54]

The Oblates, and especially de Mazenod, seemed of this view in 1856 when they called a debt that Guigues had incurred over the past three years to support his diocese. Calling this debt established Oblate dominance over the Bishop in a dispute with one of their own. The diocese borrowed 1,600 Louis—roughly $10,000 today—from the Oblate Provincial (now Father Santoni)—cash that the Order sorely needed to meet its expenses and to grow in Canada. De Mazenod took a hard line in private correspondence with the Provincial on January 20, 1856, when he warned against a "rupture avec l'Évêque de Bytown" and conceded

> qu'il a un peu trop abondé dans la pensée qu'il était Évêque de Bytown, au détriment d'une autre considération qui devait lui rappeler les liens qui l'unissent à la Congrégation et que dès lors il a donné en plus à son diocèse ce qu'il laissait en moins à notre œuvre particulière. . . . J'ai cru nécessaire de vous communiquer ces réflexions avant de vous dire quel est l'arrangement que nous avons adopté ici afin de terminer le différend qui existe entre l'Évêque de Bytown et vous autres au sujet des 1600 L. dont vous réclamez actuellement le remboursement que lui vous refuse.[55]

De Mazenod is not a perfect witness; his priority even eight years into Guigues' tenure was ensuring Oblate dominance in Bytown. Guigues' intransigence stemmed from these split loyalties. He borrowed Oblate funds to establish his diocese but did not give Oblate needs their due—at least, so the Oblates thought. Perhaps as a gesture of good will, Guigues made a parallel offer during these repayment negotiations. He wished to sell Bytown College. De Mazenod's comments to Guigues on the same day show this offer was for peace:

> Ce projet me souriait assez, il me semble concilier tout à la fois les intérêts du diocèse et ceux de la Congrégation; les conditions qu'il fait aux Oblats sont avantageuses en les mettant en état de remplir les deux fins principales de leur Institut et leur créant des ressources pécuniaires bien suffisantes pour les rendre indépendants et les placer sur un pied respectable.[56]

The independence that Canadian Oblates sought could come from College revenues, where immovable property could be complemented by tuition fees. The Oblates could train aspirants not only to their Order, but also to the secular clergy and to other orders operating in North America. The service would thus provoke

Oblate financial growth a decade and a half after their introduction to Canada.

The sale split supervision over the College going forward. The contract, signed in Marseilles on August 17, 1856, formally divided the Bishop from executive control over the College. He was relegated to the visitatorial role that he knew well. The contract stipulated that the Bishop of Bytown ceded the College to the Oblates "dans l'intérêt de son diocèse" and in order to perpetuate "les fruits de salut opérés jusqu'à ce jour dans son Diocèse par la Congrégation des Missionnaires Oblats de Marie Immaculée."[57] These terms implied that the Bishop still had a vested interest in how the College performed because it was in his diocese. The contract acknowledged the bishop's canonical duty to inspect the moral and religious education in his territory, though the Oblates (Guigues still among them) thought themselves exempt from the Bishop's supervision as bishop; Guigues was made the new Oblate Provincial on August 30,[58] which allowed him to inspect the now Oblate College under another right.[59] It was only in 1866, when the Pope declared that the Oblates must submit to bishops' regular jurisdictions, that Guigues acquired free-standing twin rights.[60] He maintained this right until his death in 1874, although no record shows him exercising it.[61] Guigues did, however, immediately exercise his right as Provincial to visit Oblate houses in the province, for Eugène de Mazenod acknowledged receipt of an official transcription of Guigues' *acte de visite* on January 20, 1857.[62]

The contract required approval from the Oblate general chapter, the Order's highest legislative authority. This approval was completed by August 27, 1856, when the Canadian Oblate Provincial Council (now about to come under Guigues' control) appointed the College's new personnel: Father Augustin Gaudet became president and Superior; Henri Tabaret, the bursar and first assessor; Alexandre Trudeau was second assessor; Nicholas Burtin and Alexandre Soulerin were members of the teaching staff.[63] Guigues remained a member ex officio of the corporation, but the contract that he signed as Bishop silenced him in the corporation's debates:

> Mgr. l'Évêque de Bytown par la convention actuelle confie aux Oblats susdits qui acceptent dans la personne de Mgr. Charles Joseph Eugène de Mazenod, Évêque de Marseille & Supérieur général de la dite [c]ongrégation agissant au titre des conditions

énoncées ci dessus 1° la direction & l'administration du séminaire & du Collège de Bytown.[64]

Guigues' subsequent declaration on August 29 as Bishop and as Provincial renounced control over the college in favour of the Oblates that he and his council had appointed two days earlier.[65] He remained, however, bound to financially support the college. De Mazenod reminded Guigues of this fact on June 23, 1857.[66]

Guigues' role in the College's 1849 charter was thus overlaid with Oblate government that brought a second visitor onto the stage. This government existed within the Province of Canada under the terms of the sister Act creating the Oblate Order. The Oblate administration created a second governing body that continued through to the reformation of the University in 1965: the house of the University, and specifically its council of the Superior and two advisors, subject to visitation through the Oblate Superior-General and the Oblate Provincial.[67] Alongside Guigues' canonical right to visit as bishop, the Oblates now had their own ability to impose order upon the Oblate Superior and any Oblate student or professor.

Legislative reform slowly kept pace with changes at the College. By 1857, one year after the sale, the College had grown to ninety students supervised by eight professors. Two curricula existed: one designed for practical application that emphasized applied mathematics; another for traditional liberal arts course of study, "Belles-lettres, Rhetoric, Mental and Natural Philosophy, a more extensive course in Mathematics, History, Ancient and Modern."[68] By 1860, these curricula were being taught to 160 students, twenty of whom were admitted gratis.[69] University College in Toronto, by way of contrast, had only forty-six students in residence in 1859–60.[70] By 1862, that number had dwindled to nineteen.[71] Growth and Guigues' declining involvement in College business required a new charter, one that excluded Guigues and that reflected Oblate power structures. Parliament recognized the new Order with a fresh charter on May 18, 1861, which instilled this new Order. The president of the College, hitherto the Bishop of Bytown, was now ex officio the Oblate Superior of the College. The Oblates appointed the Superior, so the corporations were officially linked instead of linked through practice and internal regulation. All other officers remained the same, and visitation was not altered, indicating that the Bishop of Ottawa — the original founder — continued as visitor.[72]

The hierarchy that would dominate exchanges between the University and Ontario in the 1960s was established. The College altered its character soon after the new charter. On August 20, 1861, at the College's first corporate assembly under the new charter, the assembly "prenait connaissance des déclarations de Mgr. Guigues et du père Damase Dandurand reconnaissant ne plus appartenir à la corporation."[73] The terms of the amended charter were promptly fulfilled.

Catholic visitation was not long in the offing before the Legislature altered the Bishop's right while complicating the College's charitable status by making it a university. Father Joseph-Henry Tabaret, now the College Superior, requested a legislative grant of university powers. On August 15, 1866, Parliament appointed the Roman Catholic Bishop of Ottawa an ex officio member of the new "College Senate," created by An Act to amend the Acts incorporating "The College of Ottawa," and to grant certain privileges to the said college. This supplementary charter was brought in by the member for Brome, Christopher Dunkin, himself a schoolteacher familiar with universities.[74] The College's maximum annual corporate holdings were raised from £2,000 (the 1849 amount) to £4,000. The rest of the Act granted new powers and privileges, chief of which was the Senate, populated by "the President, the Bursar, the Professors of Divinity, Philosophy, Rhetoric, and Belles-Lettres, and the Prefect of Studies."[75] This body was granted authority "to confer the several Degrees of Batchelors of Arts, Master of Arts, Batchelors of Laws, Doctor of Laws, Batchelors of Medicine [sic]."[76] The Senate was also granted "power and authority to make and pass such Statutes, rules, orders and regulations as may be deemed advisable, and to alter, vary and change the same" in order to "[carry] the provisions of this Act fully into effect."[77] The College of Ottawa became a university.

The creation of a senate severed the corporation's power to create academic policy from its body politic. It marked the beginning of the University of Ottawa's bicameral tradition, though membership in the Senate and the body politic remained essentially the same. The Senate, capable of granting degrees, took on a distinctly academic role supervised by the newly constituted visitor, the Governor General through the "Provincial Secretary."[78] The College Senate, not the body politic, was bound to report, upon request, to the Governor on the state of the College's affairs, and the statutes created by the Senate were to be "laid before the visitor" after the Senate passed them.[79] This element in the College's new charter signalled the importance of the government's decision to grant University powers. It also complicates posterity's understanding of the government's relationship to the University.

III

The close involvement of the visitor was no abstract requirement. The formulation imposed by the Legislature imitated the University of Toronto's charter, but with notable practical differences when the government did not insist upon its visitatorial powers. Its legislative claim made in 1866 and in practice did not align. Catholic norms for visitation filled the void. Whether use of the visitor was contemplated during debate on the new charter is unclear; visitors in English institutions of higher education were longstanding jurisdictions, which perhaps took their examples from Oxford and Cambridge. These universities of originally Catholic extraction, with colleges to boot, jealously guarded their powers of visitation. When Parliament sought to visit Oxford during the English Civil Wars (1642–1651), Oxford rejected the parliamentary commissioners. Only the Crown could visit.[80] Though as yet unconfirmed, it seems that these clauses were included by Parliament to guarantee a measure of control over otherwise independent charities for education.

In short, the visitor was the nineteenth-century form of today's Ministry of Education, except with a much wider ability to interfere in the internal management of the corporation's affairs. William Blackstone (then a popular jurist, even if some law scholars sneer at him today) described it best: the visitor is an ancient office inherited from twelfth-century canon law and acknowledged at common law. All corporations benefitted from a visitor, but only charitable corporations had the privilege of a personal visitor.

The creation of the College of Ottawa Senate was twinned with the first mention of a visitor in the College's civil charter. Royal oversight allowed the government to supervise the provision of education in Ottawa just as the privilege (and recognition) of the College's degrees was granted. The degree-granting assembly—the Senate—thus had to report to the Crown at regular intervals on the "progress and prospects of the University."[81] The prerogative accorded to the Senate granted a general supervisory jurisdiction over the College, vested first in the visitor and then delegated to the Senate. The Senate's statutes, submitted to the visitor for approval, were thus unimpeachable before the visitor, for they received approval before they could permanently enter into effect. Whether they were, then, the founder's statutes, or merely in conformity with the founder's will, is unclear. Visitation was bestowed, which acknowledged the corporation's charitable role, but it was with a much more systemic purpose in mind. The government arrogated supervision over the privately owned College's activities to itself, as it did at other institutions in the Province of Canada.[82]

Several nineteenth-century cases stand for this proposition, and for the claim that the Oblates and the legislators that created the College's charters were aware of the legal importance of visitors and the power that they could wield. The most prominent case where a visitor was used was at the University of Western Ontario, where, in 1886, the Crown interceded to disallow the creation of a faculty of law.[83]

More critically, albeit less clearly, the Crown exercised visitation at the University of Toronto after scandalous overspending in the 1830s. So public an incident could not have been overlooked by any observer of Upper Canadian university affairs. The Oblates would have known about it, even though no archival evidence connects the Oblates with Toronto's visitation.

The incident at the University of Toronto saw the bursar of King's College (as it was then known) not properly keep financial records, which led to a lack of accountability in the University's expenditures. When the Lieutenant-Governor of the colony (then Lord Sydenham) reviewed the College's expenditures as its chancellor in 1839, they were found so lacking in definite information that the College was ordered to undertake a special inquiry. That special inquiry admitted *mea culpa*, which triggered Robert Baldwin's proposed royal commission in 1843. Legislation to this effect died on the Order paper when the Governor, Sir Charles Metcalfe, prorogued the Legislature after Baldwin and Louis-Hippolyte LaFontaine resigned government in November 1843 in protest of Metcalfe's patronage appointments. Upon his return to power in 1848, Baldwin, now Attorney General, exerted himself through his ex officio membership on King's governing council. He created a commission of inquiry that partially explained King's lack of bookkeeping. This explanation was transmitted to the College chancellor, the Governor (now the more liberal Lord Elgin), in 1851.[84]

Baldwin's artifice in 1848 was officially confirmed when King's College was reorganized with the University Act in 1849, on the same day in which the College of Bytown was created. The process that

Baldwin set in motion through his ex officio membership on King's council was set aside for the expedient of university visitation. Lord Elgin ceased to be chancellor and instead functioned as visitor.[85] As the visitor, the governor was commanded by Parliament to issue a "Commission of Visitation ... to not less than five Commissioners," who would compile a code of statutes for the University and who would resolve differences between professors and the University.[86] Though these commissioners discharged their duty in 1850,[87] an act was introduced a year later by Henry Sherwood to amend the University's composition.[88] By 1852, Francis Hincks (now premier and inspector-general of education), introduced a university bill proposed by the Superintendent of Education, Egerton Ryerson, to deal with the issue. This bill preserved royal visitation, but made the University a provincial degree-granting institution without any power to teach courses; the University was modelled after the University of London. It only examined candidates for degrees.[89]

Hincks' intent with this bill was to centralize granting degrees in a single provincial university for Canada West. Colleges would affiliate to the University for the prestige its degrees would bring.[90] The University opposed the change, but the bill was passed over its objections.

A decade later, the University question was again brought to the fore in a much-politicized debate on the rights of denominational colleges. John A. MacDonald was by now the Attorney General and thus in charge of legislating on university business. When the Methodist Church and other religious organizations running colleges mounted an attack on the University of Toronto's privileged position, Egerton Ryerson again suggested a bill that would split the University from the collegiate in April 1860.[91] MacDonald demurred and again exercised the Crown's power to appoint visitors to inquire into the University's affairs.[92] He did so with the intention to bring in legislation only if the visitors showed that legislation was warranted at Parliament's next session.[93]

The visitors did not disappoint in this regard. They condemned the University's and College's overspending and cited their powers as visitors to suggest and implement changes.[94] The visitors' report laid blame on the University and its College for failing to implement the Legislature's wishes in 1853, which were, in part, to avoid the ills expressed in Hincks' university bill preamble:

> Whereas the Enactments hereinafter repealed have failed to effect the end proposed by the Legislature in passing them, inasmuch as no College, or Educational Institution, hath, under them, become affiliated to the University to which they relate, and many parents and others are deterred by the expense and other causes, from sending the youth under their charge to be educated in a large City distant, in many cases from their homes.[95]

The commissioners recommended that the entire system of upper education in Upper Canada be overhauled to avoid removing students from their communities. They suggested that the Univeristy of Toronto be a general examining board for the province. It could only legislate a curriculum and award degrees to students emanating from each affiliated college. In return for affiliation, the commissioners promised regular funding to each affiliated college.[96]

These recommendations were influenced by Catholics and by the Oblates who, though silent in these exchanges, no doubt communicated with their sister diocese in Kingston and its college, Regiopolis. Indeed, the Principal of Regiopolis and Vicar General in the Diocese of Kingston, Alexander MacDonnell, submitted as much to the commissioners in March 1862. He charged the University's current system of affiliation with being "all along inoperative" in no small measure because it diminished affiliates' independence without providing any pecuniary advantage.[97] This charge likely resonated with the Oblates superintending the College of Ottawa. Alexander MacDonnell was Bishop Phelan's first representative; Phelan had paved the way for Guigues' creation of the College of Ottawa. More critically, Ottawa's and Regiopolis's Superiors sat ex officio on the University of Toronto's Senate, although they do not appear to be regular attendees, hence MacDonnell's complaint.[98] Further evidence exists of coordination between MacDonnell and Guigues' Oblates in the decade leading up to the commissioners' 1863 report.[99] Ottawa was at such a remove from Toronto that its Superior could not effectively participate in the Senate's meetings.

Ottawa's long remove from Upper Canadian power influenced the visitor's jurisdiction once the Crown claimed it for its own in 1866, even if the Legislature was sitting in Ottawa at that time.[100] When the Legislature granted the College university powers, it imitated the formula contained in the University of Toronto's charter. The Crown and, through it, the provincial government, was empowered to supervise the Catholic corporation. This power, however, was not used through the College's history even though the government was willing to use its powers to correct abuses in Toronto. There were no pressing abuses to correct in Ottawa that went beyond the College's walls; the government did not exercise its powers because, it seems, the visitor's jurisdiction was interpreted as an expedient for public surveillance rather than its traditionally private supervisory role as a court of appeal at colleges and universities.

The structural consequence of the Crown's decision is unclear, which sets the stage for tension between Oblates and government a century later, in the 1960s. As the Crown donned the mantle of visitor, it putatively abolished the original founder's right. Ecclesiastical law, however, endured at the College, through the Oblate house, which continued one line of Catholic jurisdiction. This enduring religious authority created a logical loop in which the civil government claimed supervision over the College while ecclesiastical writs continued to run over and through the staff. Thus, even though the Bbishop of Ottawa, now the College's chancellor, was no longer formally the visitor in civil law, religious authority remained strong through visitation at canon law—a distinct legal system. The College found itself in the absurd position of being run by a religious charity (the Oblate house), but with a secular force ostensibly supervising its internal law. The College's governors, however, were not troubled by this alteration, and they had every opportunity to object. This lack of opposition lends credence to the hypothesis that the Crown's reservation of the visitor's role to itself did not trouble the Oblates, for it was a normal feature of Canadian universities.[101]

The College continued in this way until 1885, though the relationship between visitor and university was slightly modified alongside structural changes to the College Senate that brought it further into line with the University of Toronto format. Cosmetic changes altered elements of the College's powers to reflect the changed legal landscape post-Confederation. Those changes in no way disturbed the College Senate's status. In a way harkening unto the University of Toronto's dual structure as a civil degree-granting corporation warding over a collection of eleemosynary colleges, the College of Ottawa's Senate was established as the hinge between line faculty and the visitor. This move established the Senate more than ever as part of a university corporation that also had to act as a college council dealing with traditional faculty issues.

The changes that became law on March 30, 1885, with a further Act amending the Acts incorporating the College of Ottawa, were entirely cosmetic, which thus engrained the government's claim in the 1866 Act. The Senate was also enlarged, and the Lieutenant-Governor of Ontario (instead of the Governor General) was officially made visitor.[102] This last change reflected the new division of sovereignty between federal and provincial Crowns, where the province was accorded control over "The Establishment, Maintenance, and Management of ... Eleemosynary Institutions in and for the Province."[103] It also reveals some understanding of the visitor among legislators.[104] The closing provision of the Act upheld the Senate's prerogative to investigate the College's activities, and further stipulated that the Senate make an annual report to the Legislative Assembly of Ontario on the College's activities.[105] The new reporting structure slightly re-arranged the visitor's powers to better accord with an evolving view of government oversight into university affairs and with the College's new powers. The Legislature, itself an emanation of the Crown in (admittedly ancient) constitutional law, received reports from the university while the Lieutenant-Governor continued to perform the judicial and executive functions incumbent upon the visitor. These functions, however, remained unused. No evidence exists to suggest that the university was ever visited by the civil government and, in this way, the religious authority continued to be ascendant even as the civil power was formally expanded.

That power, however, was firmly entrenched in the College's Senate. Under the 1866 and 1885 Acts, the College Senate possessed the right to report to the governor, and to make suggestions concerning the College's affairs.[106] The identical wording of the Acts also imposed a duty to report to the visitor upon request.[107] By thus empowering the Senate to report recommendations to the visitor, the Legislature allowed the Senate to advise the visitor on its office. The Crown ensured that it need not often intervene in the College's internal affairs by expanding the Senate's supervisory role over line faculty, which thus granted the College significant control over its own affairs. These acts conferred authority to act in the name of the visitor. An appeal, of course, lay to the visitor, but even this appeal was routed through the body that acted in its name. Moreover, as acts of Parliament required the assent of the Crown to become law, the visitor *de jure* approved the delegation of his authority.[108]

The absence of real exercise of the civil visitor's power strengthened Catholic control. Even though the tension between civil and ecclesiastical jurisdictions was theoretically resolved with the Crown's deference to the Senate in the 1866 and 1885 Acts, Pope Leo XIII's 1889 charter caused the College to receive canon law, and thus imposed formal papal supervision alongside the civil power's claim to authority. This charter augmented the Church's role at the College. The canonical jurisdiction created a second ecclesiastical visitor to supervise the University's religious mission. The terms of this new visitor's jurisdiction were obliquely stated in the papal brief. The preamble acknowledged the College's excellence and standing as a civil university while referring to the Legislature:

> [A]nd the addition of museums and of all means and appliances for the imparting of a complete and thorough education, and furthermore by the ever-increasing number of students whom the fame and high standing of the institution had attracted even from distant localities, so that in the year 1866, the same College was judged worthy, by the highest legislative assembly in Canada, to receive the well deserved legal title of a civil University, and to be vested with all the rights and privileges which the other civil Universities enjoy through the authority of the civil power.[109]

The Holy See acknowledged the civil authority and invoked Canada's decision to grant university privileges to the College as a reason to bestow its own ecclesiastical privileges upon it. The onus, however, on legal strictures was different. The formal recognition of the "Apostolic See" implied governing the University according to "the established regulations and laws of Universities" that were proper to canon law, which necessitated the approval of the University's statutes by the Pope in Rome.[110] The Senate was burdened with reporting at once to the Crown as founder, and to the Holy See as patron. Each authority had an exclusive jurisdiction that recognized the other's.[111] Ecclesiastic recognition formally imposed deference to Roman Catholic dogma and canon law upon the College, which in turn created a formal visitatorial jurisdiction under canon law.[112] The papal brief reflected another level of charity, this time Catholic, that was overlaid onto the already charitable mission that the Oblates carried out for Canadians under the civil government's lax supervision.[113]

To be sure of the proper guidance of Christian souls, the papal brief co-opted the terms of the College's civil charters. Its final section enjoined the Roman Catholic now Archbishop of Ottawa as "Apostolic

Chancellor" of the College, to watch over the College and its policies. The command to the archbishop, and "the Bishops of the Province of Ottawa and of Toronto, who will affiliate their Seminaries and Colleges and other similar institutions with the aforesaid University, to watch over the preservation of a correct and sound doctrine in the same," delegated the Pope's visitatorial jurisdiction to the ordinaries whose dioceses contributed to the University.[114] The chancellor, who had a general jurisdiction over his archdiocese, was canonically obliged to ensure his parishioners' proper moral and ethical conduct.[115] The bishop's jurisdiction was once again acknowledged in the University's constitution. Submission to the Pope required submission to the bishop, not as a representative of the Pope, but in his own right as the shepherd of his diocesan flock and administrator of the Church's local property.[116] The chancellor was thus appointed titular head of the University in the civil regime, but had broader ecclesiastical powers to reform any educational or administrative error in the spiritual regime to which the Oblates paid greater attention.

Indeed, the College's new need to seek apostolic approval for its statutes mirrored the approval it required from the civil authority. The Holy See, by allowing the College to grant ecclesiastical degrees, caused itself to become the College's canonical visitor. The civil authority, moreover, appeared to recognize multiple visitors in the 1885 and 1933 Acts, where the Lieutenant-Governor was constituted as "a visitor of the said university."[117] The use of "a" suggests acceptance for a plurality of visitors. In contrast, section 14 of the earlier 1866 Act stipulated that "[t]he Governor shall, on behalf of Her Majesty, be visitor of the said University."[118] The legislator's absence any qualifying article denoted a single visitor.

Multiple visitors to the College suggested differing levels of interest and control. By the close of the nineteenth century, there were two visitors overseeing different parts of the College's charitable mission, which laid the groundwork for competing claims to authority in the decades leading up to 1965. The Crown had usurped the Bishop of Ottawa's common law to visit, granting it initial rights to supervise education at the College. This supervision may have ensured that instruction, though that of a religious minority, conformed to wider social expectations of the time. The government's failure to use or even to enforce this expedient meant, however, that the more immediate ecclesiastical supervision remained at the College. Ecclesiastical visitation worked explicitly to safeguard

Catholic souls through the maintenance of spiritual health. The Pope's 1889 charter further enhanced the Church's stake, both at home in Ottawa and abroad.

IV

The uneven division of power between civil and ecclesiastical spheres continued for almost half a century. In 1931, the ecclesiastical jurisdiction again stirred to better define the administrative structure of Catholic charities the world over. The Pope's apostolic constitution, *Veritatis Gaudium*, created a uniform governance model for Catholic universities. This so-called constitution amended the constitutions of all universities chartered by the Holy See. The civil charter was amended two years later, in 1933, to accord with the new reality.

In Ottawa, the apostolic constitution further formalized the arrangement first expressed in 1885. The governing Oblate authorities saw their hierarchal structure reproduced. Articles thirteen through eighteen of the Act gave Catholic universities a bicameral governance structure. Thus, the Council of Administration, formally created in 1933 as the body politic of the University,[119] was only constituted as an advisory body to the rector in the apostolic document. The rector's power over the University was, in ecclesiastical terms, absolute, much like that of a Superior's power over their house. The chancellor was, moreover, named the University's *Praelatus Ordinarius*—a rank identical to that of a bishop, which was no mistake, for the code of canon law recognized bishops as universities' ordinaries.[120] The Holy See explicitly granted the bishop supervisory jurisdiction as the Pope's delegate that before was read into the College's ecclesiastical charter. Whereas the Lieutenant-Governor, as civil visitor, was never called upon to exercise his jurisdiction, canonical visitation was increasingly being defined.

That ecclesiastical thread was further pulled in Oblate rules, which created a theocracy in miniature. The rules stipulated a hierarchy that descended from the Superior-General through his council (the Superior-General's assistant, the bursar, the attorney to the Holy See) and into the provinces (with the provincial or vicar along with their councillors and bursar) down into the houses with Superiors and assessors.[121] These officers maintained executive authority, and from them sprang deliberative councils. The immediate council for the Superior-General bound the executive authority in day-to-day operations, and the Council of Administration at the University of Ottawa mirrored this model:

> Ils forment le Conseil du Supérieur Général, et toutes les fois que le Droit commun ou les Constitutions exigent qu'ils donnent leur avis, ils doivent le faire, prêtant ainsi leurs concours au Supérieur général dans le but de contribuer autant qu'il est en eux de le faire, au bon gouvernement de la Congrégation.[122]

That reference to "Droit commun" gives the rules some flexibility. It allows a unique legal culture within the Oblate Order that places flesh to the bones of its bylaws. Little evidence exists to suggest that the Ottawa Oblates diverged significantly from these general rules. Rather, the flexibility existed for Oblates to adapt their devoted lives to the demands of local communities, and this flexibility might well have been deployed (as shall be seen) in the decade of the sixties to countenance devotion with more worldly university business.

The strictures of the Oblate constitution and its common law were enhanced by their association with religious belief. The Obalte vow of obedience prescribed just how much and what kind of contact with the outside world was permissible. The Constitution was explicit on this score, instructing as it regulated:

> L'obéissance ne doit pas être seulement effective, mais elle doit être affective, c'est-à-dire qu'il ne suffit pas d'accomplir ce qui a été commandé, mais qu'il faut aussi conformer sa volonté personnelle à celle de celui qui commande, et croire qu'il commande ce qui est bien; sans cela l'obéissance est imparfaite.[123]

Obedience requires a willing spirit. Each Oblate invested themselves in the power structures and in the operation of those structures. This kind of rule bound their religious life to the functioning of the little kingdom in which they existed. Obedience in that kingdom necessitated humility and deference in power relationships that reinforced a theocratic hierarchy:

> Les nôtres professeront envers les Supérieurs un tel respect et une telle déférence, qu'ils s'abstiendront de s'excuser ou de se défendre lorsqu'ils seront repris. En acceptant les avertissements

des Supérieurs, qu'ils aient devant les yeux Dieu lui-même, à qui ils se soumettent en leur personne.[124]

Obedience to ecclesiastical law was a tenet of faith, perhaps one of the most palpable in an Oblate's life. The rector of the College thus benefitted from considerable power over the Oblates of his house who worked at the College as professors or who were students. Though he was bound to take counsel, and especially in College business, where Ontarian law vested much more authority in the deliberative assemblies of the Senate and the body politic, the rector's ecclesiastical authority was nearly absolute. The counsel that civil law required the rector to take was thus balanced by an affective obedience binding Oblates to their hierarchy; Catholics were more generally bound to respect laws that applied across the Church or to their particular circumstances.[125]

The 1933 legislative charter is the best evidence for the civil jurisdiction's acquiescence to the religious hierarchy of the now-renamed Université d'Ottawa. This charter, along with the apostolic constitution, marked a shift in the University's fortunes, fortunes in stark contrast to the University's perennially unfortunate cousin, Regiopolis College. The Legislature updated the University's charter to reflect the apostolic constitution's focus on centralized control emanating from a select council of administration and to allow the creation of distinct faculties. Creating a formal council of administration and faculties further separated the degree-granting authority, the Senate, from collegiate representation, which was now conducted in faculty councils before deans, with central control exerted by an independent executive.

As these changes were effected in Ottawa, Regiopolis College grew resurgent. The Kingston College did not fare well in 1866. The College's charter went dormant over the passage of time. By the 1930s, the Archidocese of Kingston wished to rid itself of the College; the leader of the Jesuit vice-province in which Kingston was situated, Father William Hingston, was enthusiastic about establishing a Canadian Catholic university. He sought and won legislative reactivation of the old Regiopolis charter—a charter granted just as the College of Ottawa received its university powers—in 1931.[126] Kingston was once again home to a Catholic university, albeit one that would only graduate six students before its charter again fell into desuetude.[127]

The terms of Regiopolis's 1866 charter were similar to the College of Ottawa's university charter granted in the same year. Indeed, the two charters are only separated in the 1866 statute book by one other act, the incorporation of the Roman Catholic College of Saint Jerome in Berlin, Ontario. These terms were a set of basic university powers. A senate existed that could grant degrees and make regulations. The trustees at the heart of Regiopolis remained the body corporate; the Governor General was appointed the visitor, with annual returns just as was required at Ottawa. There was no regulation for faculties, nor need there have been.[128] Regiopolis was in 1931, like Ottawa in 1866, nowhere large enough to consider creating faculties. Therein, however, lay the rub. Without government funding, Regiopolis was caught between a rock and a hard place. The relative size of the College of Ottawa and its remove from the more competitive market in southern Ontario allowed it to establish a dedicated base. This base was acknowledged at home and, critically, abroad, when the Pope granted patronage in 1889. Regiopolis relied upon subscription from Canadian dioceses and from surrounding parishes. These were not forthcoming as the depression loomed and the renewed charter was simply not enough to allow the small university to survive.[129]

The College of Ottawa operated under the same structure as Regiopolis, but it amended its governance structure as it grew to suit the terms of the apostolic constitution. These terms better reflected Oblate culture and norms. Based on the terms of the 1885 Act, the College of Ottawa was governed by its Senate, which was obliged to report on the College's affairs to the government. This structure linked the College's charitable religious purpose to the government's desire to surveil the provision of higher education.

The decade of the thirties changed this view by moving ultimate authority at both religious and civil law away from the Senate to the more select Council of Administration, which was composed entirely of Oblates. Where the apostolic constitution created the rector as the ultimate authority at the College, the 1933 charter gave those same powers to his Council of Administration by making it the body politic. This council possessed a general veto over the University's officers and legislative bodies. When coupled with the papal rescript, the rector effectively possessed veto in the University's new constitution. That plenipotential power was only subject to review by the visitors, which remained the Lieutenant-Governor and the university's chancellor, the Archbishop of Ottawa.[130] While the charitable nature of the university was preserved, power incrementally moved from the *collegium* to the executive-cum-administrative council. These assemblies continued, however, to overlap, which meant that the Council of Administration sat and voted in Senate.[131] The executive branch remained exposed to some academic opinion.

The change between 1885 and 1933 was subtle. To put it teleologically, it reflected the trend in Ontarian universities away from collegiate models of governance to a more recognizable bicameral model of university government that came to be criticized in the 1965 Duff-Berdahl report.

A more measured legal-historical claim frames this change in terms of the visitor. The Church's increasing interest in and regulation of the University was accommodated by the civil power, which changed the University's structure to ensure that new ecclesiastical legal norms could put down roots. The University's governors, the rector and his assistants, formed an upper legislative assembly that could stymie the academic Senate if it wished. This potential rarely occurred at the Oblate university. The combination of Oblate house and Oblate-dominated Senate kept disputes, if major disputes occurred, between priests confined to their house.

The result of this existing informal setting for disputes was that the Senate was not often called upon to legislate. Its activities were limited to awarding degrees and making changes to program requirements.[132] These functions accorded with the Senate's jurisdiction to control the University's core mission: it alone could award degrees, create, or amend academic programs.

The Senate's changed reality, and the shift in the university's charitable mission, was symbolically represented in the 1933 Act as it conferred upon the seven-Oblate-member Council of Administration the duty to report to the visitor.[133] It was not required to submit its laws to the visitor for approval, nor was the Senate required to submit its statutes. The transfer of the privilege of reporting to the visitor represented the transfer of power from the Senate to the Council of Administration. The Council made bylaws, and its members were officers who directly managed the University.[134] Revision of the University's charter formalized practise.

Even as Catholic practice concatenated, responsibility for frontline operations shifted from the Council of Administration and Senate to the University's faculties. The 1933 Act created faculties, thus giving specialized *collegia* a measure of independence. This independence was expressed in the provision for faculty councils. This new deliberative body made faculties mini-colleges subject to the University's reforming power. These bodies united professors and faculty administrators along rough disciplinary lines. The central administration's hierarchal structure was tempered at the faculty level by these councils, which combined (and still combine) the legislative mandates of Council of Administration and Senate into one collegiate body (the councils were then composed of all permanent "teaching staff"). The faculties could further make bylaws for their government that were to be approved by the University either through the Senate or Council, depending on their subject matter.[135] The faculty councils thus held sovereignty over the executive branch of their academic unit in much the same way as the Senate held sway over the executive in preceding College charters. They controlled the elections of dean, vice-dean, and secretary, but were subject always to the approval of the Council of Administration. This approval operated in the same way as the Lieutenant-Governor's approval of the former College's statutes: disapproval was absolute and required a new decision.

The framework thus created by the 1933 Act and the apostolic constitution that preceded it created levels of administration inclined toward Catholic control. As the University grew, the fresh changes also increasingly removed central administrators from exposure to the University's front-line charitable mission. The Oblate house, oft mentioned but still lurking in the narrative's shadows, underwrote this corporate structure. The Oblates owned the university. On a more practical level, they staffed it, and these employees were subjected to Oblate discipline through their house. The two did not have formal connections. Rather, the rector was Superior of the house that contained the vice-rectors, secretary and councillors, and teaching staff and students besides. The makeup of the Council would change as the 1960s approached, but in 1933 remained solidly Oblate.

The Second World War reified the centralist gains made in the 1930s. The Oblate Superior-General was for half of the 1940s isolated in occupied or Vichy France, where communication with Allied powers was difficult. A vicar general for the Americas was appointed in 1943 as a result. This necessary movement away from central control began a gradual shift in Oblate culture toward local autonomy. Léo Deschâtelets' early years after his surprise election as Superior-General in 1947, however, reasserted central control until Vatican II, when a new Church-wide ecumenism took root.[136]

V

The two sovereignties that had arisen over the course of the University's growth in the main complemented each other but sowed the seeds for conflict if and when one asserted a disproportionate interest over the other. The civil power acquired authority from the temporal space where the University was located. The Crown incorporated the College and provided for its legal growth into a university.

These civil charters were complemented by religious law from the University's earliest moments as the College of Bytown. These norms depended on Catholic influence over the minds of the University's members. Religious discipline existed from the start. Bishop Guigues brought with him Catholic law at the College's inception in 1849. In 1856, when the Oblates took direct ownership of the College, the Oblate rules were superimposed, albeit still informally, onto the College's civil charter. Two constitutions came to govern its affairs: the civil charter, and those rules from the College's Oblate house. This duality initially settled the culture of the University into a pattern where the University's dominant qualities mirrored the Oblate corporation: religious and eleemosynary. Whereas civil control remained, the University's mission, to educate in a Catholic tradition, remained its guiding principle throughout the subsequent canonical and civil enactments.

The University's visitors, in their roles as final arbiters of internal law, could not both concurrently exercise their jurisdiction. Doing so would jeopardize the legitimacy of one or another visitor: the civil power could ill afford to run afoul of the Catholics because Ottawa was the largest university in its immediate area for all of its early history; the Church needed to co-operate with the civil power to ensure the University's continued existence. Therefore, while the civil visitor retained the ability to receive reports from the Council of Administration in 1933, the Pope and his entourage, the Archbishop of Ottawa, and the Oblate Superior-General as ecclesiastical visitors were ascendant. Within the University's constitution, then, the subject of the visitor symbolized a wider domestic reality: the Oblates of the University of Ottawa were more concerned with maintaining an ecclesiastical legal order at the University, and thus sought to mould the civil charter to their image.

CHAPTER 2

The Road to Reform: 1959–1964

> This I say therefore, and testify in the Lord, that ye henceforth walk not as other Gentiles walk, in the vanity of their mind,
>
> Having the understanding darkened, being alienated from the life of God through the ignorance that is in them, because of the blindness of their heart:
>
> Who being past feeling have given themselves over unto lasciviousness, to work all uncleanness with greediness.
>
> — Ephesians 3:17–19

The University of Ottawa in the 1960s was the last denominational university in Ontario to move from the older model of university government by a small executive council to a new, ostensibly community-based model, where a board of governors oversaw, but did not participate in, day-to-day administration. This newer view of universities emphasized the civil government's view of higher education as a socio-economic lever. Governors were drawn from all walks of life, but they were successful in their fields and prepared to bring the new, secular ideas of government into universities. These models differed by situation executive authority under the immediate control of a university's private owners via a council of administration or under the public's putative control via a board of governors. The change further reflects the increasing importance of executive control at institutions whose size no longer allowed for direct collegial governance. As a result, the idea of a university, at least in public discourse, shifted from a focus on saving souls or allowing them to flourish (in the Catholic sense) to an individualist focus on improving citizens so that they could participate in modern society: education created a prosperous and competitive economy.

V. C. Fowke, delivering a paper at McGill University in September 1958 entitled "Who Should Determine University Policy?," identified such tension in structural terms. He submitted that "two diametrically opposed concepts" existed that shaped consideration of "the main issues arising in the control of university policy." These concepts pitted "the idea of a self-governing community of scholars" dispensing charity on its terms against "the view that a university ought properly to be patterned after the modern business corporation."[1] The latter model increased efficiency and a sense of accountability to government and taxpayers. These poles set the stakes. As a "modern business corporation," the university required a board of directors separate from its servants, the academics that dispensed education. A board could inject the surrounding community's views into the university's administration. Taking in these views, however, exposed the scholarly community to a not wholly welcome influence. The danger was especially palpable to Oblates, whose religious discipline and law did not line up with the provincial government's expectations, nor did these expectations (to Oblate minds, at least) attend to the community's needs.

Cleavage between church and state is apparent in Georges Simard's works immediately preceding the University's transformation. Simard (1878–1956) was an Oblate theologian who, like his colleague Marcel Bélanger, was interested in Saint Augustine's works. His politics, as they related to the University, centred on linguistic tension between French- and English-speaking Catholics. In the early twentieth century, Simard (like many of his brothers) saw the College of Ottawa as a pillar of Franco-Ontarian nationalism. In the wake of the Regulation 17 crisis, Simard turned from nationalist to loyalist.[2] He advanced a united Catholic front. This position allowed him to express the University's Catholic (rather than Catholic)[3] position in Ottawa and in Ontario: a repository of universal truth. Simard's position was apparent in 1939, when he reflected on the role of Catholic universities. He gives the classic view of the university first: "L'université est encore une corporation de maîtres réunis en des facultés et en des sénats académiques; elle est aussi le groupement de toutes les cultures."[4] Already here, that tendency to universalize shines forth. Simard went further by suggesting that regrouping cultures is best accomplished within the Church and its calling:

> Tous les citoyens sont liés au service de leur pays. Mais ce que les uns ont à accomplir au nom de la loi commune, par surcroît ou pur dévouement, les autres peuvent y être tenus en vertu d'une obligation propre, d'un appel spécial. De cette façon chacun, pour son compte, contribue à la véritable éducation catholique et nationale, celle de la foi assumant les richesses de la raison et procurant par là aux âges successifs et aux besoins divers des peuples et des milieux l'inappréciable bienfaire de la vérité intégrale.[5]

While citizens owe their allegiance to the government sovereign over the territory in which they reside, that government only extends so far into their lives. A separate, otherworldly sovereign exists that imbues education with necessary faith to link physical and metaphysical worlds through reason.[6] That link between faith and teaching was being eroded as the provincial government insisted more and more on non-denominational universities.

The University's Oblates were aware of these future challenges and engaged with them at the Council of Administration. H. S. Armstrong, Dean of Arts and Science at McMaster University, published a report with the Canadian Universities Federation in June 1959 that reviewed the administration of twenty-eight universities in the United States and Canada. Armstrong thanked Father Henri Légaré, Rector of the University of Ottawa from 1958 to 1964, for editing his work.[7] Légaré subsequently submitted Armstrong's report to his Council of Administration's advisory Committee of University Affairs, which was created to study the University's development.[8] The committee met from 1962 to 1964. It was composed of a cross-section of the University disproportionately comprised of Oblates, whether administrators or professors: the rector, the secretary, the dean of each faculty, and Rev. Raymond Shevenell, OMI (1908–2003), then founding director of the School of Psychology and Education, Dr. J. Doyle, president of the Alumni Association, Dr. Emmett O'Grady, a professor in English, and Father John Joseph Kelly, the Oblate Director of Saint Patrick's College.[9] The committee was composed of seven Oblates and six lay persons; there were are total of sixty-eight Oblates teaching at the University in 1961 out of 342 professors.

These members received Armstrong's report because they were considering a change along the lines of McMaster's 1957 move from a Baptist university to a non-denominational university. The report examined the use of academic officers in a non-denominational institution in order to understand how best to employ them in the face of "a surge of young people" seeking admission in the 1960s.[10] These conditions were nearly the same as those at the University of Ottawa for the same period.[11] Armstrong's commentary on the general state of universities in North America acknowledged the increasing financial pressure on universities to accommodate a growing number of students.

Armstrong's paper indirectly considered Fowke's diametric insofar as the growth of students in the decade of the 1960s became its focus. The management of such growth in Canada necessitated the examination of universities' government to "streamline" administrations. The paper advocated standardization of university government while maintaining constitutional authority in line appointments. A large bureaucracy was permissible if it was always responsible to the academic community. Fowke's diametric suggested the danger inherent in this kind of responsibility. The University of Ottawa's historical move away from a purely charitable corporate model to a more limited body politic belies some of this tension. Growth necessitated a more efficient decision-making process by the 1960s; it required a more specialized bureaucracy. Armstrong foresaw Canadian "non-professional" administrators, deans and vice-deans, suffering from an increasing workload that detracted from their academic obligations.[12] He suggested increased administrative personnel to facilitate university administration, while allowing "line" appointments—university officers—to govern academic affairs.[13]

This more democratic approach to university government was anathema to the Catholic hierarchy established in 1933. The Oblate's personal hierarchal obedience was not conducive to democratic culture dependent on a large and impersonal bureaucracy. More critically, the distinction between Oblate and non-Oblate teaching staff created an exclusive group of insiders more easily benefitting from religious administrators' attentions. The perception of such a difference among some lay staff caused debate within Oblate and University circles on the composition of the University and its body politic—the final authority that represented the University's corporate personality in law.

The debate on faculty's regulations under the 1933 charter, for example, turned on the degree of central, Oblate, control; Jean-Jacques Lussier, a Catholic layperson and Dean of the Faculty of Medicine, reported on the University's prospects, which forced Oblates to confront the government's desire to create a public network of universities based on the trust model. The Oblates pushed back. They sought to keep the University in their Congregation but were challenged from without and within. The professoriate's expectations were changing as the Oblates attempted to retain control in the face of pressure caused by the University's rapid expansion and from government. These pressures were pointed up after the fact by a Catholic commission that examined Catholic colleges and universities in the latter half at of the 1960s. The commission was composed with two of the University's own, Jean-Louis Allard and Joseph E. Roach. It remarked upon the tensions that could arise after rapid expansion of the lay professoriate:

> Dans quelques institutions, celles qui sont mal administrées et celles où les prêtres et les religieux chargés de l'administration ne sont pas assez éveillés aux aspirations légitimes des professeurs laïcs, on décèle une tension malsaine entre professeurs laïcs et administrateurs religieux.[14]

Some of this suspicion certainly played out at the University of Ottawa leading up to its reform. More critically still, tensions circulated with the Oblate Order. Conservative elements ran up against priests who wanted to move forward with reforms necessary to regulate the growing institution.[15] This chapter lays out some of those internal challenges, with a nod toward the rare public manifestation of Oblate frustration.

The lack of government funds hit the rapidly expanding university hard, which created a financial crisis. Revenue did not match increasing enrolments. This basic problem was apparent in the University's balance sheets between 1960 and 1965.

Table 2.1. Comparative Table of Operating Expenses for Fiscal Years Ending June 30[16]

Year		Medicine	Science	Faculties	Admin	Total	OMI
1960	Expenses	799 879	1 210 316	1 269 425	1 059 355	4 338 975	1 109 465
	Revenues	580 352	910 875	1 532 665	731 239	3 755 131	1 543 002
	Deficit (Surplus)	219 527	299 441	(263 240)	328 116	583 844	(433 537)
1961	Expenses	842 777	1 314 392	1 479 421	1 210 091	4 846 681	1 621 650
	Revenues	666 839	987 944	1 659 212	792 819	4 106 814	2 059 417
	Deficit (Surplus)	175 938	326 448	(179 791)	417 272	739 867	(437 767)
1962	Expenses	914 415	1 367 358	1 566 833	1 154 426	5 003 032	1 187 466
	Revenues	725 399	1 133 639	1 957 145	913 168	4 729 351	1 720 443
	Deficit (Surplus)	189 016	233 719	(390 312)	241 258	273 681	(532 977)
1963	Expenses	1 108 166	1 572 017	1 914 860	1 343 730	5 948 773	1 207 450
	Revenues	1 010 098	1 403 493	2 405 934	985 377	5 804 902	1 768 108
	Deficit (Surplus)	98 068	168 524	(491 074)	358 353	143 871	(560 658)
1964	Expenses		3 114 727	2 401 263	1 546 643	7 062 633	1 490 281
	Revenues		2 947 541	2 660 401	971 550	6 579 493	1 770 442
	Deficit (Surplus)		167 186	(259 138)	575 093	483 140	(280 161)
1965[17]	Expenses		3 663 938	2 831 123	1 827 267	8 322 328	1 018 297
	Revenues		3 394 391	2 969 130	1 019 322	7 382 843	1 549 060
	Deficit (Surplus)		269 547	(138 007)	807 945	939 485	(530 763)[18]

The University ran deficits each year leading up to reform. The problem was fuelled by a worldwide contracting Oblate population, which also meant fewer revenues to the mother corporation.[19] We see this expressed in the figures above; the University had nothing to fall back on. While the Oblates were, of course, aware of the situation, little seems to have been accomplished in Rector Henri Légaré's efforts with the government during his tenure between 1958 and 1964. Rather, the Rector laid the ground for his successor, Roger Guindon, who served from 1964 to 1965, and continued in the new University until 1984, to quickly conform to the provincial government's wishes.

Even as the University took cognizance of its problems, Doctor Jean-Jacques Lussier submitted the first proposal to reform the University's government. Lussier's 1963 report sparked debate within Oblates circles about the need to leave the University to its own devices, which was likely due to the overwhelming lay population and the manner in which Dr. Lussier presented his report—the Oblates only numbered 15 percent of the University's faculty and staff.[20] The Oblate debate was not visible to the wider University community. Tensions spilled over to some lay faculty and staff, but they were generally kept within the Oblate house. The lay staff would have their own discussion, be consulted in their own time, and have at best restricted input on the terms of reform.

The discussion within the Oblate house left an incisive documentary record on the University's culture written by Marcel Bélanger, the first Vice-Rector. Bélanger's arguments were conservative: they drew on a blend of facts and canon law that seemingly could not imagine an altered paradigm in which the Oblates ceded their obligation to educate. Bélanger's stubbornness is best seen in letters to Léo Deschâtelets, the Oblate Superior-General whose career began in Ottawa at the St-Joseph Scholasticat.[21] Faculty regulation was addressed obliquely in the same correspondence, which built on Dean of the Faculty of Arts Jean-Marie Quirion's proposal to supplement the University's statutes with further regulation. Bélanger discussed the rector's dual role as president of the University and Superior of the Oblate house attached to the University, an office recognized by the old University charters, but which had since been dropped in 1933. While considering of these matters, Bélanger advocated for the reigning hierarchy and legal culture. Indeed, his comments were trenchant to the point of sacrificing his political capital as an administrator. He argued so forcefully for the minority opinion, asserting that the University should remain Catholic, that he eventually suffered rebuke from Léo Deschâtelets—from the Superior-General himself. Bélanger's running argument drew on the University's ecclesiastical obligation to remain Catholic.

Marcel Bélanger represented the minority among Oblates and adhered to that old model of corporation. (His colleague,

Georges Simard, would have approved.) Bélanger defended the concept of a university as a self-governing community, but specifically as Catholic scholars: a charity that required private control to guarantee its mission. He argued against a lay view of universities as organs for public service and, more particularly, as socio-economic levers that sought to adopt the trust model, where a civil corporation administered public money to serve an announced public end. While Henri Légaré, Roger Guindon, and other senior Oblates likely sympathized with Bélanger's position, the financial situation was simply untenable for the Oblate Congregation. The pressure placed on the University eventually forced the adoption of a practical, business-oriented approach looking forward instead of back.

This chapter specifically documents the tension between Bélanger's position and that of his Oblate colleagues, who sought compromise with the government to keep the University fully operational. This drama played out between 1963 and 1964, and Bélanger's position also reflects the Oblates' wider concern for preserving Church sovereignty in order to educate in Catholic reason and spirit. There is no question that their desire sprung from a deeply held conviction in that reason and the truths that it provided. That concern, however, was counterbalanced by a pragmatic view championed most obviously by the lay Dean of Medicine, Jean-Jacques Lussier. Lussier's view found official support among Oblates like the Dean of Theology, Roger Guindon, and Rector Henri Légaré. It was also approved by major Oblate authorities as a negotiating position with the government of Ontario. Bélanger's minority view must be read against this result: the debate between Oblates fleshes out a concern for Catholic hierarchy and doctrine.

The provincial government, on the other hand, was increasingly keen to impose the business model that Fowkes suggested would become dominant, and that Armstrong thought might be paired (more or less harmoniously) with existing academic norms. Government insistence on its view of universities was about to reach a fever pitch with regards to the University of Ottawa. Before doing so, however, minor skirmishes tested the resolve of both parties, which wound up seeping into an exchange between Horace Racine, the Liberal MPP for Ottawa East, and Premier John Robarts in the Legislative Assembly in 1964. These exchanges are the culmination of frustration between Oblate and government negotiators, all of whom were working at cross purposes toward the same putative end: a more prosperous Eastern Ontario.

I

The trouble began with Dean Jean-Jacques Lussier's proposal to reform the University's government. He presented his unsolicited report by interjecting on Dean Joseph-Marie Quirion's presentation on December 4, 1963, addressing faculty government at the Committee of University Affairs. Quirion's report was itself a reform proposal that detailed nineteen articles creating a proto-governing structure, some of which was new, but some of which formalized then current practice. Lussier's rude procedure was unannounced, and it set Quirion's recommendation back a year to February 4, 1965, and even then his suggestions were only implemented at what became Saint Paul University on July 1, 1965.[22] Lussier's interruption tabled Quirion's report to instead discuss and study a wholly new way of governing the university that, though preserving Oblate control, would have allowed much more lay influence.

Quirion's project was an Oblate attempt to meet the provincial government halfway. Though the attempt was far too inward-looking, Quirion was tasked with sampling industry-wide practices while identifying what kinds of rules existed at home. The Oblates exercised their power to bring the university in line with government expectations, but this was too little, too late, hence the parochial nature of the task.

The limited scope of Quirion's mandate is evidenced in his correspondence. His letters to other deans at the University and to other universities, such as McGill and Sir George Williams, reveals an active interest in the examples of faculty management.[23] Quirion specifically stated in a letter to the Dean of the Faculty of Law, Pierre Azard, dated December 28, 1962, that

> A la dernière réunion du Comité des Affaires universitaires, on m'a demandé d'ajouter à la documentation recueillie auprès des universités canadiennes sur les statuts des facultés celle qui existe dans les différentes facultés ou écoles de notre propre université. S'il existe dans votre faculté de tels statuts sur sa structure interne ou son fonctionnement, je vous serais reconnaissant de m'en faire tenir un exemplaire.[24]

The committee mandated Quirion to gather information regarding university and faculty statutes. Such research was too narrow for a university beset by financial and political concerns that could be alleviated by government funding. Quirion's task could have been much larger: finding a solution that the government could accept.

The text of Quirion's report does little better. It mapped Oblate norms onto the University's civil constitution. The "Projet de Statuts" created a governing structure that significantly departed from the 1933 charter. It blended religious and civil constitutions, perhaps with an obfuscatory aim. It framed the University as an institution controlled from the centre outwards by one officer, taking advice, just like an Oblate Superior in his own house. Article one granted power to the rector far beyond his statutory scope. The charter granted him power, "subject to the bylaws of the council of administration," to

> be the manager of the affairs of the University and in all cases not provided for by this Act or by the bylaws of the council shall have power and authority to act on behalf of the University; he shall, subject only to the bylaws of the council as to the place and notice of meetings, have the right to call any meeting of the council, of the senate and of the councils of the faculties and preside, if he is present, at all meetings of the council, of the senate and of the councils of the faculties whether called by him or not and vote thereat.[25]

Quirion's proposal gave the rector power of veto over any decision:

> Article 1 – Le recteur de l'université représente celle-ci dans l'exercice des pouvoirs accordés par la charte de l'université.
>
> Il est assisté par un Conseil d'Administration dans l'exercice de sa tâche administrative et par un sénat académique, dans l'exercice de sa tâche universitaire.
>
> ...
>
> Le rôle du conseil d'administration est essentiellement consultatif et ses avis, pris avec un quorum d'au moins la moitié de ses membres et à la majorité, n'engagent pas le recteur, seul responsable du bien commun de l'université.[26]

This interpretation of the rector's role ran against the charter, which accorded separate spheres of authority to the rector, the Council of Administration, and the Senate. Quirion's version instead framed the Council of Administration and the Senate as advisory bodies to a plenipotentiary. The rector further held the right to preside over Faculty Councils and Assemblies in place of the dean, with power to reject the faculties' statutes.[27] This centralist character was further confirmed in article three, which proclaimed the faculties of the University working as "mandataires de l'université, seule propriétaire et administratrice de ces biens."[28] This statement was absolutely true: it did not bear repetition in statutes, which begs the question. Faculties might have exercised more independent control over their administration than first meets the eye, thus prompting Quirion to insert this declaration. Quirion affirmed that the central authority not only had a moral right to govern the faculties, it also had a legal right.

Quirion further limited line faculty's voice in professors' respective faculties. Article four entrenched denominational mores in the faculty composition. Faculties' respective professors, students, and academic officers were not granted an electoral or deliberative franchise. The franchise was instead reserved to tenured professors and some part-time professors named by the rector on the advice of the Faculty Council under article eleven. Such reservation aligned with the Oblate constitution, which extended a vote or a voice only to those Oblates above a certain age for certain positions.[29] The rector again had power to influence the Council's composition. The only right that all professors possessed was to advise their deans at a biannual faculty assemblies.[30] The faculty assembly replicated Oblate assemblies where the Superior met with all the members of the house to discuss issues of mutual concern.[31]

These reforms made faculty governance much clearer but did so in a strictly Oblate and Catholic sense. Canonical hierarchy was privileged in Quirion's proposal, which guaranteed the government's displeasure, should the proposal be presented.

Lussier adroitly interrupted Quirion's modest, parochial reform of the University's statutes to account for the government's most pressing requirement: non-denominational control. A telling exchange with Floyd S. Chalmers, a member of the Ontario government's advisory Committee on University Affairs, betrayed the government's strategy. Chalmers met University administrators to get firsthand knowledge of the University and administrators' desire for increased funding. He generally appreciated the discussion and left with confidence in Father Légaré's management. Writing on May 7, 1962, to Leslie M. Frost (the premier who retired into a prominent position on the government's advisory Committee on University

Affairs under John Robarts), Chalmers also noted the presence of deans and vice-rectors during his visit. A vice-rector "said that no board of governors runs any university in Ontario[;] they are all run by their presidents and deans." Recognition of universities' realities, in the vice-rector's opinion, meant that academics were best placed to administrate and supervise higher education. Chalmers reports: "Business and professional men have no place on a university board and certainly not on the Senate." Chalmers was an eminent businessman, and these statements rankled him: "I refused to accept this and in the end, the point was not pursued, especially with such contrary examples as Waterloo and McMaster to be cited." These two universities had recently emerged from denominational control with boards of governors. The University delegation pressed the point, insisting that the Oblate Congregation could do that which a board of governors only "nominally" did at other universities: provide effective supervision over academic affairs in the interest of the surrounding community. Theirs was a Catholic view, brought about by the superior Church authorities, and the local situation, which saw Quebec francophone students entering the University in numbers to warrant protecting their interest. The University's point was taken, and Chalmers closed his summary with the suggestion that the University not be pressured into making a decision.[32]

Chalmers's report reflected Rector Légaré's argument against Ontario's desire to take over. In a cautionary letter of April 30, 1963, Légaré suggested that the state discriminated against the University's Franco-Ontarian population by withholding financial support under the old policy of only funding secular universities and colleges. His argument was not well received in government circles, and this gives us some sense of at least a part of the government's reaction to Chalmers's letter. Leslie Frost, writing to premier Robarts a month after Légaré's letter, on May 29, dismissed the University's intransigence as the fault of Oblate religious superiors in Quebec. In a separate letter of the same day to the editor of the *Globe and Mail*, Oakley Dalgleish, Frost exposed the government's counterargument to Ottawa's claim of discrimination: non-denominational faculties were supplied with ample funding, already a dispensation accorded because of the University's francophone character. Finally, John Robarts responded to Légaré's letter on August 1, a full three months later, to reiterate what Frost had already made public—in fact, Frost had written most of Robarts's reply on May 29, 1963.[33] The government supported non-denominational faculties in aid of the Ottawan community; general support was out of the question.

Quirion's report was informed by these exchanges because it so plainly admitted opposing views of centralizing authority. Quirion recognized the need for change, but did not propose change aggressive enough to meet government demands. The Oblates were confident, perhaps aggressively confident, in their ability to manage the University better than any board of governors. Their confidence emerged from their lives at the University; a board would in many ways just visit the University from time to time. By centralizing faculty government in the main statutes, the university's religious character, so dear to that anonymous vice-rector (though we may believe him to be Marcel Bélanger, given his conservative character), was asserted. That centralization might have been welcome news to Chalmers, and to the provincial government more generally, had it only been a secular move. As it stood, Quirion's proposed centralization was a step away from the government's desire for more businesslike government, run by businessmen like Chalmers. To Oblate eyes, this move was myopic. It ignored the threat posed by men like John Robarts and Leslie Frost, who were politic when it suited them, but who both knew when they could press the University because they had a majority on their side. Frost's rebuttal to Légaré's claim of discrimination was a case in point. Funding for individual faculties considered non-denominational drove a wedge between those faculties and traditional Oblate faculties that were impoverished simply because of their obvious religious affiliation. The government was not blind to this reality; it exploited it to foment dissention in the ranks.

Before that dissention could express itself, however, Quirion's report had to be partially presented so that it could be brought down. The University's main statutes were published in Latin as a code in 1934 following the Apostolic Constitution and the new civil charter in 1933.[34] The book prescribed the University's internal governance and little else. The faculties for the most part remained without statutes, which meant that the only rules for faculty government were found in the 1933 charter. Only section 28 was useful in this regard: "[E]very faculty established at the University shall be governed by a council."[35] The council was typically composed of every professor, thus granting the collegiate a voice in the faculty's operation. They, and not the executive, were sovereign: "The dean, vice-dean and the secretary of each faculty shall be elected by the members of the teaching staff."[36] Professors' control of the executive made the dean *primus inter pares*.

This method of appointing executives was changed in 1961 by removing faculty control over the dean, thus weakening the collegiate nature of faculty administration. The move played into Oblate hierarchical governance and foreshadowed Quirion's still more centralist proposals; it also created more efficient governance. The central administration's man could become dean much more freely. This change was likely mooted in the increased administrative difficulties of the time. Growing student numbers diverted the attention of academic administrators from academic self-government to servicing a more and more diverse population. That increased burden created liabilities that defied self-government. The university was exposed in the blunders of its administrative personnel, so the wagons were circled. Faculty government was placed under the purview of a general administration exercising direct control over elements of the faculty's affairs. The dean might have in practice remained *primus inter pares* in this new scheme, but the change in method of appointment told a different story: "The dean, vice-dean and the secretary of each faculty shall be appointed by the council of administration."[37] The move to a centrally appointed dean formally shifted the balance of power away from the *collegium*. In this shift, faculties required further definition to ensure that the balance of power was not overly upset, hence Jean-Marie Quirion's proposal. Rules were granted from the centre, along with deans, and applied universally, which was already reminiscent of a business model rather than collegial governance. The change no doubt facilitated university administration, but already there was a trend toward centralizing authority that was once vested in the closest relative to the college in the modern university, the faculty.

This concern for faculty government responded to the provincial government's concern for efficient and non-denominational university administration. The central administration increased its written administrative apparatus to make rules that hitherto went unexpressed because the University was so small, authoritative, and self-evident. The statute book was supplemented to discourage individual faculties from having too many idiosyncrasies.

Quirion's presentation of these Oblate reforms on December 4, 1963, was interrupted halfway through by a more grandiose proposition from Jean-Jacques Lussier. The Dean of the Faculty of Medicine submitted a personal study entitled "Université d'Ottawa, Une étude sur les modifications de ses structures." His report worked in Quirion's vein, which suggests that he superseded the Oblate to propose a more expansive reform of the University's administrative structures. Lussier's work balanced Oblate priorities (keeping the University under Catholic control) and the government's interest in a non-denominational structure. Though somewhat bowled over by Lussier's move, Quirion seconded the supersession of his report. This grace allowed the Committee to recommend Lussier's report to its master, the Council of Administration, as the University's basis for funding negotiations with the government of Ontario—a radically different proposition from Quirion's mandate, which seemed informed by Oblate stubbornness to centralize authority on Oblate terms. After this motion was approved, the Committee rose, and the report Quirion had begun the meeting by presenting was taken up again on March 12, 1964, destined to pass just before the University reformed.[38]

The Lussier report was only part of a wider effort that elicited serious debate among Oblate and lay members of the University, though it proved the definitive spark for serious talks with government about reform. The University's administrators witnessed a domino effect, where religious universities in Ontario one by one fell to the increasing need for government operating grants to survive the postwar influx of students. This was the case with McMaster, which Rector Légaré plainly knew. It was also the case at the Catholic Assumption College in Windsor, which became part of the non-denominational University of Windsor in 1962. Ottawa was the last of the denominational universities to hold out against an insistent government; Jean-Jacques Lussier's proposal sought a compromise between the Oblates' desire to retain control over their university and the government's wish that lay people be placed in charge. By giving even an inch to government, Lussier's proposal raised the ire of more hardline Oblates, chief of whom was Marcel Bélanger.

Bélanger's opposition to Lussier's proposal sprang from a second committee study conducted independently from the reform of faculty statutes. The Council of Administration created a task force to study the tension between the University and the province in 1963. The group was composed of Marcel Bélanger; Roger Guindon then Dean of Theology; Thomas Feeney, Dean of Common Law; John M. Robson of the Department of Physics; and Bill Boss, the Director of Public Relations.[39] These members were senior enough to confidently articulate the University's lay and religious positions. They were also widely different from the committee of which Lussier and Quirion were a part. This specialized committee was responding to the provincial government's insistence that the University's charter be reformed along the lines of the University of Windsor. Bélanger was the chair, which explains why his stubborn view was what he finally wished to enact. Such a stance explains the vehicle for Lussier's report. His interruption in another committee dodges Bélanger's controlling influence around the task force's table.

Bélanger's writ did not extend beyond measure. Roger Guindon left his thoughts on the University's situation, whether for colleagues on the task force or for the benefit of a restricted audience, on August 31, 1963. Guindon's focus complemented Lussier's slightly later emphasis: He began by emphasizing that the University and the government were faced with the same problem. The University provided a valuable service necessary to the Ottawa community. The parties differed only in what kind of control could be tolerated. To this end, Guindon (in that parochial spirit of Quirion's faculty regulations) recommended, among other things, creating bylaws that forbade "religious tests," and that enlarged the "Board of Governors," as he curiously called it, to take in non-Catholic lay persons. These measures found expression in Lussier's later report. Even more presciently, Guindon laid out the Government of Ontario's politics:

> En réalité, ce n'est pas nous mais c'est le Gouvernement—et cela depuis bientôt un siècle—qui a introduit la question religieuse dans le débat. Nous ne demandons pas d'octrois parce que nous sommes catholiques, nous ne demandons pas de FAVEUR. Nous demandons seulement qu'on nous laisse rendre service à la population de cette Province qui veut bien se prévaloir de notre institution pour y apprendre les différentes disciplines qui leur sont nécessaire{s} pour devenir de meilleurs citoyens.[40]

Guindon's rhetoric framed the Oblate University as stoic public servants. The University was beset by a provincial government that insisted upon differentiating universities based on religion. Guindon clearly[41] saw the government's insistence on non-denominational universities as another form of religious test.[42] The Oblates' challenge, on this view, was to overcome the century of government rhetoric that framed consideration of universities as denominational (not benefitting from public funds) and non-denominational (benefitting from government support).

The Lussier report appears to take up Guindon's pragmatic concerns even as it couched itself in the language of crisis in order to spur its readers to action, but also to highlight a common sentiment among lay professors. His report provided a solution to the increasing problems the University faced, not least of which was the "court of public opinion" turning against Catholics and denominational instruction.[43] Lussier alluded to "certains évènements récents ... très symptomatiques [qui] indiquent clairement qu'au moins certaines parties de la famille universitaire sont atteintes d'un grave malaise."[44] The Oblate and University community were "atteinte du même mal." The University's financial situation was dire enough to restrict growth of professorial staff to meet growing student numbers. Financial relief from the government was required to meet the influx. Lussier baldly stated that professors cognizant of this reality, and mindful of their careers, could seek to abandon the University for other institutions able to offer better pay and privileges.[45]

The pressure placed on the University was heightened by the government's expansive power. If a workable solution could not be found, Lussier estimated that the government of Ontario would move of its own accord to reform the University by modifying the charter: "[L]e gouvernement se verra obligé par la force des choses à imposer ses solutions puisque la société ne peut se permettre que de telles questions [the instability of the University's financial situation] demeurent sans réponses." The government, however, was, in Lussier's estimation, reticent to impose a solution upon the University. It preferred to see the University propose its own reform.[46] Floyd Chalmers's correspondence with Leslie Frost shows that Lussier's assumption was correct. The palpable sense of loss of control over their affairs showed just how far members of the University thought that the government would step in. With hindsight, it seems more plausible that the government would have allowed the University to founder until it came into line. Rector Légaré had rightly pointed to the political question of francophone rights: the government was unlikely to actively trample them.

The principle of private charities being left to their founder's control allowed the provincial government to sidestep the political issue altogether. It was the University's francophone and Catholic administration that would face political pushback if it did not survive to serve the French minority. Lussier adduced a similar view in his citation of Premier Robarts, who said that the University need not be placed in an "embarrassing" position. Lussier extrapolated that the University did not need to radically change its governing structure; the power politics of the time suggested instead that Robarts was only being canny. The University placed itself in an "embarrassing" position if it held out to the point of implosion.

Lussier advanced a conservative compromise that sought to convince the Oblates of the need for change: co-operation between the University and government was in order. The Oblates would have to admit laypeople to the Council of Administration and divest the Oblate house from the University.[47] Such a move would split Oblate law from the University's regulations, which would leave only canon law left to sever if the University were to become wholly non-denominational. Lussier further proposed some movement in this regard that accorded with Frost's view of government-funded faculties. Lussier suggested that the ecclesiastical and lay faculties be divided. Such a move would effectively remove canon law from lay faculties, for they were to be split into a wholly separate governing structure that only met at the very top of the University hierarchy.

The government seemed willing to accept a compromise along Lussier's lines. At the Faculty of Medicine's convocation not a month earlier, on November 16, the Dean bore witness to an enunciation of government policy in a speech by Deputy Minister of University Affairs John McCarthy. McCarthy delivered a speech that explained the social function of universities. It was a utilitarian function that presupposed "self-fulfillment of the individual" through higher education. McCarthy did, in this instance, nod toward institutional autonomy as an essential part of academic life. He immediately launched, however, into a "broader view" of each Ontario university as a player in a network, where offerings and programs could be rationalized based on institutional strengths. While universities were left to "solve the problems confronting them," McCarthy advanced a formula based on the government's desire to regularize university education across the province. Correspondence and government statements after Lussier's 1963 report reveal an increasing insistence upon the University becoming non-denominational, against Chalmer's advice from 1962.[48]

The Lussier report kindled debate on the viability of the University's government that indirectly engaged V. C. Fowke's diametric positions between civil and eleemosynary corporations. The private, religious, and charitable character of the University was reflected in its Council of Administration, which was entirely populated by Oblate Fathers. The body politic was populated by those that the corporation was designed to sustain, and they were folded into a larger eleemosynary body, the Senate. Lussier proposed gradually phasing Oblates out of the University corporation. The ecclesiastical faculties were to be created as an independent corporation affiliated with the Oblate house: "Il faudrait établir une démarcation précise entre l'Université elle-même et la Maison religieuse des Oblats de Marie-Immaculée, tout en s'assurant que la Communauté puisse continuer à jouer un rôle de premier plan dans les affaires de l'Université."[49] His proposal preserved the 1933 charter for the lay faculties while creating an independent, privately owned corporation with the papal charter and university powers attached to it by consolidating the "intérêts particuliers de la maison locale ... en une corporation distincte de ... l'Université."[50] Oblates would remain on the Council of Administration; laymen would be added, thereby increasing membership from seven to twenty, with a guaranteed proportion of Oblates. The logic of this increase was that the Council became the "homologue des 'Boards of Trustees' et tout à fait habilité à recevoir et administrer des fonds publics."[51] A trust implied money from a third party, the government, which could dictate the terms of its gift. The Oblates would be removed from government funding.

After Lussier's report passed through the Committee of University Affairs, it worked its way quickly up the ranks. The Council of Administration debated the report's merits on December 6, 1963, and found it satisfying enough to bring to the Provincial Council meeting on December 12–13. On the thirteenth, Rector Légaré and Vice-Rectors Arthur Caron and Marcel Bélanger were welcomed to the Council. They presented "la version réduite de l'étude du docteur Lussier, préparée par un sous-comité nommé par le Conseil d'Administration" in four principles:

> (1) le nombre d'Oblats dans le Conseil d'administration : 8 sur 20 ; (2) le mode de nomination du Recteur ; (3) l'établissement d'une corporation civile de l'Université d'Ottawa pour gérer tous les biens oblats (y compris les facultés ecclésiastiques) ; (4) abolition de l'obligation d'assister aux cours de religion à partir de la 1ère année.[52]

A further decision of the Council of Administration authorizing the rector to present the decision of the Council regarding the University's reform to premier Robarts, dated December 12, was also presented. Both Council of Administration meetings had resolved the questions before them unanimously.

Rising from the rector's report to the Provincial Council, the Provincial (and sometimes University) visitor Jean-Charles Laframboise asked his Council to approve the University's principles, with the caveat that the principles, especially the first two, be subject to revision, and that the reduced report be withheld from the premier until such time as the Provincial and Philippe Scheffer, assistant to the Superior-General (incidentally, ordained the same time as Léo Deschâtelets), review it.[53]

It was thus that the Lussier report became policy for a time in Oblate circles. The report brought in ideas that would eventually find their way into The University of Ottawa Act, 1965 — the idea of distinct corporations, one being a public trust and the other carrying on the religious charity; and it generated the idea of eight members of the Oblate Congregation appointed to the lay University's Board of Governors. Once endorsed by the Provincial and his council, these ideas moved from the University's private hierarchy to the civil authority, but not without serious debate on their implications.

II

Marcel Bélanger watched the Oblate Provincial Council adopt Jean-Jacques Lussier's recommendations and no doubt fumed at this result. It is easy to see why Bélanger might not have enjoyed the changes being wrought around him. By 1964, he had served the University for nearly three decades. He was created doctor of theology even as he was teaching in 1938, the year that Léo Deschâtelets was elevated to the superiorate at the Saint-Joseph Scholasticat, which taught beside the ecclesiastical faculties' installation on Main Street. Bélanger later became Secretary of the Faculty of Theology from 1940 to 1947, and Dean thereafter from 1947 to 1952. He went on to serve as the University's first vice-rector in 1952 and became Vice-Superior of the Oblate house in 1958 until the end of his term as vice-rector in 1964.[54]

This long service to the University was done in the particular legal environment dominated by concerns that were most dear to Bélanger. His early education at the Angelicum in Rome speaks to the Catholic doctrine that he preached. That university expounded a Thomistic doctrine, which would become the focal point of the rearguard action that Bélanger would fight at the University of Ottawa as vice-rector. The University of Ottawa's Faculty of Philosophy was itself one of the leading centres of Thomistic thought. His early education created a conservative mind wrought in a medieval doctrine of canon law and religious observance.[55]

Bélanger began his private commentary on the University's situation around January 1963, before the Lussier report, by appealing to the Superior-General's intimate knowledge of the Oblate house and University.

From the tenor of their letters, the two were close, perhaps sharing a political or theological affinity. That affinity sprang from shared history. Léo Deschâtelets (1899–1974) was a former pupil at the St-Joseph Scholasticat in 1919, and he worked his way up to a professorship at both the University of Ottawa in the Faculty of Theology and at the Scholasticat by 1926. He completed his education in philosophy, canon law, and theology, like Bélanger, while serving as a professor. Deschâtelets then rose through the ranks to become the Superior of the Ottawa Scholasticat in 1938 after a sojourn in Rome, then becoming Provincial for the eastern portion of Canada on November 21, 1944. He was surprisingly elected at the General Chapter of 1947 — perhaps a form of musical chairs that department heads in some universities are only too familiar with.[56] The suddenness of his election in no way affected his success at the job. He remained Superior-General until 1972 when he resigned to return to Ottawa for health reasons.[57]

Bélanger's career, though more Ottawa-focused, included a stint at a Roman university, and he circulated also in high theological circles. As a leading Marian scholar,[58] he was frequently in Rome during the early 1960s as an expert advisor to the first session of the Second Vatican Council. He was also consulted by the Pontifical Commission of Theology to help lay the ground for that Council,[59] His notes, furthermore, show him agreeing with his Superior-General at that Council.[60] Bélanger deployed this familiarity, and Deschâtelets' intimate knowledge of the University, to make his representations.

Those representations find fullest documented expression in "Les O.M.I. à l'Université d'Ottawa." Deschâtelets refers to this unsigned text in return correspondence to Bélanger on January 28, 1963. The Superior-General ascribes the work to Bélanger: they are "notes" that Bélanger left for him before his departure from Rome, where they both worked preparing for the Vatican Council.[61] Bélanger's notes reconciled the legal jurisdictions controlling the University into a consistent private law. He expounded the civil and canonical charters to demonstrate papal supremacy over the University. This mode cast the rector as the University's chief executive officer while according with the 1963 "Projet de Statuts" presented twelve months later. The rector was advised by the Council of Administration and the Senate under the heading "fonction générale." The brief then contradicted itself by alluding to the division between "l'ordre civil," where the rector administered the University under the bylaws created by the Council of Administration and the ecclesiastical structure just laid out.[62]

Bélanger's brief tried valiantly to blend Canadian law and ecclesiastical jurisdiction, but he was forced to acknowledge a strict division. His perpetual vows, and the University's status as a Catholic university, caused him to perceive canon law as preeminent. Civil law continued, for the University was bound to the lay charter, but it was only a means to operate the University in Canada: "[I]l faut s'empresser d'ajouter que ce conflit [entre les deux chartres] n'existe qu'au plan des textes, mais nullement à celui de la conduite qu'on a toujours tenue ici."[63] Bélanger appealed to a tradition with which Deschâtelets was familiar. His analysis relegated the civil constitution to legislation framing the University's existence; it was up to the Oblates, in his view, to direct that existence free from interference. Long practice naturalized the two bodies of law into a single private law. This practice of executing the two charters as though they were one was later criticized by Paul Marcotte, a professor of English writing for the Association of Professors[64] at the University of Ottawa, for benefitting the status quo.[65]

Bélanger, commenting both as a vice-rector and Vice-Superior, was concerned with status quo. His knowledge of the tensions inherent in combining two offices that oversaw distinct cultures lent credence to his commentary. The rectorate and superiorate implied different considerations in the 1960s. The former lent his talents to the administration of a civil and ecclesiastical university staffed by lay and religious personnel; the preoccupations of an increasing lay population limited the scope of the rector's religious discipline. On the other hand, the Superior oversaw discipline in a religious community. Bélanger worried that government financial aid would tempt a religious leader to forsake his religious community and its charitable purpose. Bélanger desisted from his commentary with a telling statement: "[L]e chantage des gens de Toronto et le mirage des dollars" was likely to swing the opinion of the Oblates to favour secularizing the University.[66] Materialist considerations pressed against the University's religious community.

Canonical structures that ensured the Oblate's and the University's submission to the international Church needed to be reinforced. Canon law required papal superintendence over the University's moral and religious life.[67] This internal check was complemented by the Oblate right to supervise the disposition of University property, itself regulated by canon law that the civil power did not recognize. Bélanger highlighted those dual lines of authority in order to rebut a central part of Ontario's presumption against the University. The Oblate Congregation did not have full control. The rector, who was head of a council populated by Oblate priests named by the Congregation, was a case in point. That mark of ownership was checked by the rector's nomination. Though selected by the Oblate Congregation, the chief executive, ostensibly responsible to the Council and Senate, was formally nominated to his post by the University's Chancellor, the Archbishop of Ottawa. The local ordinary selected the rector (likely via papal delegation), which recalls one of the formal functions of the visitor's ancient canonical jurisdiction. The Archbishop's recommendation was then ratified, not by Oblate governors in the Council of Administration, but by the Sacred Congregation of Seminaries and Universities, which was a central organ of papal university governance. While the Superior-General had direct reforming power over the Oblate priests on the Council, the Vatican had wider control of the University that allowed Bélanger to distinguish between the Oblate house and the University's administration.

Léo Deschâtelets paid little mind to the irregularity of Bélanger's address because he no doubt appreciated the less polished version of events that Bélanger happily provided. Deschâtelets called Bélanger's report "un exposé [...] clair, aussi net, aussi précis,"[68] and encouraged Bélanger to come forward with any problems he detected. His tone was collegial, even friendly. The frank exchange of views between the senior academic and the Superior-General was as democratic as could be and emerged from an understanding of the University as a member of Oblate and Catholic society.

Bélanger's reply to Deschâtelets on February 10, 1963, took the Superior-General up on his invitation to come forward. He submitted that existing tensions were rooted in the Superior's lack of authority: Légaré's attention was split between the religious house and the growing University. The distinction between Oblate house and University come full circle in this analysis. Oblate religious principles were routed by a Superior who could not devote his full energies to either enterprise. Bélanger devoted particular attention to the lack of democratic culture in the Oblate house. Without the ability to exchange frank views, his and some of his colleagues' frustration only grew, and not just with the administration of the University:

> Vous savez, ces conférences à la communauté oblate de l'Université me mettent toujours sur les dents, et aujourd'hui encore plus qu'au début. Sans doute, la matière à traiter ne manque pas; et c'est normal que les questions abondent dans une communauté de quatre-vingt-dix religieux. Mais, comment peut-on les traiter à fond, ces questions-là, lorsqu'on n'a pas les coudées franches qu'il faudrait pour le faire ? Il est des rappels que je ne puis faire qu'en termes voilés, d'autres que je ne puis même pas faire, afin de ne pas incriminer devant la communauté le Supérieur dont la conduite n'échappe à personne. Il est vrai que de leur temps déjà les fils de Noé ont dû marcher à reculons pour couvrir la nudité de leur père. J'avoue que ça m'embête quand même.[69]

Bélanger describes an assembly not fully addressing the issues before it. Much was left unsaid. Obedience to the Superior was due, but his moral authority over the community was eroding and there was no move on his part to address the problem. This lack of "coudées franches" may well have been due to the discipline imposed by Oblate law. Obedience, that cardinal virtue, precluded overt, active disagreement, promoting humility that could easily become repressive in the hands of an overbearing Superior.[70] The rector's misconduct, moreover, was apparently familiar to Deschâtelets; it is unlikely that a senior University officer such as Marcel Bélanger would make such an allegation against his Superior if it were not already substantiated.[71]

Bélanger further suggested that the result of this lack of moral authority was linked to that steady corruption of the University's mission as lay academic and administrative staff displaced Oblates in numbers approaching five to one. Out of 342 full-time faculty, the Oblates had 68 professors in 1961, with another 400 mostly lay sessional professors filling out the ranks. Bélanger's preface showed his motivation: he was humbly submitting facts that might upset some, but that were in the interest of the Oblate's spiritual mission:

> En prenant ainsi le contre-pied de ce qui existe [the rectorate and superiorate being joined], je suis parfaitement conscient, non seulement d'aller contre toutes les habitudes établies, mais de refuser certains principes qu'on a tenus jusqu'ici pour sacrés et, j'ai des raisons pour le croire, de troubler certaines ambitions. Je n'en démordrai pas pour autant : la primauté du spirituel est une vérité qui demande à être vécue à l'Université comme ailleurs, à être incarnée dans les rouages universitaires, à commencer par les principaux.

Bélanger was conscious that his conduct violated his vows, but his religious conviction pushed him to write. The Superior acting as rector tended too much to expose that person to worldly concerns, which corrupted the university's religious character even as the Oblate house was adversely affected. Bélanger laid these stakes out:

> La pratique du contraire a coûté trop cher ici, le traitement de faveur dont a bénéficié l'académique ou l'administratif aux dépens même du spirituel s'est avéré trop funeste à l'œuvre universitaire elle-même pour que l'on puisse se croire plus longtemps autorisé«s» à garder le silence et à demeurer dans l'inaction. Encore une fois, ce langage risque fort de paraître révolutionnaire ou du moins inopportun. Mais, c'est en conscience que je crois devoir le tenir. L'enjeu est devenu trop sérieux et maintenant trop réelle la menace d'une catastrophe pour que l'on ne crie pas casse-cou et que l'autorité majeure ne donne pas le coup de barre sauveur avant qu'il ne soit trop tard. Vous savez à quoi je fais allusion ici.[72]

The rector's divided attentions between these divergent responsibilities diminished his role. More critically, his poor example, perhaps due to an overemphasis on worldly concerns, potentially affected religious discipline in both institutions, which in turn diminished Catholic university instruction. Splitting the rectorate and the superiorate from each other would cure some of these ills by allowing further specialization and attention to the problems that plagued each organization.

Deschâtelets appreciated Bélanger's warning and his suggestions. The Superior-General's response on March 23 qualified Bélanger's commentary as "une très précieuse source d'information," one to which he would likely refer in the future: a "coup[s] de cloche," and at that one of the loudest he had heard.[73] For all this appreciation, however, the Superior-General was conscious of Bélanger's increasing transgression against religious obedience. He asked Bélanger to submit his thoughts to the Provincial.

Bélanger was concerned with the Oblates' religious health, but his worry also explains the inaction that prompted Jean-Jacques Lussier to present his report in terms of crisis rather than constructive opportunity for growth. By December 1963, the University clearly saw the problems it faced with the provincial government but had not moved on them. This may be because the rector and his principal aides were distracted by problems within the Oblate community; it may also have been paralysis brought on by the overwhelming nature of the task. Whatever the reason, the crisis was made clear in Lussier's report, and served, as Bélanger would later admit, to galvanize free debate in Oblate and University councils, although little documentary evidence exists to show such cross-pollination between Oblate and lay University members.[74]

Even as Bélanger objected to the rector's leadership and to the general state of affairs in the house and at the University, Henri Légaré began to act. Armed with the Provincial's approval, the rector informed Premier John Robarts of the University's proposal. He met with the leader of the government on December 16, 1963, and met with the Committee on University Affairs two days later. Dean Lussier accompanied the rector to Toronto for these meetings. John Robarts, himself (like his predecessor and successor) a former Minister for University Affairs, took an interest in the project. He received Lussier's complete report and remarked positively on the separation of civil and ecclesiastical faculties, even if they existed in the same corporate hierarchy. He pointedly threw a wrench into the wheels, however, by asking whether the rector had studied the recent legislation reforming other denominational institutions. These acts universally allowed denominational colleges and universities to continue so long as they federated to a new non-denominational university built upon the lay faculties that the older, religious universities had first created.[75]

The first minister's question expressed his government's levelling influence over universities. Other universities in Ontario had come into line with the province's desire; Ottawa was no different. Lussier's solution was one step removed from the government's more radical procedure, but it was that step that the Oblates did not wish to take. Légaré parried the premier's question well by invoking the eleemosynary idea: The University was a self-governing community that did not wish to have its charter amended. If the government imposed its solution, it effectively violated the freedom it had itself provided as one of the University's benefactors. Légaré did not claim academic freedom. Rather, he claimed simply that the legal personality granted to the University through successive charters precluded government interference without the corporation's consent.[76]

Légaré and Lussier were faced with the problem of precedent, which the premier was using to effect: the once-Catholic University of Windsor had become non-denominational just a year before and had done so very willingly. Through no fault of its own, Ottawa was in a bind that transcended its charter. (Assumption College had only been created a university in 1953.)[77] The Board of Governors and the Regents of Assumption University of Windsor, and the Board of Essex College had requested amalgamation under a 1962 charter to form a "non-denominational board of governors" for the new University of Windsor.[78] This creation maintained Assumption University as a non-teaching affiliated body. More importantly, it allowed the Basilian Fathers in control of Assumption to manage the transition on their terms.[79] The Board of the new University received six of its members from Assumption College.[80] In the same statute book as Windsor's charter, the University of Waterloo's charter was also amended to specify a "non-denominational" board.[81] Trent University's charter, also found in the Statutes of Ontario for 1963, was already non-denominational.[82] The Government was armed with several quick successes in 1963, and the University of Ottawa's proposal diverged from that general model the government wanted to impose across the province.

Légaré knew full well of the government's success. Roger Guindon's submissions to the Council of Administration's task force were proof enough of the University of Ottawa's knowledge,[83] and Lussier's suggestions hewed awfully close to the government's model. The significant difference was that the University of Ottawa wished to remain a single corporation under Oblate control. Légaré bought time by asserting the University's historic independence.

Two days later, however, the jig was up. Légaré and Lussier made a similar presentation to the minister's Committee on University

Affairs, with similar sticking points raised from the government side. The committee was composed of businessmen and former politicians, such as Leslie Frost, Robarts's predecessor, who was the committee's dominant member, and thus the likely chair, although nothing other than a contemptuous Oblate appraisal about the opening of the meeting leads to this conclusion.[84] Floyd Chalmers, later appointed Chancellor of York University, Robert Mitchell, and J. R. McCarthy, the Deputy Minister of University Affairs, were also present. The Rector and Dean Lussier were accompanied by Lawrence Freiman and Roger Séguin, later members of the Board of Governors, and Rhéo Brisson.

It may be that Robarts had warned the Committee about Légaré's parry because, as the report was read through completely by the Committee, Frost raised several objections to sustained Oblate control. He took aim at the rector's continued selection from a "slate put forward by the Oblates" and that the Chancellor was ex officio the Archbishop of Ottawa. This religious influence was not what the government had in mind. Leslie Frost said as much when he then put much the same question the premier had put two days before: Had the University of Ottawa consulted other university charters, particularly Windsor's? He was so ready with the question that he distributed copies of that charter to the University's delegation, which suggests forewarning. Dean Lussier responded that the University's problems were unique enough to warrant unique solutions, a weak hedge along much the same lines as Rector Légaré's before the premier.[85] Floyd Chalmers, reflecting his 1962 comments, responded favourably to this hedge, but supported Frost by disagreeing with the University's uniqueness. Chalmers instead suggested modifications to Lussier's propositions to bring them into line with reorganizations at Windsor and elsewhere.[86]

Faced with a *fait accompli*, the University was hard pressed to advance its policy agenda in Toronto. The premier and former first minister were aware of the Conservative government's accomplishment with the University of Windsor, and they exploited these gains to point the University of Ottawa toward a similar settlement.

Marcel Bélanger, still angry and still writing at the very end of 1963, after the results of the rector's presentations were known, baldly proposed the University's course of action in the face of the government's levelling desire. Francophone minority language rights were a hot enough issue in eastern Ontario that Bélanger estimated invoking these rights was enough to push against the government. He agreed in this regard with some of Guindon's remarks on August 31, 1963. He argued for creating a discourse centred on the University's unique, bilingual, character (an approach that endures to this day). Bélanger acknowledged the shifting ground: "C'est ainsi que nous pourrons contourner la difficulté créée [sic] par la soumission des autres institutions catholiques et l'approbation de l'épiscopat."[87] The University could fend off the new reality seen at the anglophone University of Windsor by asserting a unique francophone identity. Bélanger's confidence in the University's mission, and its success against the government's desires, was odd considering the stakes for both parties. His reliance on bilingualism as a means of preserving the University's charter underestimated the University's financial straits, and the government's desire to see the University reformed.

He did, however, give an accurate estimate of morale in Oblate circles. It was abysmal. This state was observed by the Provincial in a letter to the Superior-General on February 7, 1963. The changes considered by Oblate administrators concerned the University's Oblate community just as much, and a free and frank debate was something Bélanger always advocated to increase morale. In Bélanger's view, the religious members of the University granted it its culture and its excellence; high morale was thus required to make good impressions on the provincial government, the media, and the surrounding Ottawa community.[88]

The Lussier report was an example of unilateral action (from which Bélanger had been excluded) that imperiled Oblate concerns. Jean-Jacques Lussier was, after all, the dean of a growing faculty of medicine in receipt of government funds. His position was that which Bélanger may have most sought to avoid. Dependence on government funds encouraged a materialist mindset at odds with Oblate charism. Relegating religious influence to a few faculties undermined the Oblates' Catholic endeavour, which was to imbue all branches of knowledge with respect for and concern with the mystery of faith. The Rector Légaré and Oblate provincial authorities accepted relegation, in Bélanger's view, too easily. A more protracted battle, one in which Oblates had a voice, was needed to defend the faith.

On the other hand, Jean-Jacques Lussier broke a stalemate late in 1963. The Oblates were still paralyzed in 1963: their limited experience in public relations frustrated attempts to organize effective public resistance to a government more skilled in public relations. The year was thus a quiet period of reflection, but financial pressure kept climbing. Lussier's departure from an incremental approach to pacifying government was the genesis of Oblate reform; it paved a way forward for a stressed administration.

III

Even as the University's Oblate administrators found their preference, though, the government applied increasing pressure on the University's affairs. Bad news materialized when the University's powers of expropriation lapsed. New legislation was needed to realize the University's expansion. The request became a bargaining chip that signalled a harder government line in 1964. Roman Catholic exhaustion also began to creep in: the Oblate zeal for its university was not universally shared among Ontario's Catholic bishops, which may have reflected Oblate administrators' deepening financial concerns with the University. Frustration with the government's line crystallized in Horace Racine's budget speech, where he encouraged increased government funding for the University of Ottawa — an appeal that was swiftly refused by John Robarts on the floor of the house.

Armed after their year of reflection, the Oblates began to indirectly express themselves. In early 1964, debate about the University focused on its powers of expropriation; Ontario was reluctant to renew these powers after the expiration of a 1959 Act that granted them. On the face of it, the government's lack of enthusiasm stemmed from the Legislature's unwillingness to renew expropriation powers to any university. University administrators were, however, skeptical. It seemed more likely that the government was creating a new bargaining chip. If the University complied with the wishes expressed by the premier and the Committee on University Affairs in 1963, the Legislature could be induced to grant expropriation powers. Such a quid pro quo annoyed Oblates and other Catholics at the helm of the University. It also spilled over into the political arena when those aggravated administrators sought assistance from Ottawa Members of the Provincial Parliament, one of whom, Horace Racine, rose in the Legislature to address the government's handling of the University of Ottawa.

The first volley in the government's salvo came on January 14, 1964, when Leslie Frost represented the opinion of the Committee on University Affairs' on expropriation to Henri Légaré. The powers of expropriation the University of Ottawa possessed would not be continued because resentment against the power of expropriation for universities was prevalent in the Legislature. Frost stated that a legislative committee had been created to study the grant of expropriation powers, and indeed a statute had regularized expropriation powers, receiving royal assent on April 26, 1963. This bill, however, did not cover the University of Ottawa, which was subject to special legislation.

Frost's role was to articulate the government's conception of a university as a civil corporation. Indeed, as a former premier now fulfilling an advisory function in the Robarts cabinet, Frost at once represented his view of the matter and the government's. He sought to create efficiency in an integrated system; the University of Ottawa, by contrast, viewed itself apart, as a system unto itself. By standardizing governance across universities in the push to supply public money to the post-secondary education sector, the civil power became better capable of assessing the management of those corporations to which their funds were given in trust. In this way, the civil power became better placed to standardize certain aspects of educational policy.[89] Frost explained that such a policy was necessary if money was to be fairly given to each university in the province. Frost closed with an assurance that his representations to Légaré carried the unanimous will of the Committee on University Affairs and offered to draft an Act with all the government's desired legislative amendments to the 1933 charter.[90]

At issue was the government's concept of a university, which had become the determining criteria for that government's financial assistance to universities across the province. Frost expounded upon the legislative definition of "university" in his letter, which laid bare the government's objective. A university for the government's purposes meant the "provincially assisted" universities, public trusts over which the government exerted fiscal control. The University of Ottawa was left out of this crucial definition, and Frost did not mince his words. His reasoning accounted for "other universities" that "met the requirements of provincial policy" by becoming non-denominational, an obvious jab at the University's denominational character. Alongside this stick, however, Frost also dangled a carrot:

> in view of the magnitude of the problem of universities, [he felt] that there [were] overwhelming reasons in favour of extending

powers of expropriation to them and, in such case, Ottawa could be included with the rest.[91]

Even as he communicated the government's exclusive definition of "university" to the rector, Frost suggested that a more inclusive grant of expropriation powers might be forthcoming. This mixed message evoked the government's end game: wresting control of the University from the Oblates by applying sufficient financial incentive to force them to terms. By 1964, the Ontario government no longer intended to budge on accommodating the University of Ottawa's religious character. If the University would like to receive government aid to continue its mission, it would have to become non-denominational.[92]

This pressure tactic was taken further when the Act granting expropriation to the University was passed by the Legislature. Frost made good on his word. The University was given special treatment in that it remained denominational even as the Legislature granted it favour. The resistance put up by Frost and, presumably, by his colleagues in the ministry, was a sign of the times. While John Robarts was willing in 1963 to ask politely if the University had considered other options, Frost now communicated more aggressively that the University had to come into line if it was going to continue to have government support. The expropriation powers were limited. The Act was only good for five years from its coming into force, and only for certain plots of land surrounding the Sandy Hill campus.[93]

As if his thinly veiled threat was not enough, the former premier went further to suggest ways in which the University of Ottawa could make amendments to its constitution. Citing the Lussier report under the rubric "recent briefs and proposals," he alluded specifically to the suggestion, adopted by the Council of Administration and the Provincial Council, that the University make amendments to its statutes, and not its charter. Ottawa's proposal did "not ... meet the requirements of policy which have been met by other universities, notably McMaster, Windsor, Waterloo and Laurentian."[94] Indeed, the Acts creating these latter institutions moved each away from denominational control toward a para-public function. That movement toward para-public universities was a legacy from Frost's years as premier. Each of the universities he mentioned received their charters under his government. The tenor of Frost's letter coupled with his zeal in 1963 suggests that he viewed this systemic reform as a personal project.

Whether personal or no, Frost dismissed the Lussier report, thus dealing a death blow to Oblate pretensions at continued independence. His opinion seemed brutally egalitarian: "[Y]ou [the University] could not do by bylaws what should be done by statute and, therefore, the requirement for statutory amendment is necessary." Frost insisted upon statutory amendment to force the University to accede to other stipulations: to make clear that the University of Ottawa was a non-denominational institution; to withdraw the power to appoint new councillors from the Council of Administration (nullifying Lussier's central proposition); and to have the Chancellor of the University of Ottawa "selected as in any of the other universities."[95] These requirements distanced the Oblate Congregation and the Bishop of Ottawa from supervision over the University. Frost further wished to see the Irish-Oblate St. Patrick's College expressly included in the University's charter, but this proposition was not so contentious, for Henri Légaré was good friends with the Rector of Saint Patrick's, J. J. Kelly, whose background in French literature was similar to Légaré's own education.[96] Though the provincial government would not grant a third set of university powers in the Ottawa Valley,[97] it was not insensitive to Saint Patrick's plight. It supported, quite unlike its approach with the University of Ottawa, the Oblate's free choice regarding this English college—an anomaly that no doubt rankled the predominantly French Oblate administrators, regardless of personal amity. These government demands would not change through the negotiations leading to a new charter.

The Oblates took the government's threat seriously. Lorenzo Danis, Oblate director of the Association of Catholic Hospitals of Canada, exchanged correspondence with Louis Lévesque, Bishop of Hearst. Lévesque had founded the Seminary, later University, of Hearst in 1953 through a subscription campaign in his diocese.[98] The Seminary affiliated with the University of Sudbury in 1957 and incorporated as a college in 1959. Bishop Lévesque experienced negotiations with the provincial government firsthand; Danis warned the Bishop against lumping the University of Ottawa in with Catholic submission in Windsor. Danis wrote on March 5, 1964, "à l'occasion du changement apporté au statut de l'Université de l'Assomption, à Windsor" in order to comment on the implications of Windsor's recent shift for Ottawa:

> Quelques-uns de mes confrères Oblats, désirant obtenir pour l'Université des octrois provinciaux plus considérables, sont prêts

à déclarer la non-confessionnalité de l'Institution. Ils prétendent que, par le document mentionné, les évêques de l'Ontario ont indiqué la voie que l'Université d'Ottawa devrait suivre.

Evincing discontent within Oblate ranks, suggesting despair tending toward disobedience, Danis asked that the bishops desist from using their "autorité pour séculariser l'Université d'Ottawa."[99] The relative positions of bishops, priests, and Catholic orders, however, doomed Father Danis's supplication. He highlighted the break between Ontario's Conference of Bishops and some of the University's Oblates. In so doing, the Oblate quietly asserted his congregation's ownership of the University. Such an assertion, however, did not account for the bishops' superintending authority over a university incorporated by papal charter.

Bishop Lévesque deftly replied on March 11 with a sidestep that confirms the ecclesiastical structure over the University. Using the College of Bishops as a crutch, the Bishop pointed toward his colleague, the Bishop of Ottawa, who was Chancellor of the University, saying that, regarding the Universities of Windsor and Sudbury, the

> action d'ensemble des évêques de langue française de notre province, le premier porte-parole ne saurait en être, je crois, que Son Excellence Monseigneur l'Archevêque d'Ottawa, mon très cher métropolitaine et votre chancelier magnifique.[100]

The Chancellor of the University, vested in the Apostolic Constitution of 1931 with a general supervisory jurisdiction over the University as *Praelatus Ordinarius*, was the bishop to whom Danis ought to have addressed his appeal. Lévesque notably fails to contradict Danis's observations, which raises the question: Might he imply that the College of Bishops was giving up on the University's ecclesiastical character to preserve its core educational mission? Lévesque had witnessed the 1960 Jesuit capitulation in Sudbury, where the University of Sudbury pooled assets with other denominational universities to create Laurentian University. Indeed, his college had come with Sudbury to the new Laurentian. The University of Ottawa's resistance to government control may have fallen on deaf ears.

These straits were confirmed in the Ontario Legislature's debate on the provincial 1964 budget and on university matters. Speaking in the evening session on April 30, 1964, the MPP for Ottawa East,

Horace Racine, addressed the "entirely inadequate" funding provided to the University of Ottawa.[101] Racine argued for fairness between comparable institutions. He worked against Leslie Frost's legislative definition of universities as only meaning provincially funded institutions. His argument for fairness took up Roger Guindon's and Marcel Bélanger's views of the public relations problem. The government could not discriminate against the francophone minority in eastern Ontario by hampering the University's growth. Fairness was then due to the University not only because it did "for this province exactly the same job as the other universities, in a way which is not inferior to that found in similar institutions," but also because the francophones the University served would be disadvantaged if Ontario did not provide adequate support.[102]

Racine's argument for fairness was not simply hortatory. He also argued from precedents acknowledged by Leslie Frost in private dealings with the University. The University's Faculties of Pure and Applied Sciences and Medicine received provincial operating grants beginning in 1949 to protect the University's bilingual character. The University's religious nature was a necessary adjunct in this scheme that, Racine argued, only depended on the francophone population at the University. Religious affiliation played no part in the government's granting scheme. On this view, minority rights could be upheld, even if denominal status was a consequence: "[N]ursing, psychology, civil and common law, library science, arts, commerce and philosophy are [not] in any way more denominational than science and medicine."[103] Racine's was the logical middle ground that informed the Lussier report. The only faculties legally bound by the ecclesiastical charter were the Faculties of Theology and Canon Law, which existed to serve ecclesiastical needs. The government's concern was in large part with the papal charter, which imposed an obligation on the religious faculties to conform to dogma. The other faculties, however, were not so keenly affected by this religious law. Such a reality had played itself out at Saint Michael's College when it affiliated with the University of Toronto in 1881. The Archbishop of Toronto, John Joseph Lynch, required and won exemptions from Toronto's curriculum so that it could teach Catholic doctrine in history and philosophy.[104] Differences between lay and ecclesiastical faculty were more pronounced in the 1960s, when the non-denominational faculties were increasingly populated by lay professors and students. As the other faculties for all intents and purposes taught secular subjects, the government's test was skewed in favour of the government's end: secularization and control in the public trust model.

Racine's view thus accused the government of only seeking to support faculties that were beyond a doubt non-denominational, rather than examining other faculties to establish their character. Such a presumptuous model sought to control the University through fiscal means:

> Of course, science and medicine are the most costly faculties in any university. But the grants we give to the University of Ottawa do not even cover operating costs of these two faculties. This means that in order to continue to produce medical doctors, scientists, and engineers for the benefit of the province, the university must tap the other faculties and institutes of part of their actual revenues and cramp their overdue developments. Is this fair when we proclaim our need for a greater number of professors of French, for a greater number of librarians, nurses and psychologists? As one of my friends told me one day, the actual grants from the government of Ontario to the University of Ottawa appear like "golden chains" which gradually could bring the institution to the verge of bankruptcy.[105]

Those "golden chains" were only too real.[106] Racine exposed an enduring tension at the University of Ottawa between faculties studying humanities and those in sciences and adjacent disciplines. The relative importance placed on these latter categories by government caused fiscal imbalance, which created a funding model that played into the government's hand. Sciences were given higher priority because they could achieve their funding and development goals with government grants, whereas faculties without grants had less likelihood of meeting development goals. The easiest solution to continue to receive what grants the University could get became one of drawing resources away from faculties that did not absolutely require them, even if they then stagnated, and granting them to two faculties that had a significant opportunity to grow[107] — and this, in a University that was expanding its physical plant to meet increasing enrollments. Meagre government grants only forced the University deeper into a financial crisis.

Racine's peroration brought fairness into perspective by analogizing the provision of higher education to the government's funding of hospitals. His analogy characterized universities, whether publicly funded or not, as akin to the independent hospital corporations that were funded by the Hospital Tax Act.[108] This Act provided uniform standards for funding hospitals that, in Racine's view, was as a fair model for universities:

> In accord with the Ontario Human Rights Code, hospital problems are solved according to hospital norms established by the civil authorities, regardless of race, creed, colour, nationality, ancestry or place of origin. No one has ever thought of excluding any hospital from the benefits derived from this Act because it was operated and controlled by a board of nuns, Catholic or otherwise.

Racine placed higher education on par with health care. Under this levelling gaze, he brought human rights into the mix to show how the government might be offending not just francophones, but also Catholics whose university was targeted for its religious character. The better way, in Racine's analogy, was to treat universities as service providers. In so doing, they would be required to meet minimum standards in exchange for government subsidies. Such a view spoke to a wider religious and humanist view of education. While the provision of health care was immediately remedial, higher education allowed individuals to situate themselves spiritually and morally in the world, which was an essential virtue in creating a full human being in the Roman Catholic understanding of the University's culture.[109]

Racine's speech was supposed to close debate in the house. After the vote on this aspect of the budget, however, Premier John Robarts rose in reply. Technically a violation of parliamentary procedure, the premier may well have risen for the opportunity to articulate government policy against a considered speech that evoked longstanding religious and linguistic tensions. Robarts simply asserted the government's historical policy of refusing support to denominational universities. He reiterated the recent experience of other universities in Ontario that shed their religious governors. The University of Ottawa was not the sole university subject to the government's policy. This view was meant to turn Racine's argument for fairness on its head, but the logic of that view instead perverted the equality that Racine advocated. The premier's inflexibility bore out Lussier's astute observation that, if the University could not find solutions to its woes, "le gouvernement se verra obligé par la force des choses à imposer ses solutions puisque la société ne peut se permettre que de telles questions demeurent sans réponses."[110] Racine sought to preserve the university's character. The government's view of equality discriminated against any institution that was owned and governed by a religious organization. Only non-denominational universities were treated equally, which is to say that only one kind of university benefitted from government funding. Racine nuanced his approach to equality by relying at once on the new Human Rights Code (enacted in 1962) and also on the Hospital Tax Act, where each demonstrated government commitment to the kind of system that Racine wanted enacted for universities.

Racine's speech was a stirring example of the injustice created by government focus on legal equality across universities over equity that could consider each Ontarian university on its merits. The frustration expressed by Lorenzo Danis to Bishop Lévesque may similarly stem from a deep sense of inequity, albeit directed at religious authorities rather than government.

IV

The University's inaction through the first half of the 1960s guaranteed that Racine's vision for provincial university funding would never occur. The rector was beset by problems not just among his professors, but also at home, in the Oblate house over which he was Superior. These problems caused some measure of paralysis that is attested in Marcel Bélanger's correspondence with Léo Deschâtelets. The Oblates were not unified in their approach to the government's demands, and that lack of unity led to a weaker defence in the face of a very insistent government. Whether, of course, that defence would in all cases amount to anything against a civil power determined to carry the day is another matter. John Robarts's and Leslie Frost's comments to and about the University during this period suggest that the government was simply intent on having its way in order to secure a stable and controllable system of post-secondary education in Ontario.

The government's discourse in this regard betrayed an uneasy relationship with the history of higher education in the province. While the government might not have consistently subsidized education in the nineteenth and first half of the twentieth centuries, the growing economic pressure for higher education in postwar Ontario necessitated government involvement. As Horace Racine correctly pointed out, the province's most egalitarian option for oversight of higher education was to move in the same direction as it had with hospitals—another growth industry about to receive full public support through the federal Medical Care Act. Government regulation of minimum standards for higher education would have allowed universities of all stripes to coexist. John Robarts and Leslie Frost instead articulated a policy that existed since time immemorial: denominational universities did not receive government patronage. There were, however, notable exceptions to this policy: the University of Ottawa's Faculties of Science and Medicine had received funding since 1949. Premier Robarts had the luxury of conveniently ignoring such facts in a game of power politics. The growth of the University of Ottawa was outstripping the Oblate's ability to finance their institution.

In such circumstances, it is surprising that Rector Légaré did not act more quickly. It took a layman's brusque intervention to galvanize the University and its Rector. Légaré's inaction may well have been due to divided attention between the University and the Oblate house, as Marcel Bélanger suggests was the case. That retrogressive outlook is, however, fraught from the start. Though he represented a minority in the house, Bélanger's access to the most senior Oblate in the Congregation allowed him some sway. He took full advantage of the influence that he had, but this, to mixed results. Léo Deschâtelets eventually tired of Bélanger's direct address (and he was perhaps warned that his communication with Bélanger rankled other members of his flock). The dissenting opinions Bélanger expressed would need to be tried within the local Oblate house and in the University more generally.

This seething dissent, contained only in some correspondence, may have caught the rector's eye, as Bélanger claims, and thus distracted him from managing the University at this critical juncture when voices of reform were making themselves heard in more local councils. Roger Guindon, Dean of the Faculty of Philosophy, hewed more closely to the lay view articulated by Jean-Jacques Lussier. The Dean of Medicine's view sought a middle ground between the government's levelling desire and the Oblates' reticence to give up full control of their university. Lussier's report was a bold move up the middle that ultimately failed, and perhaps even opened the University up to further government attacks. Demonstrating a willingness to accede to some of the government's demands emboldened the government to push all the more against the Oblates.

Légaré's approval of the Lussier report and its rush through the Council of Administration thus appear to be the final scramble before the chilling realization of defeat set in. At root, the report sought to maintain the University of Ottawa's civil charter, a move designed to maintain the Oblates in some control simply by expanding the Council of Administration and relegating the ecclesiastical faculties to a new part of the corporation. The report became the basis for negotiations with the provincial government, even though Marcel Bélanger organized an articulate minority lobby that would continue into 1965.

The Road to Reform: 1959–1964   93

Figure 2.1. Father Henri Légaré, OMI, first dean of the Faculty of Social Sciences and president of the University of Ottawa, standing on the stairs of Tabaret Hall. Taken between 1958 and 1964.
Source: Fonds: Miscellaneous Documents Collection. AUO-PHO-NB-38AH-6-30. Credit: Unknown.

Figures 2.2 and 2.3. Portraits of Father Roger Guindon, OMI, president of the University of Ottawa.
Source: Fonds Alumni Relations. AUO-PHO-NB-98-72-06-15-1 & -2. Credit: Jon Joosten.

Figure 2.4. On October 26, 1966, a historical plaque commemorating the founding of the University of Ottawa was unveiled at Tabaret Hall on Cumberland Street by Her Excellency, Madame Georges P. Vanier, the Chancellor of the University. Participants in the ceremony shown left to right included: the Very Reverend J. C. Laframboise, OMI, Provincial of the Oblate Province of St. Joseph; Mr. Fernand Guindon, MPP (Stormont); Rev. Dr. Roger Guindon, OMI, Rector of the University; Madame Vanier; the Hon. James A. C. Auld, Ontario's Minister of Tourism and Information; and Dr. G. F. G. Stanley, member of the Historic Sites Board.
Source: Fonds Office of the President. AUO-PHO-NB-3-88. Credit: Unknown.

Figure 2.5. Father Jean-Charles Laframboise, OMI, president of the University of Ottawa taken between 1946 and 1952.

Source: Fonds: Miscellaneous Documents Collection. AUO-PHO-NB-38AH-6-3. Credit: Unknown.

Figure 2.6. Portrait of Fernand Landry. The photo was used to illustrate invitations to the June 12, 1990, convocation ceremony where he received an honorary doctorate.

Source: Fonds: Office of the President. AUO-PHO-NB-3-48. Credit: Unknown.

Figure 2.7. Portrait of Bill Boss, director of the communications services. Date unknown.

Source: Fonds: Communications Directorate. AUO-PHO-NB-6-251. Credit: Unknown.

Figure 2.8. Members of the Board of Governors.

Standing, from left to right: Unknown, Jules Bélanger, OMI, R. N. Séguin, Roger Duhamel, Unknown, Père Cousineau, J. Charles Laframboise, OMI, Unknown, Léo-Paul Pigeon, OMI, René Lavigne, OMI, J. Paul Dugal, Arthur Caron, OMI, Unknown, Aurèle Gratton. Seated: A. J. Major, Unknown, George Addy, Roger Guindon, OMI, Gérald Fauteux, Lawrence Freiman, Unknown, J. P. Gilmore, ca. 1965.

Source: Fonds: Communications Directorate. AUO-PHO-NB-6-82. Credit: Unknown.

Figure 2.9. Portrait of Andrew H. Robinson taken between 1964 and 1968.
Source: Fonds: Communications Directorate. AUO-PHO-NB-6-320. Credit: Unknown.

Figure 2.10. Photograph of Père Arthur Caron, OMI, standing in front of a building. June 5, 1937.
Source: Archives de l'Université Saint-Paul. AUO-PHO-NB-38A-2-600.

CHAPTER 3

Reforming the University Government: 1964–1965

> Let no man beguile you of your reward in voluntary humility and worshipping of angels, intruding into those things which he hath not seen, vainly puffed up by his fleshly mind,
>
> And not holding the Head, from which all the body by joints and bands having nourishment ministered, and knit together, increaseth with the increase of God.
>
> — Colossians 2:18–19

The government mistrusted Oblate authorities because they operated in secret.[1] That kind of mistrust had deep roots in a province of anglophone Protestants. The University had to negotiate with Leslie Frost, the retired premier of Ontario, and he perfectly exemplified those roots. Frost was a devout member of the United Church,[2] and his piety allowed him a measure of empathy toward religious institutions. John Robarts was no pious man, but his business-like, laid-back governing style left Frost, a prominent member of the government's Committee of University Affairs, in substantial control of negotiations with the University of Ottawa.[3] Placing Frost in this position put an old-boy conservative in charge of negotiations with

Catholic officials steeped not only in Canadian legal practice but more fully in the formalities of canon law. This encouraged misunderstandings and missteps from Frost and from the Oblates, not least because funding a francophone Catholic university was a liability for the governing Conservatives. Investing public money required faith on the government's part that it would not be appropriated to scandalous (religious) use. The government's aversion to religious scandal grew from historical roots in the linguistic as well as religious divisions between Upper and Lower Canada.

These roots found definite expression in the nineteenth century amalgamation of colleges under the University of Toronto's umbrella. The Victorian and Edwardian push to frame the University of Toronto as the University of London's colonial cousin dogged the University of Ottawa throughout its history. Though Henri Tabaret was at one time a member of Toronto's Senate,[4] the College of Bytown was constantly out of favour (like all unaffiliated Ontarian colleges) due to the University's rapacious consumption of the surplus that ought to have existed after the University had appropriated cash from the Permanent Fund, established in 1853 to maintain the University and Ontarian colleges.[5] One Catholic college, Saint Michael's, benefitted from the University of Toronto's expenditure. Though that college was an inspiration to Bishop Guigues in 1855, just before he sold his work to the Oblates, its affiliation with Toronto in 1881 guaranteed Saint Michael's a prosperous future.[6] The University of Ottawa, on the other hand, had been specifically enjoined not to affiliate with any college in Ontario in its 1885 supplementary charter.[7] That injunction left the University of Ottawa out in the financial cold, just as it had been in its collegiate years. The result was that, as the University of Ottawa attended to local linguistic debates in the opening decades of the twentieth century,[8] Saint Michael's was considering becoming a larger Catholic institution.[9] The relative difficulties suffered by the University of Ottawa in its adolescent years complemented the Catholic university's historical suspicion of the University of Toronto. Such suspicions were heightened by 1964, when the Oblates were running the only Catholic university still resisting submission to generous provincial funding.

Oblate and Catholic authorities were sensitive to some of this mistrust, but, if Marcel Bélanger's correspondence is given its due, internal disputes in the University's central administration hampered its ability to effectively deal with government. These disputes only promoted unease between government and the University at a time when negotiations were becoming increasingly necessary for the University to remain open.

The Oblate sensitivity did not, however, preclude their scheming. By 1965, it was apparent to Oblates that a new legislative charter was required. This new document allowed the University of Ottawa to continue as a civil corporation with no religious faculties—the ecclesiastical faculties, the papal charter, and the 1933 legislative charter remained with a renamed University of Saint Paul. As this transition occurred, the Oblates left many of their fathers and brothers in positions throughout the civil faculties transmitted to the new corporation. These monks, and especially their Superior, Roger Guindon, carried Catholic values into the new university that the Oblates counted on using to promote "Christian principles."[10] They sought to accomplish this mission with the help of a handpicked Catholic Board of Governors. Their subterfuge would ultimately fail, but it was a plan that allowed the Oblates to cede the jewel in their crown according to canon law. This chapter sketches that pressure in Oblate and lay terms: parallel lines arriving at the same conclusion.

The Oblates sought to sidestep Ontario's desire for a non-denominational corporation. Their former stubbornness could not remain in the face of lay opposition within and without the University. A supple resistance was more appropriate. Roger Guindon was the likely author of such a policy. The government had, throughout the 1960s, but most especially in 1963–1964, gone out of its way to apply pressure to the Catholic university. The pressure spurred the Oblates to action, but it was ill-conceived. By 1965, the University's negotiations with Ontario broke down when, just as Communications Director Bill Boss predicted, its combative submission to the McCruer commission, appointed to inquire into civil rights in Ontario, went public. There could be no discussion once the government had been publicly attacked for impugning linguistic and human rights. Indeed, that kind of dogmatic response to Ontario's pressure was a caricature of Catholic inflexibility. It was time to change tack, and Guindon played into the government's hand such that, by June 21, 1965, the University of Ottawa was radically changed, even as Oblates still controlled the central administration.

In the face of mounting internal discord and external pressure, the Oblates resorted to a traditional mechanism for pressure relief: visitation. This device was employed like modern-day program reviews.

Every seven or so years, a senior Oblate (typically the Provincial or his deputy) would attend at the Oblate house for several days, question the fathers and brothers, and inspect the books to ensure that Oblate rules and Catholic dogma were being respected. With Bélanger's reports of strife and, perhaps, of scandal, visitation seemed due. Stanislas-A. LaRochelle, Léo Deschâtelets' Assistant General, was appointed to this role in the Superior-General's stead. He was asked to provide reliable information about the University to the Provincial Council, the Superior-General in Rome, and the Vatican. This general visitation relied on two jurisdictions. Oblate and papal control were being exercised over the University under separate constitutions, the Oblate bylaws and the ecclesiastical charter of 1889. Both jurisdictions required information in order to properly decide the University's fate, and each had distinct control over the University to different degrees. LaRochelle's information thus paved the way for an independent review of the claims at once being made by University authorities, such as the rector and Jean-Jacques Lussier, and personal commentators, such as Marcel Bélanger. LaRochelle's findings led, in part, to a change of leadership that was, if Marcel Bélanger may be accorded representative weight, much needed.

Bélanger was, however, shunted aside in this change. His final attempt to influence the Superior-General was a step beyond the mark, though his point was taken. Légaré was sent away to become Bishop of Labrador–Schefferville in Quebec. Whether penance or a promotion, Légaré was out, and his former positions, Rector and Superior of the Oblate house, were split. Even as Bélanger was removed from his University duties, he gleaned some reward for his outspokenness by acceding to the superiorate. He was under the rector's authority, but he was able to implement the kind of free and frank exchanges that characterized his letters and that he wished to have had with his peers. Bélanger lost his seat as vice-rector, thus paving the way for a less conservative approach to the University. These moves in Bélanger's regard complemented personnel changes at the University proper. Roger Guindon, a young dean of theology, was promoted to the top job at a time when the energy of his youth was most needed.

Such energy was needed because lay troubles contributed to the change in leadership and signalled deeper tensions against the Oblate administration that were more fully actualized after the reform. Two lay camps existed: Catholic supporters and detractors. Conflict between the administration and lay faculty before 1965 contributed to the feeling of mistrust that Marcel Bélanger pointed up in 1964. The vice-rector's concern was reflected in Paul Marcotte's submission to the Duff-Berdahl Commission on university government, which conducted interviews at the University in February 1965. Marcotte wrote on behalf of the Association of Professors and he delivered a frank appraisal of the Oblate administration and the lay culture surrounding it. His positions were fair, but the association Marcotte represented nevertheless worked in the lay interest. Other professors, acting individually, supplied further evidence of grave concern for their academic units.

This correspondence suggests that Oblate administrators were overwhelmed. They dropped requests and mishandled staff's grievances. These slips created a culture of mistrust between lay and religious sectors that, ultimately, impacted unity of purpose even as it reflected the broader mistrust between Oblate authorities and the provincial government. The Oblates, due to their constitution and vows, held a common purpose; lay faculty theoretically did as well by virtue of their attachment to the University. Low morale engendered by a sense of detachment from the true ruling class at the University eroded lay faith. Lay professors increasingly felt divorced from a involvement in administrative business. The feeling manifested itself as cynicism.

That cynicism contributed to reform. With lay professors clamouring for additional resources on the one hand, and the government insisting on a non-denominational university in exchange for funds on the other, the Oblates had little choice. The University of Ottawa Act, 1965, was passed without fanfare in the Legislature, and came quickly when the University, considering its financial straits and utter lack of headway in negotiations with government, found the government's offer acceptable. Conversely, the government was not willing to budge on reforms, which reflected some of the University's lay faculty's opinions even as it was designed to reflect a broader consensus among Ontarians.

I

Stanislas-A. LaRochelle's official visit in 1964 called out the Oblate community's hitherto-concealed opinions. Views generally diverged between members of the Oblate house and the University's Council of Administration in a pattern that mapped onto Marcel Bélanger's complaints to Léo Deschâtelets. The Council wanted to move from ecclesiastical control to a mixed governance model as proposed by Dean Lussier. This position offended Oblates with a more straightforward (and imperialist) view of their educational mission in Ottawa. LaRochelle, whose presence elicited this controversy, had to mediate it in some wise, but he quickly faded from view. His report ultimately saddled the Council of Administration with the burden of strict obedience to canon law as the Council became increasingly cognizant of the University's dire straits. Roger Guindon rose from this maelstrom. He showed empathy that came to serve him in good stead when, just after the visitor completed his observations, he was elevated from dean to rector. His views became the new University's backbone as he positioned himself (wittingly or not) as the compromise candidate to replace Henri Légaré.

LaRochelle's visit prompted change in leadership. Léo Deschâtelets appointed LaRochelle because LaRochelle (like Deschâtelets) was familiar with the University. Indeed, LaRochelle had visited as Provincial in 1951.[11] He had also, perhaps over the course of some other visits while in Deschâtelets' service, published his thoughts on the difficulties of visiting houses in an international order:

> En pratique, il y a beaucoup de flottement, voire des oublis, sur les situations respectives. De plus, les diversités d'opinions ne rendent pas toujours facile le travail de la Visite. Il arrive qu'un groupe crie à la ruine des bonnes habitudes, tandis qu'un autre s'impatiente de la lenteur des changements. On rencontre des styles de vie plus ou moins conscients, des structures mentales, personnelles ou régionales, qui semblent constituer d'inquiétantes installations. On peut avoir exagéré la syntonisation de la vie religieuse avec la sensibilité moderne; exagéré aussi la submersion de l'apôtre dans l'actualité. Après des années de course à l'idéal, à la perfection, on en arrive parfois à se résigner à un humanisme trop terrestre, à un processus progressif de nivellement, sans courage dans l'ascèse, et sans élan vers le divin. Des rappels du Visiteur, au *sursum corda*, retentissent parfois comme des désapprobations directes, peu agréables à entendre. Pourtant, il faudrait pouvoir compter sur des interventions internes, pour réaliser les réformes opportunes, plutôt que sur des révolutions venant du dehors.[12]

The visitor's role, in LaRochelle's mind, was to mirror the visited community's spiritual foibles. Conflicts about changing manifestations of spiritual engagement on earth within tight-knit communities were aired to this third party, who took a global view of the Order's objectives and laws. Reminders from the visitor thus came as exhortations with the force of Oblate hierarchy behind them. The *sursum corda* to which LaRochelle referred encouraged the visited to lift their eyes from worldly concerns. By thus refocusing on the Order's spiritual goals while accounting for local particularities, individuals could again generatively express their apostolate.

LaRochelle's 1964 visit did focus on these concerns, but his dual mandate required a wider view that encompassed lay members of the University. Oblate and papal constitutions were to be upheld in an event that involved thorough perusal of the University's records and interviews with Oblates and lay faculty. Though the visit was Oblate-forward (no surprise, given Oblate political dominance), the opinions of lay faculty lent perspective to tensions in the Oblate house: Will the University remain under Oblate control, or will the Congregation and the Church cede their controlling stake to the government of Ontario? This question needed firm answer from a third party capable of understanding the University for its strengths and weaknesses, and LaRochelle was capable of convincing Oblates of his conclusions. LaRochelle's experience and his position in the Oblate hierarchy secured for him and for Deschâtelets the moral authority needed to cut through Oblate dissenting voices that may have sprung up when he remarked in a postscript that "Cent copies de cet Acte de Visite de 1964 ont été distribuées aux Oblates de l'Université."[13] His religious peers received a copy of his report, and the community's reaction was fierce.[14]

The visitor had a fact-finding mandate concordant with his views on visitation. His activities do not suggest that he undertook any kind of delegated decision-making or reforming power, with one exception. He commanded the University to above all respect canon law. Canadian law was to be complied with only to legitimate canonical decisions at civil law:

> À l'administration centrale, on distinguait jusqu'ici l'action personnelle prise par le Supérieur, après vote délibératif ou consultatif de son Conseil, et l'action collégiale de la Corporation civile, présidée par le Recteur, avec vote décisif. Le Conseil doit se régler, jusqu'à nouvel ordre, d'après les prescriptions canoniques, puis légaliser au besoin ses actes, au regard de la loi civile, en

procédant selon la charte civile. Il s'agit seulement de protéger la foi civile des actes canoniques; il ne s'agit pas de trahir une cause ecclésiastique au bénéfice de la foi civile.[15]

The Canadian distinction between Oblate faith and corporate identity and the University's civil structure did not comply with canon law. LaRochelle identified this failure as a failure of the Oblate vow of obedience. Lack of obedience to Catholic law was a lack of respect for the faith that affected the University's governors personally, but also impacted the minds and souls beneath them. The manner in which the University created its private law—not simply its content—had to accord with Catholic values.[16] Hence Dean Quirion's 1963 proposal to reform faculty regulation in favour of increased executive power.

LaRochelle's fact-finding mission thus deviated slightly from the visitors that preceded him. He surveyed the scene, and he found things at the University wanting. His pronouncement to obey canon law was the death knell for Oblate control even as Oblates stirred to save their enterprise. It demonstrated to the University's Oblates and their superiors just how removed from front-line operations the Oblates had become; they had to solve a temporal problem with a civil authority, yet their vow of obedience to Oblate and church norms complicated any potential solution. The civil power actively eschewed Catholic norms.

This tension between ecclesiastical regulation and civil demands became apparent in meetings with the visitor. Oblates of all stripes used this forum to debate. LaRochelle summoned the community to first meet him on April 24, 1964. He met the Oblates "de la rue Laurier," who were connected with the University. Laurier Street (East) still houses the University's central administration building, Tabaret Hall, and the plot immediately west of this building remains home to an Oblate mission. These University Oblates met under an agenda that is suggestive of the threat to the Oblate enterprise (and of LaRochelle's mission):

Statu Quo?
Réduction de l'entreprise ?
Université Catholique ?
Nouvelle administration ?
Propriétés et chartes ?
Guerre froide ?[17]

These topics are fairly standard based on the discussions LaRochelle had with senior Oblates, like second Vice-Rector Arthur Caron, Henri Légaré, and Roger Guindon. They are also standard in connection to the discussions between the University and the Oblate Provincial Council about the Lussier report, and again between Marcel Bélanger and Léo Deschâtelets. Each evoked a particular thread: Bélanger advocated the "Statu Quo" or, failing that, a "Reduction de l'entreprise" to more humble roots that maintained University's Catholic status. The University, with Légaré and Guindon at the forefront (though Arthur Caron figured into this mix), was considering a rearrangement of its "Propriétés et chartes" as well as a new administration that took the government's lay view into account. These various threads culminated in the visitor's inquiry—as impartial an assessment of the University's future as could be had from inside the Catholic hierarchy, and LaRochelle was careful to meet his brothers several more times to set the record straight. He clarified to Oblates that Lussier's report did not advocate removing the Oblates from power. Quite the contrary: Lussier designed his report to meet Oblate expectations.[18]

LaRochelle could see the pieces moving across the Board as he presented his findings at a May 4 meeting of the Oblate local council that expanded on some headings from April 24. He took the opportunity to chastize local Oblate administrators and command them to obey canon law. He deferred to university authorities, to the "Recteur, aux Doyens, au Sénat académique, au Conseil d'administration locale, au Trésorier, voire au Supérieur provincial des Oblats," in Pauline humility, to implement this command.[19]

LaRochelle's deference, however, seems only to have extended so far. His report spurred the Council of Administration to act; the visitor sat beside his colleagues as they did so. The Council's agenda considers the University's future that, though again no fuller record exists, still better shows the University's slow movement away from conservative opposition to embracing reform, even though canon law is supposed to reign supreme. The Oblate house and University are treated as separate units in these points, which recognizes their legal separation in Canadian law. Discussion of the twin functions of the Superior and of Oblate control over the University are placed side by side, which further evokes that separation.

These discussions led to action. A member of the Council proposed to modify bylaw 1 of 1936 to increase the number of councillors on the Council of Administration. This modification firmly shifted the

University away from the "statu quo" toward a "nouvelle administration" because it contemplated adding lay councillors. This move would (it was feared by some) lead to an entirely non-denominational university. Other discussion points only confirmed these fears. This new governance structure would see the current Chancellor, ex officio the Archbishop of Ottawa, removed from his largely ceremonial position. With him went a public link to the original founder, Bishop Guigues, that promoted a Catholic image. These kinds of discussions militated for "modifications à la charte pontificale" and to the "charte civile" in line with Lussier's suggestions.[20]

It is little wonder that the Council moved to act on LaRochelle's bleak report. Only ten percent of personnel (professors and administrators) in the civil faculties were Oblates; a meagre four to five percent of teaching hours were conducted by Oblates. In contradistinction, the central administration was almost entirely Oblate, a vestige of what must have appeared to professionally trained lay faculty as a dying power, a view toward which the visitor expressed sympathy: "[L]e corps académique laïc voudrait, ici comme ailleurs, pouvoir influencer un peu plus les décisions prises par l'Administration Oblate. Il est facile de comprendre la position des laïcs."[21] While easy to understand, the visitor, after rehearsing the many options for administrative reforms, played on that fear of allowing laymen into the administration. Their lack of administrative skill and religious faith would endanger the University.

Roger Guindon supplied a rare first-person view of these councils and of the visitor's report. His correspondence and notes revealed "un vote secret présidé par le visiteur," where an almost unanimous Oblate house favoured continued religious control that allowed only limited lay participation in university government.[22] The visitor's deference to this vote found its way into his final report with his prescription for the University's private law and again in his closing exhortation: LaRochelle laid out a public relations strategy that stressed the University's position as a guarantor of francophone minority rights in Ontario. This position had already been suggested by Roger Guindon (and Guindon might here embellish the record somewhat). The future rector's administration adopted the strategy, particularly with its briefs to the Royal Commissions on Bilingualism and Human Rights.[23]

For the present, Guindon gave his opinion on the composition of a new Council of Administration that ran against sentiment in the

Oblate house. He proposed including lay people as a follow-up to "trois questions" from the visitor. This proposal showed Guindon's receptivity to the lay faculty's feeling of disenfranchisement as Vatican II was on its way to declaring that the faithful were co-responsible for the Church. Guindon's suggestions acknowledge this impending change, but LaRochelle's command to obey canon law imposed a deliberative process for those changes. Guindon envisioned a Council of Administration of twelve members dominated by a seven-Oblate majority.[24] Marcel Bélanger would be the Vice-Rector of Ecclesiastic Affairs, a position proposed for him by Jean-Jacques Lussier.[25] Bélanger was "[un] [e]sprit lucide, même s'il est un peu lent, il peut apporter une contribution indispensable à condition qu'il se sente respecté dans un dialogue franc et ouvert."[26] Guindon reasoned that Bélanger represented continuity on the Council, for he had valuable administrative experience, and a conservative disposition fostering prudent decision making. Emmet O'Grady, a professor in English, would lead the civil faculties, with Laurent Isabelle, another lay professor, as Vice-Rector, Student Affairs.

Guindon's correspondence is indicative of a reforming spirit that was quickly promoted to high office. Shortly after LaRochelle reported to the University's Oblates, the Provincial Council brought Guindon in to lead the University through final negotiations with the government. A dramatic two-day meeting beginning on May 14, 1964, considered the University's future with reference to its leading personnel. Negotiations with Ontario had begun under Henri Légaré, but his term as rector was elongated (five years) and tenuous (as correspondence between Marcel Bélanger and Léo Deschâtelets has shown). The financial crisis that took hold during his administration, low morale, and government pressure on the University made change necessary.[27] Roger Guindon stepped onto the scene with an articulated vision that LaRochelle no doubt communicated to his brothers on the Provincial Council. Even as some of the moves between May 12 to 14 were retrograde and negatively affected the University's ability to move forward with reforms, Guindon's appointment could not be interpreted otherwise: reforms were going to take place. The diplomacy Guindon evinced in his sensitivity to lay professors' concerns stood him in good stead to mediate between government and Oblates, a mediation that set canon and civil law more obviously against one another.

The meeting at which Guindon was nominated began with discussion of LaRochelle's report. The visitor submitted some preliminary questions for the Council's information. These questions arose from his visit, and the Council of Administration had debated similar questions just before the Provincial Council meeting.[28] The question raised little controversy; they set the stage for the following day, where Oblate and Catholic law was invoked to censure Henri Légaré's independence from the Oblate Provincial when the rector moved forward with negotiations in 1963. As this censure unfolded, tensions around the table predictably rose. Lussier's proposals, though approved in principle, were again discussed. In something of a *caveat emptor*, Roger Guindon's alliance with Lussier was this time made clear, even if the Provincial and his Council were not prepared to accept the proposed reforms.[29]

The meeting continued on May 13, this time beginning afresh with questions from the Provincial about the inclusion of laymen on the existing Council of Administration and about the creation of a new corporation for part of the University. These questions again mimicked LaRochelle's inquiries at the University, where Guindon had commented in real terms on the composition of an expanded Council of Administration. The Council balked at these proposals and substituted their own:

> 1) [O]n ne connaît pas de façon suffisante les implications financières d'une telle décision, cette étude étant encore à faire pour que l'on puisse savoir exactement où l'on va.
> 2) aucune décision formelle n'a été prise par le Conseil d'Administration de l'Université sur la création d'une nouvelle corporation, comme il appert par les termes mêmes de la question posée : "Êtes-vous favorables à la création ..." ;
> 3) aucune demande explicite et formelle n'est présentée au Conseil provincial par le Recteur en Conseil ;
> 4) enfin, deux membres du Conseil d'Administration de l'Université – les RR. PP. Marcel Bélanger et Jean Moncion—se sont officiellement dissociés – post factum – des expressions d'opinions ou des décisions dont il est question plus haut.
> 5) Le R. P. Provincial en Conseil est fermement d'avis qu'il y a lieu (selon le numéro quatre du procès-verbal) de réaffirmer le caractère traditionnel, catholique et bilingue de l'Université.[30]

Catholic law plainly carried the day in a punctilious way. Just as LaRochelle had commanded the University obey canon law, the Provincial and his Council could not countenance a move away from the Church, even if this move was by degrees. Lack of information in this case coupled with conservative sentiment to block reform. The Provincial sought consensus within the Oblate Congregation at the University to avoid fractious politics; traditional Catholic law further dictated that the University continue its mission as it had always done. The civil authority was due mere lip service.

The Provincial Council supplied these reasons in order to defer to the rector-in-council while instructing him in his duties. Légaré had exceeded his jurisdiction because he had not obtained consensus from his council, which tended toward proposing illegal alienation of Oblate property.[31] His 1963 presentation to the Provincial Council, where the Lussier report had been approved in principle, was attained. The formulation of the "Recteur en Conseil" spells this excess out. While the rector had total authority over his house and the University corporation, his power to act unilaterally was curbed in much the same way as the Crown's in Canada. Oblate government was strictly hierarchical, from rector up a clearly defined chain. Each officer in this chain held a council to advise them on the exercise of their office. Consensus from these councils was essential to Oblate policy creation.[32] Thus, the Provincial Council noted dissent to the rector's policy *"post factum"* to support the conclusions that there had been excess of jurisdiction, and that pressure had been applied to certain members of the Council to toe the line. The Provincial and his council applied the Oblate constitution to the rector's actions to find excess. All of this was, however, cautionary, and directed against Légaré. The point was moot, for the University had not made a formal request to alter any of its structures.

As the Council rejected this proposal for reform, it followed the visitor's recommendation by creating a "Commission spéciale" to study the possibility of separating the superiorate and rectorate into distinct offices. The commission was composed of Marcel Bélanger, René Latrémouille (ord. 1932–d. 1982), and Louis-Philippe Vézina (ord. 1941–d. 1987). The Council's actions may be the result of Bélanger's complaints to Deschâtelets, and perhaps to the Provincial. Bélanger's influence guaranteed at least some conservative stubbornness that agreed with the Provincial's desire to keep the University firmly in the Catholic fold. This fact-finding commission looked into the "structures de l'Université" in order to ascertain how it might divide the Superior and the rector's functions. The Provincial required further information to make a decision, but the University's lay population and Oblates like Henri Légaré and Roger Guindon viewed the Ontario government's demands with more urgency. The commission's recommendation was held over until the installation of a new rector.[33]

That decision came later in the day. Roger Guindon was called before the Council to be consulted about the "nomination du prochaine Recteur":

> Après avoir attentivement exploré l'état d'esprit qui règne présentement à l'Université tant chez les religieux que chez un grand nombre de laïcs, il paraît grandement préférable et sagement prudent au Conseil provincial que l'on procède à la nomination et à l'installation du nouveau Recteur avant de faire au T.R.P. Général la présentation des membres du Conseil d'Administration. [...] Cette manière de procéder aura le grand avantage de permettre au Recteur et à son Conseil d'affecter des laïcs à des postes administratifs importants à l'extérieur du Conseil d'Administration et, on l'espère, de satisfaire au moins partiellement aux exigences et à l'attente de plusieurs. Elle manifestera la bonne volonté de l'autorité oblate, tant provinciale qu'universitaire, à l'égard des laïcs qui se dévouent à l'Université et qui ont à cœur son plein développement.[34]

The Council's interest in the University's morale was palpable, and played to Guindon's proposals, if they could be formulated according to canon law. More laymen would be included in the administration. Once the University's bureaucracy was populated with senior lay administrators outside of the Council of Administration, the Oblate Council itself would have better knowledge of its lay population.

Guindon's archival footprint is limited, but from what exists, his openness to lay points of view and to reform allowed him to gain the confidence of lay and Oblate branches of the University. The opening paragraph of Guindon's doctoral thesis, "Béatitude et théologie morale chez Saint Thomas d'Aquin," was indicative of Guindon's ability to balance a new openness with more traditional concerns:

> Le souci du « retour aux sources » marque la vie intellectuelle de notre époque. C'est un signe excellent de vitalité et une garantie de progrès. Un arbre coupé de ses racines peut rester debout. Pour qu'il vive et progresse, il faut que la sève monte sans cesse et porte la vie jusqu'au bout de ses branches. Dès que cette

circulation se ralentit, l'arbre se dessèche et commence à mourir. Or ce phénomène du développement dans la continuité doit caractériser la théologie entre toutes les disciplines.[35]

All the ills inherent in reform are captured in these opening lines. Guindon's appreciation for the deep roots of Catholic intellectual history and their instantiation at the University of Ottawa made him an attractive candidate. He received unanimous support from the Provincial Council after this discussion.[36] He was installed on October 28, 1964,[37] and went on to serve as rector of the reorganized University of Ottawa in 1965.[38]

The end result of LaRochelle's visit was Roger Guindon's promotion. Henri Légaré, in part because he did not consult his peers, was censured for derogating from appropriate legal forms. In this censure, we see the Church asserting its sovereignty while viewing the civil authority only enabling its legal existence in Canada. This position did not accord with the government's desire; it calcified the Oblate position and forced the incoming administration to press again against the government when University authorities had already determined that the Lussier report would not suffice. Even so, however, the Provincial and his Council were open to reforms brought about with the consent—the unity, as we shall see—that would allow the Oblates to move forward without rancour. The requirement for unity mimicked the visitor's view of his office. LaRochelle served only as a mirror; his advice ultimately had to be implemented with grace. This objective was fleeting and idealistic, but it was necessary to have a more solid base before proceeding with reforms that would alter the Order's long presence in Ottawa.

II

Marcel Bélanger was characteristically irrepressible through all of this. He weighed in on these changes by forwarding a copy of a document originally given to LaRochelle to Léo Deschâtelets on May 26, 1964. Bélanger's decision to inform the Superior-General of his perspective was ill received: the first vice-rector had, to a large degree, carried the day with his complaints. Légaré was out; the Provincial was considering splitting the rectorate from the superiorate; and LaRochelle had uncovered the disobedience that so thoroughly upset Bélanger. This latest letter was cheap politics. The rectorate was weak as Légaré left office and the relatively youthful Guindon entered. Bélanger was the first vice-rector, with a steward's obligation during the transition. His letter ignored the obligation by making the rector's job difficult at the moment when unity was plainly required to weather the transition.

Bélanger was thus to be taken with a grain of salt, both by Oblate authorities and in the light of history. His influence eroded because of the well-known intensity of his beliefs. While true to his Thomistic roots, this position led Bélanger down the path of disobedience and downright unpleasantness. His letter to Deschâtelets argued *post factum* dissent to which the Provincial Council had already given effect. Deschâtelets' 1963 warning to Bélanger had, however, been clear: Oblate authorities in Canada were better seized with complaints about Oblate practices in Canada. If the Superior-General wished for information, his power of visitation had just been exercised, and Bélanger had already submitted his brief to Deschâtelets' right-hand man, who would report to the Superior-General. Circumventing the visitor raised questions about Bélanger's sincerity and about his reliability. These questions came to bear when he was removed from the University's administration.

Bélanger's May 26 letter was a bright light in his self-immolation. He revisited the circumstances leading to the Provincial Council's adoption of the Lussier report—circumstances already reported to LaRochelle and discussed by the Provincial Council. Bélanger's allegation did not differ: he was intentionally excluded from the Council of Administration's decision-making process. He was, as Deschâtelets likely knew, in Rome preparing for the Second Vatican Council and returned on December 6, 1963. It was only then that he was informed of Lussier's December 4 presentation to the University Affairs Committee, and the effect of Jean-Luc Pépin's "tirades ... sur la 'désoblisation' de l'Université d'Ottawa." Pépin was a Member of Parliament for Drummond—Arthabasca and Parliamentary Secretary to the Minister of Trade and Commerce,[39] and his public statements, where he denounced the denominational character of the University, "avaient divisé les esprits" in the Oblate community even as they emboldened the lay professors.[40] The MP's statements coupled with Lussier's expression of internal division to galvanize the Oblates to such an extent that, on December 7, the rector was reported to have taken "la conférence du mois" to discuss with the community the "situation financière de l'Université."[41] This meeting came a day after the

Council of Administration adopted Lussier's report as a negotiating position for the University.

Even five months later, Bélanger remained irked by his exclusion from debate on the Lussier report. He attacked its legitimacy:

> On m'a assuré que ces derniers [les membres de la Comité des Affaires Universitaires]—du moins, ceux qui n'avaient pas trempé dans la rédaction—n'auraient pas eu la chance de faire au préalable et privément une étude un tant soit peu sérieuse du projet. En outre, on leur aurait donné à croire, au cours de l'échange de vues qui suivit la lecture du mémoire en assemblée, que les autorités de l'Université comptaient sur une recommandation expéditive du projet de la part du Comité des Affaires Universitaires.

Lussier submitted the report without notice. He had also interrupted debate on Quirion's proposed bylaw reform. These were affronts to a parliamentary procedure that suggested an insidious and "hâtive" approach.[42] Worse still, Bélanger charged his colleagues on the Council of Administration with outright encouraging Lussier's approach in order to rush Lussier's report to approval at the Council of Administration, which met on December 11 to decide whether to present the report in Montréal to the Provincial the following day. Bélanger had missed the agreement in principle on December 6 as he flew home. The Council, perhaps particularly the rector, presented him with a *fait accompli*:

> Ce matin-là, on ne nous donna pas le choix : il n'était aucunement question de reprendre la discussion, on ne nous demandait que de chercher à nous mettre dans l'optique des gouvernants de Toronto pour leur rendre agréable la supplique qu'il était question de leur présenter.[43]

The rector, who was in the chair,[44] and his allies pressed for adoption. Their argument was fraught (though it is an argument endemic to the University to this day): external factors created a crisis that forced the University to move in a specific direction. Without strong opposition, this language of crisis took hold.

The rush and the language of crisis were opposed by procedurally minded members. Dr. Lussier, present to answer questions, was dismissed early in the meeting so that the Council could discuss an Oblate procedural concern. Did the rector exceed his jurisdiction by presenting the report for adoption without first consulting the Provincial? Members were not convinced of his power, and Légaré "se montrait manifestement accablé par la consigne qui venait de lui être donnée d'avoir à soumettre son plan d'action au Conseil Provincial avant de s'aventurer du côté de Toronto."[45] The Provincial's advice was needed before the University could even consider reform, which ultimately affected Légaré's position.

That specific challenge to Légaré's authority was effective, and it slowed the pace of reform somewhat, even if the Provincial Council allowed the University to approach the Ontario government. It left an enduring stain on the Lussier report, which some Oblates mischaracterized as a threat rather than a useful compromise. Events after December 12, 1963, proved that the government of Ontario would not back down; events after May 14, 1964, when the Provincial Council removed Légaré and brought in Guindon, showed that neither would Bélanger. His conservative voice could jeopardize Roger Guindon's early tenure by fomenting dissent within the ranks. His gratuitous letter to Deschâtelets revealed that disregard for authority, which made him a liability. There was little need to rehearse these events in mid-1964. The events that he described, while novel in this account, were already substantially known to the Oblates. Bélanger could only be writing with insidious purpose.

Such was the view of Bélanger's peer, Second Vice-Rector André Guay. In a letter to the Provincial, Jean-Charles Laframboise, dated June 8, 1964, Guay agreed that Marcel Bélanger should not be named to the Council of Administration, "étant données toutes les circonstances."[46] Those circumstances remain obscure, but they may be inferred. Bélanger was an outspoken member of the Council. He ruffled many feathers, not least of which the outgoing rector's, but likely also the Provincial's, with his May 26 appeal to the Superior-General. He had circumvented Laframboise and did so without regard to Deschâtelets' warning to keep dissent within the prescribed hierarchy. Guay, who had recently become the Oblate Congregation's attorney general to the Holy See, further suggested that Bélanger held considerable political capital within the Church. Bélanger had already deployed his familiarity with Deschâtelets by appealing to the Superior-General's intimate knowledge of the University. His influence as a Marian scholar and a member of the preparatory commission for Vatican II in Rome could embarrass the Congregation at large.

The nature and frequency of his correspondence with Deschâtelets demonstrated some of this political capital, but it also showed how he had become exhausted in the eyes of others.

Léo Deschâtelets confirmed Bélanger's ejection from the Council of Administration to the Provincial on June 19, 1964. With this confirmation also came the instrument creating a new Oblate house, with statutes appended for its regulation: the superiorate was separated from the University rectorate, and two Oblate houses were accordingly constituted for Oblate staff and Oblate management, respectively. The rector took charge of his own house, "la Maison de l'Université d'Ottawa," in which the members of the Council of Administration resided. The Superior retained control over all fathers and brothers working at the University in a house styled "Maison Centrale de l'Université d'Ottawa." A line of authority was created to ensure proper management. The rector, as the head of the University's house, now delegated authority to the Superior, so he maintained indirect control over Oblates in the other house.[47]

The Provincial retained final control over both houses. Laframboise constituted their membership eight days later, on June 27. Marcel Bélanger was removed from the Council. He instead became Superior of the Oblate house, a position he would hold until 1967.[48] Bélanger would go on to serve as the University of Saint Paul's first vice-rector at the reform in 1965.[49] Until then, the way was clear for Roger Guindon and his Council to negotiate a non-denominational charter on as favourable terms as possible.

As he left the administration to take up his new responsibilities, Bélanger likely felt some sting. He had an ardent desire to maintain the Catholic University, and the creation of a new secular institution for the civil faculties was a personal defeat. Ironically, Bélanger's defeat was something of a success in the post-conciliar Order that would emerge after Vatican II. The Catholic University, while greatly reduced, would continue for a time in its civil faculties as much as in its ecclesiastical ones. The shift, however, was too much for the dogmatic Bélanger, and he stumbled through the post-conciliar end of his life.[50]

His stumbling left its mark on the Oblate record. Bélanger erred again as Superior when he dejectedly wrote to Léo Deschâtelets on March 29, 1965, to inform him that, due to the "désoblatisation," the Oblates of the University would take it upon themselves to seek "leur idéal de catholique résistants." As Superior, he would not oppose such organized disobedience.[51] Bélanger's threat was clear: he was himself disobedient as Superior for not enforcing the vow of obedience in his house.

Deschâtelets was irritated with this breach. His April 9 response from Rome was written in a cramped hand on card-size stationery that evokes the image of a man whose time is precious. The note tersely acknowledged receipt of Bélanger's letter; an unsigned letter of April 27 communicated Bélanger's apology to the Superior-General. Reference to "Congrès marial interbational [sic]" places the author's identity beyond doubt. (Bélanger was a respected scholar of the Virgin Mary.[52]) Bélanger explained the term "catholiques résistants" that he deployed in his March letter: "C'était justement l'issue entrevue par ceux qui étaient venus me confier leur intention de rester fidèles à des principes en n'entrant pas dans les voies nouvelles."[53] Bélanger, apparently chastened, saved face by withdrawing his earlier statements. Those who approached him upon his return played upon his conservative sympathies, which elicited that strong statement to the Superior-General.

As Bélanger faded, so too did the canonical visit, which concluded with a meeting with the Deschâtelets in Montréal on August 28, 1964, where Bélanger's statements saw one final resurgence. Provincial Jean-Charles Laframboise, visitor Stanislas-A. LaRochelle, Attorney General André Guay, and Provincial Vicar Philippe Scheffer discussed the University's future with the Superior-General. This high-level group held executive power over the Oblates of the University. The visitor represented both the Congregation and the Holy See. André Guay was a senior figure in the Superior-General's council and at the University. The Provincial and Philippe Scheffer were for the province. The Superior-General was, of course, for the Congregation. The Provincial wrote and signed minutes for this meeting with some personal commentary, for the benefit of University Oblates.[54]

The meeting articulated a combative policy against the Ontario government. The Oblate response to the government's refusal to grant the University funds concluded that the University of Ottawa, to preserve its core mission, must shrink in size under continued Oblate ownership, a point ironically advanced by Marcel Bélanger. The University would be reoriented toward teaching religious and humanist subjects in order to preserve its mission, "la formation chrétienne." The Pépin incident was cited as evidence that the francophone population of Ontario wished the Oblates to remain university administrators. Bélanger's outspokenness was paying off at this council, where Laframboise noted:

> Les Oblats n'ont pas le droit d'abandonner à l'Etat ou au public l'institution qui leur a été confier, même s'ils n'ont pas ou n'auront pas les moyens financiers de rivaliser avec les universités civiles ou publiques. Ils ne peuvent s'y résigner que si l'Église en juge autrement.
>
> D'autre part, si le public se montre insatisfait de ce que l'Université d'Ottawa peut offrir avec ses moyens limités, il ne lui est pas défendu de prendre les mesures pour avoir une institution neutre bilingue.

The Oblates' tenacious control of the University was borne out of apostolic charity. The Oblates believed that the Franco-Ontarian population, at least of Ottawa, would continue to support the University. Theirs was a public relations strategy several years in the making. It framed the University not quite as it was, but as its owners wished it to be.[55] The irony was that the Oblates were beholden to the Ontario Legislature for their University, and through it to the Crown in right of Ontario. Ontario's immediate control over the University's existence was a legal reality the Oblates sidestepped in favour of Catholic dogma. They also placed much faith in the primacy of canon law, which again ignored Ontario's critical role incorporating the university. The civil charter and civil degree-granting powers could only continue with the Legislature's support.

That stubbornness would be short-lived. Not even a year later, in April 1965, the University was finalizing its petition to the Ontario Legislature for a new charter. Cardinal Joseph Pizzardo, secretary to the Congregation for the Doctrine of the Faith, wrote to Marie-Joseph Lemieux, after he received news that the forthcoming Board of Governors would not even be overwhelmingly Catholic. He fell back on the ancient Pauline view of the subject and ruler in order to accept this doctrinal failure:

> Il s'agit en effet d'une institution qui, par ses origines comme par sa destination, doit rester rattachée, de fait pour le moins, à la Saint Église. Mais cette préoccupation d'ordre religieux et moral doit vivre dans nos âmes et rayonner de notre action, sans qu'il faille la déclarer aux autorités publiques.[56]

Paul likewise instructs in Romans 13:1–5 to "let every soul be subject unto the higher powers," where those powers always spring first from

God. The Ontario government, ignorant of its obligations in Catholic cosmology, imposed its rule. The challenge was not, in Pizzardo's dispensation, to resist that authority as Laframboise wished. Pizzardo instead proposed Christian charity going into the new Order. Catholics would have to lead by example.

This resigned view was, however, yet to come: in 1964, Laframboise further rationalized continued resistance against the Ontario government in retrogressive Catholic terms. The final paragraphs of the Provincial Council's minutes framed the University as a sacrifice for the mystery of faith:

> L'Université d'Ottawa sera toujours un problème pour la Congrégation. Mais pour que la Congrégation donne dans l'Université un témoignage chrétien, elle doit accepter de ne jamais arriver à des solutions précises, complètes et définitives. Comme tout apostolat, celui de l'Université doit vivre en tension. C'est un mystère, une lutte continuelle comme celle de l'Église même. C'est la rançon de l'incarnation.
>
> Les problèmes financiers n'existent plus quand on a un idéal clair et élevé. La divine Providence n'abandonne pas ceux qui cherchent le royaume de Dieu dans la lumière, la vérité et la confiance en elle.[57]

The University was, just like an apostle, so totally committed to the faith that these senior Oblates viewed it in lapsarian terms. These terms expressly excluded the civil power because it was a manifestation of fallen, imperfect man. The University was a Catholic city upon a hill, except only the covetous eyes of the government were upon it.

III

Lay discontent has been lurking at the periphery of my consideration of Oblate troubles. It is unrealistic to think these tensions arose *ex nihilo* as Roger Guindon took up the rectorate; Guindon's new tenure seems instead the catalyst for an outpouring of dormant opinion from corners of the University. Oblates felt stifled under Henri Légaré's tenure; the lay community also felt repressed. As I have suggested, lay opinions on campus may have been doubly downtrodden by their exclusion from the University's highest council even as they formed an overwhelming majority of the teaching staff in the

1960s—numbering roughly five to one. Several letters expressed this discontent from different corners of campus. Bill Boss, Guindon's director of communications, was most notable (if only for his public profile as a journalist before returning to his alma mater), but Robert Keyserlingk, a professor of history and a staunch Catholic, also commented on morale at the Faculty of Arts. Fernand Landry, the Director of the School of Physical Education and Recreation, gave an ultimatum to the rector that highlighted the University's financial straits and their effects on staff. D. M. Baird, an aspirant Dean of Science, gave an overview of morale at the Faculty of Science. These witnesses speak to wider irritation with Oblate governance on the eve of reform.

Such irritants drove a wedge between the powerful and the subjects in the little republic that the government could exploit alongside the University's financial situation. The University of Ottawa was only truly governed by a small theocracy. The Congregation debates about the University's future assumed the supremacy of canon law and, at the last, on a resolution to carry the faith regardless of pressure from a gentile government. That government likely knew something of this cleavage.

Ontario could easily exploit this wedge and differences between religious and lay opinion because the Oblates, including a much more publicly sympathetic Guindon, were extremely political in their academic administration. They deployed politics of exclusion. The Oblates consulted essential players on files while leaving out broader swaths of the University community.

This conduct is nowhere more apparent than in the University's preparation for its submission to the McCruer Commission examining human rights in Ontario. Guindon had sought legal advice from his colleague, Dean Thomas G. Feeney of the Faculty of Law, before he was officially installed as rector. A first draft of Feeney's brief came to Guindon on July 24, 1964. This opinion essentially reproduced the Oblate line. Feeney said that the University submitted its brief

> especially on behalf of the University of Ottawa which incongruously receives some support for two of its faculties—Science and Medicine—but none for most of its faculties, schools and departments and, therefore, most of the professors and students of the University of Ottawa are, it is submitted (as are the professors and students of the other recognized colleges and universities that do not receive grants), discriminated against through a distributive

injustice in the distribution of that part of the tax revenues of this Province which is going to the support of higher education.[58]

Feeney's charge runs along the lines of Oblate discussion in 1963–1964. The government of Ontario discriminated against Catholics because it did not allocate a proportional amount to support Catholic education even though Catholics attending the University of Ottawa (for example) continued to pay taxes in partial support of other universities. This charge was rounded out at the close:

> The University of Ottawa has submitted to discrimination in quiet confidence. In the quiet confidence that the British sense of justice will prevail and see to it that a great institution will be preserved. We do not abandon hope. We believe we will not perish, but perish we will before we surrender our character and abdicate the responsibilities of that obligation and duty accepted over 100 years ago: to strive for the highest excellence and morality in education.[59]

This combative final paragraph lays down the gauntlet to the McCruer Commission, which Bill Boss described as "essentially the former Chief Justice of Ontario and his research staff."[60] It was a commission operating out of Queen's Park—the same building in which the premier and the Minister of University Affairs worked. The University's charge against the government, at least in this first draft, was an affront that found its home at the University's University Affairs Committee in November 1964, which, though populated with some lay staff, was mostly composed of Oblates.[61]

Discussion at the University Affairs Committee excluded Bill Boss. A layman, Boss was no stranger to public opinion. He was a journalist of high repute after serving as a war correspondent during the Second World War and the Korean War.[62] On December 10, 1964, a day after the McCruer Commission confirmed receipt of the University's submission, Boss wrote Guidon to express his blunt opinion: he was "all the more surprised that [the brief's] preparation was so far advanced before [... his] view was sought."[63] Indeed, some confusion exists on the face of the record. Boss indicates that he was informed of the University's brief through Roy Laberge, who had handed a detailed summary of his objections to Boss some days before. If indeed Boss was not informed of the University's very public move, it is at best explained by an enthusiasm to proceed. That enthusiasm was, however, tainted with the visitor's command to obey canon law, which was reiterated by the Oblate Provincial Council's adoption of a combative stance against government encroachment. Feeney's brief was an opening salvo in a fresh battle with the government along these more conservative lines.

From Boss's perspective, the University's submission seriously undermined the University's chances of success. His surprise explains his blunt appraisal: "In short, my own view is that the entire project requires rethinking *ab initio*."[64] The University's brief was so fraught because he found "it difficult to reconcile the tactics implicit in the preparation of a document along these lines with the position I had understood the University to be advancing in Toronto."[65] That position was the co-operative stance taken in Légaré final years as rector. The University apparatus had continued working to advance reform along the lines of Lussier's proposal. Boss went further, again perhaps out of surprise, to characterize the report as "ax-grinding" that was "not worthy of a university."[66] Boss's deep concern with the University's submission to the McCruer Commission was, however, too little, too late, which may have been the point of keeping him out of discussion. The Council of Administration's position under the Oblate Provincial Council and under Catholic authorities in Rome influenced its confrontational position. The move was an act of faith going beyond the ambit of human rights policy. Unless a layperson possessed that faith, as Thomas Feeney seems to have, the University's move had no rational basis.

Four days after Boss's memorandum, Robert H. Keyserlingk Jr. submitted further evidence of lay discontent, this time on less obviously political terms, which was the problem. Lay professors felt they did not have skin in the game. Keyserlingk noted, "much unrest among members of the teaching staff." He attributed the unrest to "the almost complete lack of contact and communication between the university itself and its teaching staff." This disconnect had been a topic of discussion in the wake of LaRochelle's visit, but the problem was engrained in the way the Oblates administrated. Only in the post-war boom, however, as the University grew exponentially, was the problem becoming apparent. Traditional Oblate hierarchy was effective if the vast majority of professors were Oblate; lay personnel were not empowered, and this lack of involvement in university government meant that they were being "lured" away from the University by "higher salaries" offered elsewhere—salaries that were, in part, paid for by government, though Keyserlingk did not mention this fact.[67]

From the Oblate perspective, Keyserlingk also offered a ray of hope that encouraged the Provincial Council's faith-based approach. Keyserlingk opined that "[t]hose here are men who are dedicated, but the university appears to ignore this fact... So many professors appear to have a completely passive and sceptical attitude towards the university because they feel neglected and hurt."[68] Marcel Bélanger expressed this same concern about his Oblate brothers' relationship with Henri Légaré. The University's academic staff—those personnel interacting with students and the public—felt neglected by an administration that was governed apart. The professors had access to faculty government and to the academic senate, but those voices paled next to the elite Council of Administration. More to the point, the Oblates governed themselves out of the public eye. Most lay professors could not even view (let alone participate in) the decision-making processes that were so essential to Oblate life.

These secretive processes were compounded by a slow-moving administration that threatened at least one entire department. Fernand Landry, the Director of the School of Physical Education and Recreation, followed up on a Council of Administration decision regarding the School made on December 18, 1964. The School's request had first been presented a year earlier, on January 10, 1963, asking for additional resources to continue its operation. With this request came the ultimatum that the School's professors would not renew their employment if no action was taken. The Council's response promised resources, and Landry (at least) took it on "bonne foi." None were, however, forthcoming. The School resubmitted its request after this failure. This time, Landry and his colleagues requested immediate action and unanimously restated the School's ultimatum: barring effective remedy, the School "devra avec les regrets les plus sincères et les plus profonds cesser d'exister à l'Université d'Ottawa."[69]

Financial difficulties certainly complicated the University's expression of commitment to its teaching staff, but there is also a lurking sense that the Oblate administration was simply overwhelmed. The strain of administering a university in financial crisis and negotiating a balance between Oblate and civil authorities divided administrators' attention. This hypothesis may explain the failure to deliver the School's funds; that failure, whatever the reason, engendered mistrust between the School and the administration that led to so stark an ultimatum. The professors were struggling on limited resources to deliver a quality education, and they were not compensated fairly for their work. This sentiment was exactly what Robert Keyserlingk described in his colleagues at the Faculty of Arts. Though Landry's professors did not quit en bloc, they had to wait until 1967 for more resources.[70]

D. M. Baird's ambitious letter to Guindon of March 19, 1965, bears further witness to discord between central administration and line staff. Baird wished to replace the Dean of the Faculty of Pure and Applied Sciences, Paul L. Dugal. He supplied a "general description of what I think should be done in this Faculty in what I consider to be an urgent situation" in application for the job. His appraisal was a theme across these letters: frank. Baird depicted a faculty removed from the University and its "logical partner," Arts, a counterpart that could supply scientists with a well-rounded humanist training. He did not give reasons for the division, although a religious divide was most likely. The Faculty of Arts, humanist in orientation, was also directed by Oblates who subscribed to Thomist teaching.

The morale of Baird's faculty was, furthermore, eroding because it was removed from the central administration. Bill Boss's Department of Public Relations did not efficiently manage the faculty's needs (Boss was, perhaps, distracted by reining in his Oblate masters). So specific a problem led, in Baird's opinion, to a more general issue. Students and faculty lost influence as the corporation grew top-heavy with professional administrative staff: "[T]he University should be built around the Professors and the students they teach with the view that the fundamental purpose of the University is to make wisdom and learning available to those who desire it."[71] Non-academic staff were supposed to be subordinate to academic needs. The University of Ottawa's regime instead promoted the disconnection between administrators and the administered. Ultimately, this inversion of the constitutional order (a diminution of the collegiate model whittled down as the University grew) significantly affected morale in Baird's faculty. It also impacted professors' and students' relationships with their university.

That fraught relationship was captured best in Paul Marcotte's submission to the Duff-Berdahl Commission that visited the University on February 15, 1965. Sir James Duff and Robert Berdahl were appointed by joint resolution of the Canadian Association of University Teachers and the National Conference of Canadian

Universities and Colleges. They were to report on the ways in which universities were governed across Canada.[72] The University and the Association of Professors both received invitations to submit briefs to the Commission in January 1965.[73] Paul Marcotte was chair of the Association's Committee on University Government. He, along with Donat Pharand, the Association's president and a professor in law, made clear to the rector that the Association would present a report. Guindon did not immediately respond. He instead circulated a cryptic memorandum to his Council that called for a discussion of the professors' report at its next meeting:

> Le comité des professeurs suggère une "présentation conjointe."
> Le moment est assez "embêtant."[74] (Original emphasis)

The University did not have a brief. Its resources were committed instead to drafting that brief to the McCruer Commission on human rights that Bill Boss condemned. Without anything to hand, Guindon neither endorsed nor rejected the APUO's report: time constraints did not allow the University to make a thorough enough study.[75] The professors would submit on their own.

The University's refusal to present a joint report left the Association of Professors to make another frank appraisal of life on campus. Marcotte's and Pharand's efforts were diplomatic but made their point. If the University had participated with the professors, the resulting 155-page commentary might have been less blunt:

> It is possible that during the infancy and long adolescence of the University of Ottawa, informal, personal and relatively unsystematic methods of administration may have served their purposes. It would seem as if during earlier decades, The Civil charter of the University of Ottawa provided the basic frame of reference within which such methods of administration operated. The result was that a "traditional way of doing things" emerged, hardened and was promulgated. Few written statements of either policy or structure existed. Everyone connected with the University seems to have known everything about their "home-away-from-home." Such, briefly recapitulated, was the happy condition of our Victorian and early Twentieth Century academic and Administrative progenitors.

That "traditional way of doing things" tended to exclude the lay faculty that had been hired at a faster rate than Oblates could be inducted and trained. While the University was small, the Oblates could staff many of the positions from their ranks. That staff was already steeped in traditions and rules that informed University government. They remained with the University throughout their careers and, sometimes, even received their degrees from the University before becoming professors. The new lay staff did not benefit from this long acquaintance with the rules and traditions at the University, so:

> When changes came they came not like single spies but in battalions. Oral tradition could not and did not keep up with the tremendous influx of new staff. The result is that many people feel as if they are working in a wilderness of uncertainties, in a gloomy darkness of confusion. Most people, professors, and some younger administrators, feel that they are ignorant of the basic structure and fundamental modes of operation of their university. Like people living in a great metropolis, they know their own job and their own bailiwick, but are ignorant of most of what transpires around them. It must be observed, however, that the Council of Administration is aware of this problem. To solve it, they have set up committees to prepare written documents calculated to transform oral tradition into written law and to update and streamline both the structure and the operational policies of the whole University. The document entitled, "Structure de l'Université d'Ottawa," included above, and the "Professor's Manual," which should be completed by early Spring, are two examples in point. It must be observed further, that, some Faculties—the Faculty of Pure and Applied Science and the Faculty of Arts are examples—already have working, written documents outlining their inner structure and their rules and regulations of operation. However, many members of such Faculties are unaware of the existence of such documents and of parts of their contents.[76]

The University of Ottawa was plagued by the problem of informal administrative practices that mirrored the shift from oral to written legal traditions in English history in the eleventh and twelfth centuries. An increase in foreign subjects required the University's canon- and Oblate-based law to become codified, but the Oblates were not prepared for such a move. The result, as was seen with the "Project de status," was a codification process influenced by Oblate concerns within the central administration. Though well intentioned, Dean Lussier's more radical suggestion for total reform better reflected lay opinion. Marcotte was careful to note the University's lack of funds, which had diverted the administration's attention from political engagement, faculty, and students.[77] The Commission took the professors' submission without recorded comment on February 15, and it was welcomed by the administration.[78]

These lay examples of discontent flesh out the Oblates' impasse. They were cornered by government and increasing internal pressure against a wall of Catholic law and beliefs. Oblates like Bélanger had promoted such influence through 1963, though Bélanger himself took the point too far in 1964. Lay professors, representatives of the overwhelming majority of the University's teaching staff, pushed against Oblate preoccupations. They exhibited discontent creeping toward the central administration, apparently too preoccupied with concerns external to the University. Though these concerns were necessary, given the pressure from government and Rector Légaré's push to adopt the Lussier report without his superiors' consent, they ultimately distracted from the business of running the University: in large measure a fraught exercise in keeping professors content.

IV

As the year turned over, the Oblates were surrounded. Financial need was compounded by pressure from the government to become non-denominational and from lay professors who rightly wanted adequate resources for their enterprise. The provincial government, for which this process was old hat, played a zero-sum game. The conditions for reform were absolute: the University would cede its civil faculties to a new corporation, called the University of Ottawa, which would continue the Oblate legacy. Though there was ongoing disagreement within Oblate councils over the final terms of The University of Ottawa Act, Ontario insisted that it be passed in the Legislature's current session, before the assembly rose for summer recess in June. That insistence was rich. The government purported not to intercede in Oblate affairs, yet pressed the Oblates to move quickly.

Roger Guindon called Ontario's bluff in 1965. The University was concerned that government influence was growing pervasive. Guindon sought legislative protection against such control by insisting on section 8 of the proposed charter (now known as The University of Ottawa Act, 1965): "The management, discipline and control of the University shall be free from the restrictions and control of any outside body, whether lay or religious."[79] Thirty years after the fact, he diplomatically described his suspicion:

> Durant les négociations qui ont abouti à ce texte, mon refus d'accepter, comme tous les autres, d'exclure les restrictions et le contrôle de tout organisme religieux, impatienta le sous-ministre. Je lui expliquai que des organismes non religieux pouvaient imposer des restrictions et des contrôles à l'université. À titre d'exemples, j'ai mentionné les orangistes, les associations canadiennes-françaises, les chambres de commerce, et même... le gouvernement. Je tenais à fermer toutes les voies par lesquelles un organisme extérieur pourrait tenter d'infléchir la destinée de l'université.[80]

If the Oblates could not retain control over the University, the government of Ontario could not get any more formal power over the corporation. Guindon's assessment continues some of the Oblate bitterness at having to give up their jewel; it was also prescient. The University experienced the government's increasing financial influence. Guindon rightly attempted to circumscribe such influence by asking the government to consent to legislative protection against undue interference. Such considerations weighed heavily in the Provincial Council, where approving the transfer of power in principle ran up against the desire to preserve Oblate power in Ottawa. Guindon's proposed section 8 mollified some staunch opponents.

The Oblate approvals necessary for this change themselves were sites of dogmatic and repetitious opposition. Guindon's administration knew reform was at hand. The Council of Administration was quick to pass a resolution after the rough treatment it gave the government before the McCruer Commission. It requested approval from the Oblate Provincial Council to surrender the civil faculties—arts, social science, law, science, and medicine. The Provincial Council rejected the University's request on February 5, just weeks after the McCruer Commission visited Ottawa on January 12, 1965. The Council rejected this first request for lack of information. The Council blocked reform until the University showed absolute necessity to surrender its faculties. The University returned exactly a month later with the required data. The University's proposal was approved in principle on March 5.[81]

That approval in principle found its way to Rome for further discussion. Only one meeting, between representatives of the University of Ottawa and Saint Patrick's College on March 31, is recorded in Ottawan sources, although several must have taken place in Oblate and Vatican circles. At issue was how the College might incorporate to achieve legal personality apart from the University of Ottawa. This point was a matter between Oblates that revealed the University's reticence to make further demands from the Ontario government. Saint Patrick's would have the University's support if it wished to mention its incorporation in the University's new charter. Petitioning the Legislature for such mention was, however, Saint Patrick's business.[82] The University would not brook further negotiation. At the close of this meeting, Léo Deschâtelets, who was present only to hear the results, indicated to the University that the Oblate Congregation had already sought the required approval from the Sacred Congregation of Seminaries and Universities. The Congregation approved the transfer and the new constitution on March 24, 1965.[83] This final step paved the way for The University of Ottawa Act, 1965.

The final settlement, though not what the Oblates thought they could stomach, was not far off the Lussier report's mark. When the Act received third reading on June 21, 1965,[84] all of the necessary Oblate approvals had been met. Though the University had been pushed into a corner, it had at least nominally agreed to the changes. Such agreement allowed the priests to bow out with grace into a newly named university, the University of Saint Paul.

The passage of The University of Ottawa Act 1965 marked a substantial change in the University's government. A much firmer separation of legislative and executive power was imposed.[85] The rector was destined to be the chief executive and a member of the Board. He would not, however, be the Board's chairperson, nor would he command a council of brothers bound to him by religious law.

The Oblates made the best of their new reality. They gave Ontario exactly what it wanted: a public university free from religious control. They did so only to install their own man, Roger Guindon, as rector.[86] This move ensured a measure of Catholic spirit going into the reorganized university, which the Oblates sought to buttress by appointing Catholic members of Ottawa's community to the Board of Governors.[87] That combination of Catholic religious Superior and Catholic Board would, it was hoped, translate into continued Catholic influence at the University. This hope burned in Catholic hearts because, as the new first vice-rector, Maurice Chagnon (a layman), assured Roger Guindon, there had been "un changement récent d'attitude de la part du gouvernement dans le sens d'une plus grande tolérance."[88] That relaxed climate allowed Roger Guindon to promise his Archbishop that all would be done to make ninety percent of the new Board Catholic, with sixty-six percent francophones: "Cette solution de problème de l'Université d'Ottawa semble non seulement sauvegarder mais promouvoir les intérêts de l'Église dans l'éducation universitaire."[89] The Oblates rationalized the change with the promise of continued control through the Board of Governors and through their rector.

Many of the Oblates who stayed on in the civil faculties, Roger Guindon included (though he was a theologian), fell under the new Board of Governors' jurisdiction. They existed also, of course, in the wider Oblate community, in which Oblate laws still applied. With Guindon at the head of the new university, that discipline was a sword with which the Oblates still sought to influence their old creation. Guindon's personal obligation to the Oblate constitution required obedience to his superiors, and he remained a Superior in the religious law governing Saint Paul that dominated a university composed of exclusively ecclesiastical faculties. His obedience was "affective,"[90] which gave the Oblates sovereignty not only over the man, but over his mind and soul.[91] So tied to the faith, Guindon was a vehicle through which the Church could exert influence even as he possessed wide discretion over the University's internal affairs.

Guindon's religious obligations were supplemented just as the University of Ottawa reformed under more general Catholic undertakings in the wake of the Second Vatican Council. The Oblates, like many Catholic orders, redrafted their constitution and bylaws to mention education. This project, called for since 1947, but only undertaken in 1966, incorporated the tenets of a reformed Roman Catholic Church into the Oblate Order. Where the old constitution did not mention universities,[92] the new was explicit:

> 29 - Dans les écoles, collèges ou universités qu'ils dirigeront ou dans lesquels ils enseigneront, les Oblats seront des hommes académiquement qualifiés et unissant harmonieusement dans leur vie culture et foi, progrès et tradition. (Gravissimum, 8)

> Ils porteront auprès des étudiants comme du corps professoral et des parents d'élèves un témoignage authentiquement chrétien et missionnaire et s'efforceront de susciter chez tous le sens de leur responsabilité dans l'Église et le monde.[93]

This new bylaw prescribed the Oblate strategy going forward at the University of Ottawa. Catholic values could not be taught through institutions; the faith had to be led from examples set by teachers and administrators. Such an example had to "put on the armour of light" in order to spread a renewed gospel (Romans 13:12).

V

Roger Guindon put that armour on straightaway. His speech to the University's final convocation on May 30, 1965, highlighted the continued presence of Oblates in the work that they had started:

> [T]he government recognizes as we do that the inexhaustible search after truth, which is the raison d'être of a University, unrolls from the scientific, intellectual, spiritual, and cultural legacy of the past. But, ladies and gentlemen, the inherited values of the Western World are so permeated with the Christian doctrine that it, alone, renders Western civilization intelligible. This context precludes a neutralism that attempts to define culture without a definite philosophy of man, a set hierarchy of values and a system of principles shaping our way of life.[94]

The theologian claimed such a space for his faith that all branches of knowledge were covered by Catholic panacea. The University of Ottawa, though non-denominational, would continue to be imbued with the faith that, Guindon claimed, the Province of Ontario had agreed to: "That a Christian atmosphere shall continue to pervade the University of Ottawa is clearly indicated in the sections of the new charter dealing with the objects, the management and the Senate of the University."[95] He referred the audience to section 4 of The University of Ottawa Act, 1965, which commanded the University "to further, in accordance with Christian principles," its community's interests. This section would receive considerable attention from the University and from the government of Ontario in the coming years. For the present, the gauntlet had been laid down. As May became June, the University changed, imperceptibly to most students, from Oblate-owned to lay-controlled.

The Oblates staked their claim in the new organization along lines designed to mollify the conservative likes of Marcel Bélanger. Even as he participated alongside some of his Oblate colleagues in the Second Vatican Council, his position did not change a bit. The Church must ensure the University's continued adhesion to Catholicism. The only real way to do so was through continued Oblate control. This was the position of Oblate councils in 1964 from Rome to Montréal. It was the position that Bill Boss descried at the end of the year when he laid eyes upon Thomas Feeney's arguments for the McCruer Commission. In the end, Oblate stubbornness amounted to naught. The public relations campaign against the government worked with backroom resistance to government demands, but the Oblates won substantially the same charter as that granted to the University of Windsor. The civil faculties would be sold to a new university corporation that inherited the name and the history of its predecessor.

The Oblate administrations under Henri Légaré and then Roger Guindon were so preoccupied with this crisis and the politics it entailed that they were unable to fully treat lay concerns within the University. This was, in part, a failure of imagination. The Oblate community was more or less appraised of developments. The new lay staff were not, nor could they wholly be so informed. The congregation's secrecy prevented free circulation of information. This was most notably the case when Stanislas-A. LaRochelle circulated copies of his visitor's report to members of the Oblate house for discussion. No mention was made of lay personnel receiving copies. The Oblate visitor was preoccupied by Oblate problems. He had interviewed lay professors (he certainly entertained Jean-Jacques Lussier several times), but the results of his interviews treated the lay staff as objects of study, perhaps as statistical evidence of the problem facing his congregation.

It is small wonder, then, that Jean-Jacques Lussier had produced his recommendations for change. The 1963 document is the most strident example of lay discontent. Lay people were not members of the Council of Administration. This was the cardinal ill that the government of Ontario rectified. The Board of Governors created on June 21, 1965, was almost wholly lay, even though Roger Guindon planned to appoint a majority of Catholics. Such a plan satisfied Catholic authorities enough to concede defeat, but only in part. Guindon survived with others to promote religious interests at the University of Ottawa.

His remarks, however, at that final convocation of the Oblate-owned University of Ottawa set the tone for the fight ahead:

> When the complete history of the University of Ottawa is written in an indefinite future, this day will, I am sure, stand out as one of the epochal dates in its development. Certainly, not because this happens to be the first Convocation that it is my privilege to attend in my capacity as rector. Indeed, the future historian might be inclined to say that it was the last Convocation that it was my privilege to attend as rector appointed by the Order of the Oblates of Mary Immaculate, which founded this University 117 years ago.[96]

CHAPTER 4

Contract with Saint Paul: Meshing the Old and New

> And this I pray, that your love may abound yet more and more in knowledge and in all judgment;
>
> That ye may approve things that are excellent; that ye may be sincere and without offence till the day of Christ;
>
> Being filled with the fruits of righteousness, which are by Jesus Christ, unto the glory and praise of God.
>
> — Philippians 1:9–11

The new relationships created by The University of Ottawa Act, 1965, were in large part left to be defined by contracts between the new University and its old body corporate, now know as the University of Saint Paul. On July 1, 1965, Saint Paul held all the assets required to create a new university; the University of Ottawa — a hitherto non-existent corporation — needed to purchase these assets to continue the University's teaching mission with government funding.

The transmission of assets was a first test of the new relationship between government and university, for the government's acquiescence was required before payments were made to Saint Paul. The nature of government supervision, its insistence on reviewing the fair market value of transactions to Saint Paul, and the University's rapid acquiescence to government demands frames the government as a visitor in all but name. Though the term was never mentioned in connection with the new University corporation, the power to visit lurked in the background. Where no visitor was mentioned in a charity's charter, law filled the void by recognizing the person or entity first donating to the corporation as visitor.[1] The government behaved as though it had made the first donation. A closer look at the results of negotiations between the universities and between the University of Ottawa and government, however, might suggest the opposite view: Saint Paul may have retained a right to visit the University of Ottawa.

This argument's germ lies in The University of Ottawa Act. Though the Act nowhere mentions visitors, it modified the legal requirement to contract for real value—to contract with consideration—so that the new University of Ottawa could take its teaching obligations up without interruption. Sale for "nominal consideration," as the Act said, with payment in full to be negotiated at a later time, placed Saint Paul at a disadvantage. Its assets were already alienated when payment came due in 1967. The sale created a *fait accompli* for Ontario. The administrative expedient created the potential for government interference in negotiations between the universities because, strapped for cash, the University of Saint Paul would be much more amenable to unfavourable terms after control over its civil faculties had already been transferred to the University of Ottawa. The government would use dollar diplomacy to further force the Oblates' hands.

Such dastardly dealings could be considered bad faith, and bad faith entails a legal remedy. The history of the government's dealing with the University of Ottawa's contract negotiations between 1965 and 1967 suggests the remedy: Saint Paul is the visitor of the University of Ottawa, with all the corporate powers that such a right carries with it. The government forced Saint Paul to accept a vastly inferior sum for the sale of its faculties. It did so by inserting itself in contract negotiations between private parties. The government's conduct, then, fulfills a modern view of bad faith:

> [T]he concept of bad faith can and must be given a broader meaning that encompasses serious carelessness or recklessness. Bad faith certainly includes intentional fault. ... Such conduct is an abuse of power for which the State, or sometimes a public servant, may be held liable. However, recklessness implies a fundamental

breakdown of the orderly exercise of authority to the point that absence of good faith can be deduced and bad faith presumed. The act, in terms of how it is performed, is then inexplicable and incomprehensible to the point that it can be regarded as an actual abuse of power, having regard to the purposes for which it is meant to be exercised.[2]

The government's intervention in the universities' negotiation broke down the corporate authority on which the parties negotiated. The University of Ottawa was, as Roger Guindon went to lengths to point out during this period, a free corporation; it was statute-barred from any external control, which included government interference.

The government's brutal diplomacy was not long in the offing. The provincial government allowed the parties to negotiate a deal before injecting itself into negotiations by withholding payments required by the University of Ottawa to resolve the debt of purchasing Saint Paul's faculties. The government's tack placed the University of Ottawa in an awkward position. It sought a fair price for the property it received, which was a requirement included in the first contract between the universities. Both sides negotiated as equal partners. The government began to exert financial influence after a fair price was agreed upon by defining what it considered a fair price. The power politics of the situation influenced Oblate and Catholic opinion, especially in the wake of the University's comments to the McCruer commission. The universities interpreted the government's action as continued bias against religious institutions—a human rights abuse to which a charge of bad faith could attach.[3] Ontario was, perhaps, getting its revenge for those impolitic words. Nothing in the government's conduct disabused the universities of their conclusions. The University of Ottawa remained vulnerable to the civil power.

The government's view was, in fairness, warranted even if its actions seem underhanded. Dual sovereignties remained alive in the new corporation. Continued Catholic presence was going to carry a more ecumenical, yet no less potent, religious influence over the now non-denominational corporation. Oblates worked in the lay faculties and there was an Oblate at the helm. The executive influence Roger Guindon wielded, coupled with Oblate insistence on francophone and Catholic Board members, tipped their hand. Oblate intentions were made clearer still in the first federation agreement, which was negotiated between Oblates and Catholic Board members. The Board of Governors agreed to it as their first official act in July 1965. The contract created the federation between the University and Saint Paul's by sharing academic powers. It also bound the Board to hiring practices that ensured Oblates an even footing with lay persons, and it established the joint Faculty of Philosophy, which taught in a Thomist tradition. These measures demonstrated to a waiting provincial government that Oblate intentions to cede their corporation were anything but sincere. They also reflected lay expectations of the reform. Faculty characterized the contract as a form of Oblate control over a non-denominational institution.

Roger Guindon's public discourse, beginning in 1965, a continuation of the pre-reform media campaign, pushed back against government intervention. The University could not, however, operate completely without influence; it was theoretically independent, but in practice was already developing a "de-humaniz[ed]" aspect, as Guindon pointed out in his first convocation speech.[4] Government bureaucracy added a layer of complexity that always looked to popular politics, and this complexity diminished the weight of oral agreements between government and Oblates. Written agreements now took precedence. It limited the flexibility of what might be agreed to, and of who could be trusted. Such a change was one for which the Oblates were wholly unprepared. The University received its new charter on the promise that Oblates would continue to have a voice at the University, not least by having members on the Board of Governors. Once granted, however, the government unilaterally extended its control. Correspondence between the University and government on this point revealed that such extension was based on a potted view of Catholicism. Old Ontario prejudices were alive in the government's dealings with the University. Government agents countered this private picture by arguing that the University was a public trust, which gave Ontario the rhetorical space to set its own terms against what the two universities had agreed.

Both sovereignties exhibited their aims. The government proceeded on the apparently implicit assumption that the University's new charter altered its culture enough that it would fall wholly under state sovereignty. The Oblates used sympathetic agents within the new university: Roger Guindon was much more likely to negotiate with the Oblate Rector of Saint Paul, Jacques Gervais, on favourable terms. When the government's assumption was not born into fact, the government refused approval of the sum agreed between the universities. The situation came to a head when Roger Guindon met with the Minister of University Affairs, Bill Davis, in a mediated session at Rideau Hall with the University's chancellor, Pauline Vanier, in 1966 to resolve the impasse. The difficulties could not, however, be completely sorted. The following year, General Jean-Victor Allard, second Chair of the Board of Governors, exchanged terse correspondence with the minister and his deputy, the retired Leslie Frost.

As these negotiations were running, debate over merging the Faculty of Philosophy with the Department of Philosophy in the Faculty of Arts sparked a crisis that further tipped the University's hand and imperiled negotiations. Faculty and department formally taught the same subject, but their approaches were radically different. One taught in the Thomistic vein of Catholic scholarship and theology. The other taught a broader, less affiliated tradition. The Faculty was a jointly administered faculty in which Saint Paul had the upper hand; the department belonged solely to the University of Ottawa. Each ferociously defended its corner, and that defence continues today in minor skirmishes.

The issue in 1965 and ensuing years was fusing the faculty and department. From an administrative perspective, it made sense to do away with duplicate academic units. The department quite rightly saw the faculty's move as a power play that aimed to stamp out a secular branch of inquiry. This dispute rapidly became the focal point for brewing lay discontent. The force of repressed unease was unleashed in an episode that saw the University badly embarrassed in front of the government.

Each side, moreover, had proponents at the highest levels. The Deans of Philosophy and Arts, Jacques Croteau and Jean-Marie Quirion, were Oblate. Further up the chain, Roger Guindon was accompanied by Oblate University Secretaries: Gérard Gagnon (1918–2009), who served a year in 1965–1966, and then Roland Trudeau (1909–2003), who served from 1966 to 1974. While these senior administrators were a minority in the upper councils, their presence was influential for past Oblate contributions and experience. No one knew the institution better than the Oblates who had governed it for a century.

Tensions between the faculty and department prompted wider discussions about just how the University could read section 4 of its charter. The University's legislative mandate read:

> The objects and purposes of the University are,
> (a) to promote the advancement of learning and the dissemination of knowledge;
> (b) to further, in accordance with Christian principles, the intellectual, spiritual, moral, physical, and social development of, as well as a community spirit among, its undergraduates, graduates and teaching staff, and to promote the betterment of society;
> (c) to further bilingualism and biculturalism and to preserve and develop French culture in Ontario.

Much of this section was boilerplate. That reference to "Christian principles" was a holdover from Oblate stubbornness. It is likely that the government and Oblate Congregation interpreted this meaning differently in early 1965 before the Act passed. In late 1965 and in ensuing years, that difference of meaning proved critical to relations between the University and government on the one hand and the university and its academics on the other.

These incidents solidified mistrust between the University and government. Negotiating the federation agreement fleshed out the University's understanding of its charter, which was at odds with the government's stated intention. Oblate influence was not to continue over the University.

I

After the reform, Roger Guindon made his intentions clear. His public discourse worked in the same vein as the public relations campaign he had proposed in 1964. More senior Oblate councils had also endorsed the campaign in 1965: the University of Ottawa was victim to a capricious government that represented a hostile "other" to the University's francophone Catholic audience. That message was reassuring to students and faculty of similar persuasion. To others, the rector's comments were unwelcome news of continued religious influence. The priest's view thus divided his colleagues even as he sought Christian unity of purpose.[5] Guindon's efforts thus tried to address tensions inherent in the new governing structure even as he was building a beacon for his brothers' faith. His speeches, principally at convocation, but also at several other instances in the University presses and to the faculty, were occasions to set out his denominational interpretation of the new charter. In so doing, Guindon aimed to establish a continuing religious feeling at the University by highlighting the humanist quality of education, and by stressing the need for a historically accurate continuation of this humanist tradition at his University.

The presses, *La Rotonde* and *The Fulcrum*, were quickly put to work in August 1965. In a short statement that appeared on August 16, Guindon described "Le caractère permanent de l'Université d'Ottawa" by downplaying the modifications to the administrative structure. He instead held up a conservative goal accomplished by the reform: "Ces modifications du corps administratif n'ont qu'un seul et unique but : permettre à l'âme et au caractère de s'épanouir davantage." There is no better admission of Oblate intent. Guindon interpreted the statutory objects and purposes of the University, which were stated in section 4. The University had an essential Christian character that needed to be conserved. He went further to address the institution's new non-denominational nature:

> Certains ont prétendu que l'Université ne sera plus catholique, mais chrétienne, ou encore neutre ou laïque. Ce sont là des formules ambiguës. Il est vrai que l'Université n'est plus régie par une charte pontificale ni par les autorités religieuses des Oblats de Marie Immaculée. Mais cela ne signifie nullement que désormais des limitations ou des restrictions seront imposées à la liberté religieuse des catholiques. Semblable discrimination contredirait les textes explicites de la charte. Si celle-ci comporte quelque restriction, c'est au contraire à l'endroit du sécularisme ou du laïcisme qu'elle le fait pour autant qu'ils s'opposent aux principes chrétiens.[6]

Guindon's passive voice takes careful aim. Those who heralded a changed Order were simply wrong. The charter encouraged Catholic expression in part because of the University's history, but also because it forbade secular domination. Guindon's reading was consistent with the Oblate's intention as they drafted their petition to the Legislature. Secular readings of the University's charter that celebrated the move toward "non-denominational" governance misunderstood the term. The word permitted all denominations (especially Christian ones, of course, though this is a perfunctory distinction for the 1960s) to take part in university life. The Oblates had not seriously contemplated a loss of religious feeling. Guindon framed secular agitation as a dangerous ambiguity that weakened the University's identity and, thus, its competitive edge. The University's catholicity was at stake. Guindon promulgated the same message in the English newspaper on August 13 under the headline "The Enduring Character of the University of Ottawa." Both articles headed off interpretations of the Act that may be hostile to the Oblates.

Roger Guindon put a wider press to work in October. He defended the University's confessional character to Claude Ryan, editor of *Le Devoir*. Ryan had characterized the University as nondenominational in that secular persuasion. Guindon parried such characterization with section 8 of the charter:

> The management, discipline and control of the University shall be free from the restrictions and control of any outside body, whether lay or religious, and no religious test shall be required of any member of the Board, but such management, discipline, and control shall be based upon Christian principles.[7]

The University could not be controlled by any outside institution, whether lay or religious. It always benefitted, however, from its history in its community. The University had made its affiliation to francophone and Catholic interests clear in the lead up to reform. Limits on the University's management were themselves limited by the University's history. Such a limit was proof of the University's continuing Christian character. Section 8 provided "une affirmation *positive* de *l'autonomie* et de *l'inspiration chrétienne* de l'institution."[8] The University was, in Guindon's estimation, not non-denominational, nor was it denominational. It was simply Christian and was mandated to conduct itself under that head.

Convocation was the most public instance for interpretation of the new Act, and Guindon wasted no time. He opined at the new university's first convocation on October 24 about the University's changed structure, yet similar mission and culture. He did so with an expansive statement that described the University's place in the welfare state:

> La chose est certaine : le haut savoir et les institutions qui le dispensent ont insensiblement échappé à l'empire absolu d'autorités indépendantes et, bon gré, mal gré font dorénavant partie de l'engrenage social. Toutefois si le fait lui-même est incontestable,

les dimensions et les modalités de cette imbrication sociale n'en restent pas moins du ressort de chaque institution.[9]

This Oblate had learnt the lessons of 1964. Outright competition with the government of Ontario for control over higher education was impossible. The absolute control of any one authority was now gone and replaced by a board of governors that ostensibly embraced the University's surrounding community's values. That private jurisdiction, which once existed at law and in practice, where government would not interfere in the affairs of the University, paired with the government's function as almsgiver.[10] At the University of Ottawa, the battle was lost after much resistance. They fought for its independence against a government wielding massive powers, acquiescing at the last only to define itself by "l'inventaire des avantages spéciaux qu'elle possède et, plus particulièrement, de ses valeurs géographiques et humaines et des traditions qui lui ont forgé une personnalité propre."[11] Guindon defined the University against the provincial government's expectations. As the controller of "l'engrenage social," Ontario had admittedly broad powers. Using them to further trammel with the University's distinct identity, however, brooked political backlash. Guindon's offered interpretation was the same fighting offer presented to the McCruer Commission.

Oblate vim was fatally undermined by a concern for the University's own staff, and Guindon was fully aware of the impending crisis. It had been signalled to him just before the reform from several lay quarters: the Faculties of Arts and Sciences, Bill Boss, the Association of Professors, and the Department of Human Kinetics. These lay sources, though not all dissatisfied with the Oblates' religion, all attested to the Oblate failure to connect with lay professors. The rector used convocation to aim at this difficulty:

> Il va de soi, Mesdames et Messieurs, qu'une université qui se veut ouverte à tous les courants de la vie sociale, doit s'éprouver au contact d'idées et de points de vue différents des siens afin d'éviter l'ankylose de ses méthodes et de ses procédés. Pourtant, le fait demeure. Nonobstant la compétence de chacun dans le domaine de sa spécialité, les administrateurs et professeurs qui nous arrivent d'autres institutions et d'autres pays sont souvent étrangers à notre histoire et à nos traditions. Le seul poids de leur nombre, destiné à s'accroître de plus en plus, pourrait bien,

malgré toute leur bonne volonté, compromettre la personnalité distinctive de l'Université d'Ottawa.[12]

The foremost danger to the University was a corps of heterogenous and mobile professors. Their increasing presence in Ottawa blurred the University's character. Guindon drove that wedge deep. Lay professors arriving at the University were expected to conform to a culture that, Paul Marcotte tells us, could not effectively market itself to this new generation of academics.[13]

Guindon held the charter up as a document empowering the search for and defence of identity from external interference in Ontario's competitive non-denominational environment. That search, however, was one for the servants of the University and their pupils. The central administration could not, as Stanislas-A. LaRochelle observed in the visitatorial context, command an identity or culture. Guindon sounded a klaxon against the loss of the University's distinctive faith:

> Without prejudice to any ulterior decision that might be taken by the University Senate, upon whom the full responsibility for academic policy devolves; and also without prejudice to the intrinsic value of such research, I shall venture to suggest that the adoption of such a point of view can easily lead to a downgrading of the student, a kind of dehumanizing of the institution and a breaking-up of the university itself into various self-centred [sic] units that just happen to share the same campus.[14]

Academics and students now had to find their faith. Guindon portrayed teaching and research as communal pursuits. Though in the main tailored to individual goals, these activities required wider support to make them real contributions to knowledge. The danger of siloed academic units was a focus on a single discipline, with its own biases, that undermined a Catholic approach to higher education. Guindon acted to prevent that danger when, on December 8, he wrote to a fellow Oblate to publicize openings for "qualified Oblates in every discipline on campus":

> The soul and spirit of the University have not changed and all indications are that, relieved from the administrative and financial exclusive responsibility, the Oblates are going to continue to inspire the life of the institution.[15]

The Oblates' continued involvement with the University was not necessarily the University's path. Indeed, the path he wished to follow was one where the Oblates continued to influence the administration while receiving government funds. Competition for government resources steadily pushed the University from its former focus. Saving souls took a backseat to a brash (and fleeting) need for excellence.

Guindon's second convocation as rector of the new University on October 23, 1966, maintained the dangers of that desire for excellence, a defiance of the conventional that today invites scorn from some of the University's members. It was the one hundredth anniversary of the University of Ottawa's acquisition of university powers. The Oblate strategy was at work. Guindon argued that the twin sovereignties formerly animating the University through dual charters was preserved in the new Act, in the federation of the old and new universities, and in the culture that carried over with the transfer of students and academic staff. The University's name brought with it a history:

> En cette collation de grades académique publique de l'Université, je ne pourrais passer sous silence le centenaire de l'octroi, par le gouvernement des Canadas-Unis, d'une charte universitaire à l'institution que j'ai l'insigne honneur de diriger aujourd'hui.

The University's historic place in Ottawa linked the new corporation to the old. Guindon fleshed out the Oblate interpretation of section 1 of the Act, which transferred all references to the University's name to the new corporation:

> Rien n'arrive, tout se fait. Or, ces réalisations qui pourraient mériter à notre université plus qu'à toute autre le titre d'Université Nationale, sont le fait de la Congrégation des Oblats de Marie Immaculée. Bien que je sois moi-même membre de cette Congrégation, j'en fais état sans hésitation et sans gêne. D'abord parce que j'occupe le poste de Recteur par le libre choix des gouverneurs de l'Université, selon les dispositions de la nouvelle charte. Ensuite, parce que tout autre que moi, quels que soient son état de vie, sa langue ou ses croyances religieuses, se croirait tenu en cette circonstance d'exalter le rôle joué par les Oblats en des accents que je ne me permettrai pas moi-même. Enfin, parce que la vérité historique a ses droits et qu'il importe qu'on la dégage

> de l'enchevêtrement des passions, des préjugées et de toutes les attitudes étrangères à la plus élémentaire reconnaissance.

So simple a statement of facts carried with it a claim for Oblate eminence. The obedience so central to the rector's life was one that he wished upon his colleagues and students. Acknowledge the Oblate work; acknowledge its spirit in Paul's teaching. Those who do not might as well have been damned:

> Du reste, il n'y aurait que les esprits superficiels qui croient que l'histoire a commencé avec leurs vingt ans et se piquent d'un anticléricalisme précoce qui pourrait en prendre ombrage. Je suis certain, par contre, de répondre à l'attente de cet auditoire en anticipant sur les éloges que la postérité fera de ces pionniers dont la largeur de vue a dessiné d'une main ferme les grandes lignes du seul esprit national vraiment authentique.

An antanagoge:[16] The rector calls out the faithless, some of whom are surely in his audience, only to quickly reverse tack to praise the entire audience as the faithful; those before him are imbued with an authentic national spirit, which included an appreciation for history and religion's place in it.

That national spirit was, moreover, bilingual and bicultural, and in that culture lay salvation. Guindon stressed that the Oblates' work to date expressed such redemptive excellence:

> L'œuvre des Oblats fut une œuvre d'amour. Ils on[t] aimé leur Université parce qu'ils ont aimé et le Canada et l'Eglise et qu'ils on[t] compris que la grandeur de leur patrie exigeait à la fois le rapprochement des cultures et les lumières de la vérité chrétienne. Ils ont aimé leur Université et, pour elle, ils on[t] dépensé sans compter et se sont dépensés eux-mêmes jusqu'à la limite de leurs ressources. Ils ont aimé leur Université jusqu'à en passer la direction à d'autres mains, mais non sans avoir tout d'abord obtenu la reconnaissance officielle de son caractère original, celui d'institution bilingue et chrétienne.

Guindon deployed legislative and gubernatorial authority to legitimize the Oblates' continuing presence. He jabbed at government and secularists within the University. These last were preoccupied with expunging the University's religious history. Guindon's modesty while describing the Oblates' achievement addressed these preoccupations. He claimed that history spoke for itself. Such facts explained the University's new charter, and why that charter stipulated that the University be Christian and bilingual. It was a product of its place, at once in the Church and in Canadian society.[17]

Guindon's teleologic reasoning explained the University's modern role as a function of Oblate norms. His explanation provided an intellectual space in which secularist views could be dismissed. The Oblates represented that French, Christian character included in the charter. A person's failure to recognize this origin story created disunity; disunity undermined the University's mission. Contrary interpretations or interpretations that ignored this fact were ahistorical or impassioned. Guindon and his upper-level colleagues could dismiss such views.

This normative limit was further expressed in 1967, when Guindon delivered a speech at a special convocation, held on February 17, to mark the hundredth anniversary of Confederation. The rector again explained the transfer of culture. He refined his view by interpreting the Legislature's intention with The University of Ottawa Act, 1965:

> The external structures of institutions are bound to evolve like all things that are temporal. The essential character, that is, the identity of the institution, should endure through the vicissitudes of the society that it means to serve. The determination of the new Board of Governors and of the new Senate to preserve the traditional identity of the University of Ottawa appeared clearly when they set this day apart to honour the founders of this centre of learning, their aims and the special mission which they entrusted to the following generations. Over and above the common aims of all education enterprises, two elements of this mission stand out, both confirmed by The University of Ottawa Act, 1965, of the Ontario Legislature namely, a tolerant Christianism and an authentic Canadianism, based upon the mutual respect and understanding of the two founding races.[18]

Guindon drew on the new government only to reference the old, celebrated for their enterprise by the Board and Senate. His reading framed the new Board and Senate as assemblies created to promote bilingualism and Christianism. The University of Ottawa Act did not represent the University's culture. It was the legislative vehicle for culture already extant. Institutional mores carried over, and indeed Guindon cast this platitude as the founder's intention, which brought with it a host of assumptions about the University's government.

He expressed this theme to the new faculty members in a foreboding speech on September 6, 1967. Guindon once again teleologically rehearsed the University's mission as a function of its history, but this time with a fresh metaphor:

> Les organisateurs de cette rencontre m'ont demandé de vous brosser un tableau rapide de ce qu'est l'Université d'Ottawa. Ce qu'elle est aujourd'hui, c'est ce que l'ont faite les générations de ceux qui lui ont consacré leur vie depuis 1848. Il arrive {aujourd'hui} parfois qu'on perde le sens du passé. Tout semble se centrer sur l'"événement" [sic], au risque d'oublier que chaque "événement" a été préparé silencieusement par les générations précédentes. Les institutions, un peu comme les arbres, se développent en prolongeant leurs branches, en multipliant leurs feuilles et en s'enracinant de plus en plus profondément dans le sol qui les nourrit. Or, l'Université d'Ottawa est une réalité tout à fait propre à la vallée de l'Outaouais qui constitue le lien entre les provinces d'Ontario et de Québec.[19]

Guindon's metaphor appropriately harkens unto Saint Paul's dictum to the Israelites in Romans 11, where Paul allegorizes the branches and root of the olive tree to faith. The Oblates are the University's root; the professors and students branches. The branches may be broken off for lack of faith and grafted onto the tree for those faithful returning or coming to God. The roots of faith extend deep; they touch God's power.[20] So was the history of the University the wellspring of its institutional power. The roots extended to the physical location, the Ottawa Valley, where the University played a role developing the region. From its roots, the branches were incidents in the University's history, individuals, which sometimes required trimming, and sometimes required grafting. Following from Paul's allegory, Guindon implied that derogation from the University's history, its roots, might necessitate trimming. As Paul remarks:

> Boast not against the branches. But if thou boast, thou nearest not the root, but the root thee.

> Thou wilt say then, the branches were broken off, that I might be graffed in.
> Well; because of unbelief they were broken off, and thou standest by faith. Be not high-minded, but fear:
> For if God spared not the natural branches, take heed lest he also spare not thee.[21]

Guindon characterized willingness to forget as a loss of faith. Boasting against the branches was merely an attempt to distance the self from the branches in favour of the root, in this case the University's power structure. The root, however, did not permit such false faith, and rejected the unbeliever. Such faith was, in Guindon's estimation, axed upon belief in the University's history and tradition. Failure to acknowledge Oblate efforts could lead to the unbelievers being broken off the tree.

These kinds of pronouncements coming from the rector boded ill for a non-confessional university. The priest was positioning the University's rhetoric in terms of its past to flesh out an embryonic future mandate. Religious mores may have been formally expunged from most corners of the University of Ottawa, but its culture remained alive in the Oblate professors and administrators who carried the Catholic light a little further.

II

Guindon's comments up to 1967 were made alongside a strained back-and-forth between the Universities of Ottawa and Saint Paul over how federation between the two would take place, and over how much that union would cost Ottawa. The strain, as already discussed, stemmed from government interference at the end of negotiations. The tenor of that interference, not entirely spelt out in the extant record, nevertheless was received in the most unfavourable light: Ontario carried on prejudice toward Catholics. That prejudice violated the spirit of the contract, which was negotiated between the universities as private bodies. Correspondence from the Board of Governors and from Roger Guidon demonstrate the early cordial relations between universities. It shows also how the Board of Governors conceived its role in part as a facilitator for a culture already present.

Much of this view existed because the federation agreement transmitted most of the old university's assets and human resources to the new University of Ottawa. Saint Paul avoided additional costs, while Ottawa's operating costs were supposedly defrayed by grants from the provincial government. Saint Paul's Council of Administration, now without Roger Guindon at the helm, but Arthur Caron, the first vice-rector, discussed the sale of the University's assets to the soon-to-be-constituted University of Ottawa on June 10, 1965. Caron proposed that

> la présente Université d'Ottawa vende à la nouvelle Université d'Ottawa 1965 ses biens, tels que déterminés dans le contrat, moyennant compensation basée sur la valeur actuelle du marché; (b) que l'on demande au Conseil provincial l'autorisation d'obtenir du Saint Siège un indult d'aliénation à cet effet.[22]

The motion was adopted, and permission sought from the Holy See. The contract was signed on June 25, 1965. The agreement subjected Saint Paul to the University of Ottawa's academic authority in most matters.

The contract was meant to be a starting point for discussions in that Oblate informal style, though Saint Paul's administration also intended to receive market value for its assets. The general agreement on which the parties could build kept the university open from semester to semester.[23] Further negotiations would establish the cost of each faculty and detail payments. Section 43 was clear:

> Nature de cette convention : Il est entendu que cette convention ne constitue qu'un contrat préliminaire pour établir les principes généraux qui devront gouverner les contrats détaillés qui seront préparés pour le transport des biens et pour préciser et donner suite aux diverses clauses de ce contrat.[24]

The transfer of the faculties was an act of good faith. For Oblates it was, perhaps, charity. They placed themselves in a financially vulnerable position. Until the sale was finalized and money exchanged hands, the Oblates had given up their bargaining power for professors' and students' sakes. The universities assumed that they were free to negotiate as independent bodies.

Such an assumption was reasonable because the universities were privately incorporated and because their negotiations focused on establishing an academic division of responsibilities. Saint Paul's degree granting power was placed in abeyance. Only two faculties at the University of Saint Paul continued to grant degrees from Saint Paul's charter, Theology and Canon Law.[25] Saint Paul's civil degrees were granted under delegated power from the University of Ottawa's Senate. This structure preserved Saint Paul's obligations under the 1891 ecclesiastical charter.[26] The new institution was further obliged to consider the grant of the same lay degree in Theology or Canon Law as the old university if a candidate for that degree was presented to it.[27] Such a delegation of power framed the sale as an academic matter that, though within the Board of Governors' jurisdiction, touched on how powers were divided between both universities' Senates. Saint Paul bound itself to college status; Ottawa surrendered a portion of its Senate's independence to confer academic degrees in order to win greater powers. Ottawa's Senate, however, was not yet created in June 1965. The contract gave special powers to Saint Paul's Senate to fill the gap up to October 31, 1965.[28] The power to grant degrees for both institutions was thus vested for a time in a single Senate. Discipline, however, over students at the old university remained with its Council of Administration.[29]

The sale of faculties was the most palpable instance of cultural transfer. The material faculties were given to the Board of Governors and Senate of the new corporation. With these facilities came employment contracts and teaching obligations.[30] The unwritten rules of the old university that Paul Marcotte alluded to in his brief for the Duff-Berdahl Commission came with these people. All documentation about the lay faculties and general university administration up to 1965 came with them. The first part of the Act fleshed out. The transfer of documents and people brought the University of Ottawa with it.[31]

The Faculty of Philosophy, however, only partially migrated to the new university, much to some professors' chagrin. It became jointly administered. Saint Paul nominated its officers, the dean, the vice-dean, and the secretary to Ottawa's Board of Governors. The Board appointed those nominees. The old university was further empowered to, after a year's notice, exercise all powers over the Faculty of Philosophy, which included awarding civil degrees.[32]

The old university further benefitted from grandfather privileges that gave it influence over the larger corporation. It actively participated in the recruitment of new professors and administrators "en tâchant d'intéresser à l'œuvre tous ceux auprès desquels elle peut exercer une influence."[33] The old University remained Oblate; its writ ran most obviously with Oblates that could be assigned teaching duties. Oblates who took up such duties at the new university were further recognized as individual representatives of "la longue association des Oblats de Marie Immaculée à l'œuvre universitaire," and were accordingly granted collective rights. Their salary was paid to Saint Paul, and Saint Paul's rector authorized their nomination to any employment before it became effective.[34] These privileges recognized the role the Oblates continued to play in the transferred faculties. They also created a further revenue stream for the old university. Such collective recognition, moreover, laid the bedrock for some of Roger Guindon's speeches. The University of Ottawa's contractual recognition of its legacy allowed Oblates to claim stewardship over the new institution, which is exactly what Roger Guindon did in ensuing years on behalf of his congregation.

The contract's final stipulation was that the Board of Governors unconditionally agreed to ratify the contract once the Board was officially created on July 1, 1965. By this term, the Board was mandated to hold its first assembly at eight o'clock in the evening on July 5, 1965, something the Board had planned at its preliminary meeting on June 8 in the rector's office, to approve the contract without amendment.[35] Roger Guindon was designated rector of the new University on June 8. The Board's Chair, Gérald Fauteux, was chosen alongside Guindon. The Board formalized these decisions on July 5 pursuant to its contract.[36] The members agreed, moreover, to approve the contract even if they were absent by approving the meeting's minutes.

The meeting on July 5 thus had its routine from the contract. Roger Guindon and Gérald Fauteux were confirmed. M. L. Frieman, an Ottawa businessman who had been with Father Légaré at the 1964 meeting with the Committee on University Affairs, was elected as the Board's vice-chair.[37]

Gérald Fauteux took the night of his election as opportunity to endorse the past in romantic and religious terms. He pointed up the University's "manifest destiny as the truly great and bilingual institution of higher learning and research on this continent."[38] This was hyperbole, to be sure, but he also set the gold standard for Roger Guindon and his team. That manifest destiny was complicated by the challenges of competitive higher education in Ontario:

> We have accepted it, knowing that this is no mere matter of bricks and mortar, dollars and cents or of administrative efficiency.

> Our task is to maintain the ramparts and the underpinnings of an important bastion of democracy and knowledge so that the scholars within may quietly pursue, or vigorously debate, the truths and principles on which the forward march of man and society depend.

That "forward march" was one to which the Catholic Fauteux could subscribe in the wake of Vatican II. It was also in lockstep with Oblate and Catholic public relations after the sometimes vicious strife of 1964. Canadian Cold War rhetoric valued religious expression. The existence of diverse religious belief differentiated Western democracies from the Soviet Union. Practising Catholics demonstrated the liberal ideal; a free Christian university with a Catholic past exemplified that liberal ideal. The Board's investment in the Catholic public relations strategy highlighted this point. Catholic faith was in the Board, and the Board's faith in Catholics was paramount as Oblate and lay administrators searched for Fauteux's lofty standard:

> Greatness in universities is an elusive quality born of their scholarship and research, their generation and transmission of knowledge, the adequacy of their facilities, the stimulus of their intellectual climate, as much as of their contribution to mankind of graduates prepared, each in his own way, to write their page of history.

Inspirational words that Roger Guindon could get behind. The Oblate focus had always been on individual souls. Fauteux modified his emphasis to suit non-denominational rhetoric. Inscription on Clio's tablets was reserved for the worthy. Education's individual focus was an act of faith combined with the creation of individual ideas:

> Universities are testing places for ideas which stand or fall on the merit scholars discover in them. They are active, restless, critical, and impatient—both with themselves and with society. It is good and healthy when they are so.[39]

Even as he cast his description in non-denominational terms, Fauteux maintained the charitable discourse so dear to Oblates in the new Board. The Board's mission was to manage the institution's money to protect scholars. Such a managerial stance pursued greatness, but it was a technocratic position. Fauteux had the Board facilitating scholarship, not directing it. Such was the constitutional position of the Board, after all. It was also a charity from each of its members, for they were not remunerated for their work. That charity conveniently lined up with Oblate ambition.

Fauteux left the door open to interpret the charter in the old university's image. His speech did not strictly apply to the University of Saint Paul. It did, however, define the Board to which Saint Paul submitted in federation. The Board's inclination towards the charitable ideal that animated the old university showed that University's spirit living in the new corporation.

These contractual provisions, and what came of them, showed the close ties the Universities maintained. The Board was mandated by agreement to approve the contract as one of its official acts, and to appoint a rector, something it had already contemplated. This last deprived Saint Paul of its rector. Roger Guindon was placed in the ironic position of having signed the contract on behalf of the new University, and hosted the Board in his former office, only to be removed from that office and transported, to use the language that applied to the lay faculties, to the new corporation, where his office would henceforth reside. A more obvious display of cultural transfer is difficult to imagine. While he was only rector of the old University for a year, Roger Guindon's experience in Ottawa imbued him with the culture of the place he was called to direct. This was a further irony, perhaps, as he moved away from his home in the Faculty of Theology to control the lay faculties. The transfer of documents buttressed his administration and its goals, which were (privately) admitted to be religious.[40]

III

Problems surrounding the Faculty of Philosophy proved excuse enough for the government to push against Guindon's view of business as usual. They also created the conditions for a final Oblate claim to sovereignty over the University of Ottawa in terms quite similar to the visitatorial jurisdiction. Oblates were, of course, much more familiar with the concept than government agents. When tensions at the Faculty of Philosophy came to a head, its opinion was that the University of Saint Paul had a general right to supervise the University of Ottawa. Such a view could not help but be influenced by the tenor of negotiations through 1965–1967.

As the University negotiated with Saint Paul to take over the new faculties, it also sought to define its Christian character, as that phrase appeared in The University of Ottawa Act, 1965. This was a primordial preoccupation for the remaining Catholics at Ottawa: their agreement to reform the University hinged on meaningful continued participation in the University's government. Though it is unclear to what extent the government originally agreed to this goal, the extent of Oblate influence plainly disquieted government and lay staff alike when it focalized on changes in the Faculty of Philosophy. The University implemented these changes in moral and legal terms that continued Christian (if not wholly Catholic) discourse at the University in accordance with Guindon's view of the University's objects and purposes. His speeches evinced this view, which at times read like sermons. Saint Paul sought to evince something similar in what became the hinge between the universities: the Faculty of Philosophy.

By the time the amalgamation was completed in 1967, it was a pyrrhic victory for Oblates. In the intervening years, the Department of Philosophy deployed its rhetorical skill to attack its counterpart Faculty's legal existence at the University. It challenged Saint Paul's right to nominate the faculty's dean, vice-dean, and secretary. Their argument alleged that this right exceeded the University's powers under The University of Ottawa Act. The Faculty replied that its ability to nominate officers did not translate into a direct appointment.

The Faculty relied upon its history at the University. It was forced to defend itself most specifically by the Association of Professors, who took exception to the Oblate drive to meld Faculty with Department. The Association safeguarded the interests of its members in the Department by framing their concerns alongside the Department's: the sections of the federation agreement that gave Saint Paul power over University of Ottawa processes violated the University's charter. These concerns eventually made their way to the Attorney General of Ontario when a professor in the department, Andrew Robinson, sent a letter detailing them. He acted alone, but the Association and Department may well have privately lauded the attempt. Robinson's complaint compromised the universities' negotiating position with the government for funds to pay Saint Paul just as Ontario was becoming difficult in July 1966.[41]

The question of the Faculty of Philosophy's status was debated in the upper administration as a purely religious question in March 1965 before the University received the new charter. Conservatives wanted to shield the Church from too much exposure to secular ideas. Others advocated an openness out of necessity. If the Church could not expose its students and professors to divergent opinion, it risked losing ground at a university that now admitted all faiths. These lines replicated tensions before the reform; Roger Guindon's speeches showed the need for unity. Vatican II, which promulgated a new Catholic view of higher education, further informed the debate by promulgating a much more open theology premised upon interfaith dialogue. The postmodern marketplace of ideas had arrived at the University of Ottawa as it opened itself to non-denominational control.

Arthur Caron argued that the Church shelters its candidates to the ministry from external ideas. The Oblates' attorney general to the Holy See predictably reinforced canon law ideas. The faculties constituted by the Church for this purpose were theology, canon law, and philosophy. Rejecting the Faculty of Philosophy violated the Vatican's grant, for the Catholic university must maintain its mission to maintain its status:

> Ce serait, à mon sens, abdiquer notre responsabilité, forfaire aux engagements que nous avons pris et tromper la confiance que l'Église a mise en nous si nous allions abandonner une faculté et un enseignement ecclésiastiques à la discrétion d'une institution et d'un sénat académique officiellement et juridiquement sécularisés qui échappent à l'autorité et à la juridiction de l'Église.[42]

It was imperative to keep candidates to the ministry under ecclesiastical control. Doing anything less would violate the Church's control over its subjects, which was based on voluntary submission to canon law. This was a campaign of hearts and minds and Caron wanted to diminish future priests' exposure to corrupting ideas.

Jacques Croteau, the Dean of the Faculty of Philosophy, took the more open stance at the heart of the Oblate sale. The Faculty of Philosophy needed to integrate with the Department of Philosophy because it otherwise would lose ground to the secular professors who were clamouring for more autonomy in a soon-to-be autonomous university. The maintenance of two separate centres of philosophy would lead to the then Service Department at the Faculty of Arts teaching a full range of courses; the monopoly the Faculty of Philosophy enjoyed over advanced undergraduate and graduate teaching would disappear.

Along with this monopoly went teaching Christian philosophy. Croteau further argued that the separation of civil and ecclesiastical courses of instruction would lead to a decrease in Church influence through loss of students, especially graduate students, and through loss of teaching positions to laymen, some of whom could be hostile to the Church.[43]

These two senior Oblates feared lay dominance. Caron wished to simply limit exposure, but this conservative position did nothing to promote a Catholic worldview. Croteau, a man of his time, correctly surmised that it was not enough to hold the line. Separate education for clerics institutionalized them: they were unprepared for ideas circulating in the real world.[44] Catholicism could not spread if it did not engage more fully with the world, and engagement started with its priests. A short three months would pass before Vatican II brought Croteau's view into effect, with its "Declaration on Christian Education" commanding further co-operation between servants of the Church and lay authorities:

> [I]t is the task of the state to see to it that all citizens are able to come to a suitable share in culture and are properly prepared to exercise their civic duties and rights. Therefore the state must protect the right of children to an adequate school education, check on the ability of teachers and the excellence of their training, look after the health of the pupils and in general, promote the whole school project. But it must always keep in mind the principle of subsidiarity so that there is no kind of school monopoly, for this is opposed to the native rights of the human person, to the development and spread of culture, to the peaceful association of citizens and to the pluralism that exists today in ever so many societies.[45]

The Church allowed the state to complement its efforts, or perhaps it complemented the state's. Here, the Church was careful to guarantee, as *Université d'Ottawa* did to the Royal Commissions on Bilingualism and Human Rights, that minority and plurality interests remained unaffected by the state. This was a characteristically Catholic view grounded in a Thomistic take on Aristotle's distributive justice.[46] Even minorities had a stake in common resources. The state may not monopolize education, but the Church must also resist such monopolization in the interest of its members and for all of humanity.

The Vatican Council also specifically addressed the individual's relationship to higher education. While Croteau might not have had the fresh policy to hand, he was certainly privy to the tenor of discussion in the Council, and more broadly to papal policy, which were both cited in the "Declaration" as sources for the Church's new direction:

> The Church is concerned also with schools of a higher level, especially colleges and universities. In those schools dependent on her she intends that by their very constitution individual subjects be pursued according to their own principles, method, and liberty of scientific inquiry, in such a way that an ever-deeper understanding in these fields may be obtained and that, as questions that are new and current are raised and investigations carefully made according to the example of the doctors of the Church and especially of St. Thomas Aquinas, there may be a deeper realization of the harmony of faith and science. Thus there is accomplished a public, enduring and pervasive influence of the Christian mind in the furtherance of culture and the students of these institutions are moulded into men truly outstanding in their training, ready to undertake weighty responsibilities in society and witness to the faith in the world.[47]

The purpose of an ecclesiastical charter—whatever it might have been prior to 1965—was to now valorize the individual in states and societies increasingly tightening the reins on advanced education. Imbuing subjects with critical faculties allowed them to meld faith and science in the intensely personal process of self-discovery. The Oblates of Saint Paul (and those at Ottawa) had to respect academic freedom, but they were also commanded to hold the faith to their teaching; the Faculty of Philosophy, which fell under the University's ecclesiastical charter, had to be independent and uphold one of the Church's own, St. Thomas Aquinas. These dual responsibilities boiled down to that single mission: imparting critical abilities to students.

The tension inherent in the twin objects that informed this mission was that essential tension between civil and ecclesiastical functions. Philosophy was a secular discipline with government funding. The Faculty's preoccupation, however, was religious. The private will of at least one of Saint Paul's founders was clearly expressed in Vatican II's policy, and it directly interpolated the Church's servants. Oblates in both universities were subject to this stricture, including the rectors. Roger Guindon was busy after Vatican II doing his best to let Catholicism shine forth. He was also claiming a space for the Oblates and Christianity in the new university. Croteau sought to claim much the same space with the Faculty as Guindon did in the University. Mingling lay and religious professors watered down the faculty's religious character but afforded its members the opportunity to share Christian knowledge through the university-wide introduction to philosophy or logic courses.

Croteau's argument won the day. Arthur Caron's concerns were noted, and the Oblates proposed to transfer the faculty to the new university while retaining control over its officers. Such residual control would ensure that the Faculty could carry out its ecclesiastical obligations in the non-denominational university. The officers of the Faculty and the faculty council were thus required to maintain the ecclesiastical charter even in the new non-denominational corporation. The memorandum to that effect recognized the new approach:

> CONSIDÉRANT qu'il est dans la pensée de l'Église que les étudiants ecclésiastiques participent davantage à la vie d'étude de leurs confrères laïques et qu'ils aient, compte tenu des objectifs spécifiques de la vie sacerdotale, un niveau semblable de formation et de culture.[48]

The predominantly Oblate faculty divided over this question in a March 2 consultation on the Faculty's orientation. Of those professors present—Fathers Sylvio Ducharme, Léonard Ducharme, Marcel Patry, Clemens Stroick, and Jacques Croteau—only Father Stroick, the leader of Ottawa's German-language parish, dissented from the change.[49] Vatican II carried the day and the faculty would become a mixed lay and religious body.[50]

The immediate effect of this agreement among Oblates was that, after the passage of The University of Ottawa Act, 1965 and the federation of the universities, the faculty was without a physical home. Neither corporation knew what to do with it. Jacques Croteau described the homelessness of a Faculty seconded to Saint Paul but administered by the University of Ottawa in a July 21 letter to his superior, Jacques Gervais. He requested that the faculty continue to operate out of Saint Paul, noting that it would pay for its accommodation.[51]

The Dean couched his request in the discourse the Oblates at both universities would deploy to justify merging Faculty and Department. The Faculty bridged the old and new universities, which allowed Oblate influence to continue into the new University. Citing the new charter, Croteau presented the potential for a bridge between civil and ecclesiastical institutions:

> [T]ant du point de vue juridique que géographique, elle fait comme la jointure entre les deux institutions fédérées. Et à cet titre elle incarne d'une façon plus tangible que les autres Facultés et Ecoles l'esprit qui a présidé à la mise en œuvre de la fédération.
> Cet esprit en est un d'union, d'entraide et non de séparation. Je ne vous apprends rien en disant que les Oblats plus immédiatement responsables de la restructuration ont eu à cœur de trouver une formule qui tout en satisfaisant aux exigences du ministère de l'Éducation assurerait toutefois la continuité de l'œuvre poursuivie par les Oblats à l'Université.[52]

Croteau's representation of the Faculty of Philosophy made it eminent in the competition for resources and attention at the new institution. He supplied a further religious argument for resources from which the government recoiled, but to which the rector of Saint Paul was receptive:

> Or la situation pr{i}vilégiée de la Faculté de Philosophie, rappelée plus haut, permettra de réaliser cet idéal d'une façon exceptionnelle. C'est dans la Faculté de Philosophie plus que dans toute autre que les Oblats auront le plus de chances d'e{xc}ercer une influence chrétienne par l'enseignement et d'être par là présents au cœur de l'Université d'Ottawa. C'est encore à la Faculté de Philosophie que les occasions de rencontre entre laïcs et clercs seront fréquentes et assidues. Elles favoriseront la compréhension et l'estime mutuelles souhaitées par le Concile.[53]

The Oblates were working to keep control over their former holdings. Saint Paul's Oblates were receptive to Vatican II's decisions. Oblate governors at University of Ottawa were equally receptive: Roger Guindon signalled his cognizance of the Council in a 1965 Christmas letter to the Archbishop of Ottawa, saying: "Vous pouvez compter sur nous pour la mise en œuvre du Concile Vatican II. Nous continuerons d'être vos diocésains."[54] Guindon and Croteau had similar aims.

The Department had other ideas about its future and took offence to not being consulted at all before merger was suggested.

This was Oblate insouciance at its finest. Edgar Scully, the interim chair, said as much when he invoked "democratic process" to protest the University's decision to transfer the Department on July 22, 1966. He wrote to his dean, Jean-Marie Quirion, an Oblate defending a lay department from his colleagues. According to the Department, the Oblates did not respect such a process because of their private governance, which worked through "authoritarian control," a weightier charge, and one levelled against the Oblates that had made up their minds before The University of Ottawa Act, 1965 was introduced in the Legislature. Scully couched his charge as a representation of the opinion circulating in the now lay-controlled Faculty of Arts, heightening the stakes:

> [I]t appears to be a genuine expression of the spirit that prevails in the Faculty of Arts. Not only that, it appears to be a true expression of an irresistible trend in academic life to-day to the extent that it has been loosed from what is regarded as authoritarian control.[55]

Such control mimicked Bélanger's misgivings about the Lussier report in December 1963. It also reflected Robert Keyserlignk's thoughts about low morale in the Faculty of Arts. The merger's unilateral imposition violated lay expectations to fair treatment. Daniel Dineley, a professor of science, buttressed Scully's assertion a year later in his 1967 report to the Vice-Rector Academic, Maurice Chagnon: "One also hears rumours from the younger faculty members in the Faculty of Arts of actions smacking of restriction of academic liberty."[56] This was a restriction banned by the Church after Vatican II. It also violated the faculty's expectation, especially after the reform, that the governing culture at the University would change.

Scully's colleagues took issue with the Church's contradictory aims. They were most concerned about Catholic doctrine in the Faculty's curriculum. It was heavily Thomist, which was only one part of Vatican II's edict. Teaching doctrine now existed alongside academic freedom. Insistence on Thomism violated lay professors' academic freedom. The Departments' professors viewed the Faculty's program

> as a disguised version of the old, or at best as new patches on old clothing. They view[ed] it as a straightjacket that would prevent

> a truly free approach to Philosophy, an approach that would enable the individual professor to teach Philosophy in the light of his own convictions, interests and inspiration. Specifically, they recognize[d] it as a Thomistic program of Philosophy orientated toward Theology, which would render it impossible to introduce the student to Philosophy by way of any philosopher who did not fall within a Thomistic framework, or who could not be ordered within the context of the problems proposed. They [were] firmly convinced that Thomism should cease to be imposed from above, and be left to fare for itself in the market-place where it will stand or fall on its own merits.[57]

Content and process were at issue. The Faculty's teaching regimen relied too heavily upon one worldview. The Department could not accept such a curriculum, especially when its imposition came from on high. Even here, the Department's disagreement was not absolute. Perhaps in recognition of Oblate fiat, the Department instead appointed a two-man committee to review the faculty's curriculum and to propose an acceptable mixed curriculum.[58]

The existential threat to the Department was severe enough for them to not rely only upon a revised curriculum. The embattled professors went on the offensive by disputing Saint Paul's ability to nominate the Faculty of Philosophy's officers. The Department argued that nominations gave the ecclesiastical corporation too much control over one of the non-denominational corporations' faculties. They were willing to merge only if the dean of the Faculty of Philosophy was nominated by the University of Ottawa without involvement from Saint Paul. This proposal, of course, ran counter to Oblate wishes. Scully was, however, clear with his dean, and through him "the Senate, the Rector, [and] the Board of Governors," that "forcing a decision on the Department" would be

> imprudent not only because it would be construed as contrary to a measure of democratic process in university government, but because the position of the Department represents the expression of a widespread spirit in academic life that will not buckle under any kind of pressure.[59]

Appeals to democratic principles were convenient only if respected; the politics played on the Department were a microcosm of the ongoing power politics between government and University in 1966. Like the University in its struggle with the government, Scully would buckle before long, but not because of any pressure. The decision was not his to make, nor was it his Department's. The University owned the Department and the Faculty, and it would impose its will after a protracted and embarrassing struggle.

Scully's letter quickly reached the rector on August 2, 1966, and the Faculty of Philosophy was apprised of the situation thereafter. Jacques Gervais asked his council to draft a legal position to respond to the Department's legal challenge, and it returned an almost unanimous report to Saint Paul's Council of Administration on September 8, 1966. The Oblate-dominated Faculty considered the historical place of Saint Paul in relation to the University of Ottawa, but this time went further than Roger Guindon ever could. The Faculty claimed supervisory power over the new corporation that did not exist anywhere in the charter or in the federation agreement. Such a claim may have been purely moral, had it not appeared in a legal opinion, but alas, the Faculty did not retain counsel. Its members may well have substituted a moral claim for a legal one.

The claim, however, built on the 1965 debate within the Faculty, between Oblates, on the Faculty's place in the new corporation, and its federation with the old. It also responded, albeit obliquely, to government pressure in 1966. The Oblates had temporarily ceded their civil faculties, which fulfilled the basic criteria to recognize a visitor's jurisdiction. Property had changed hands with the intention of establishing a charity; negotiations, moreover, were going so poorly with the government entering the mix that Saint Paul might have recognized the inevitable imposed devaluation of its property. The Department's aggressive challenge to the Faculty's ties to Saint Paul forced the Faculty to claim a right of supervision in its defence. Saint Paul ceded its faculties with the intention to continue its religious tradition into the new University. They could not control the lay faculty's response, and there were indications that lay professors were convinced, as was the government, that the character of the University would change with the new incorporation. The Faculty said:

> The right which Saint-Paul University has to nominate for appointment by the Board of Governors, the Dean, the Vice-Dean and the Secretary of the Faculty of Philosophy does not in itself present an anomaly in a context of Federation. To be fully aware

of this, one has only to refer to certain precedents and analogous rights held by other federated institutions of the Province of Ontario. (For example, Assumption University in respect to the one Faculty of the University of Windsor, the Faculty of Arts and Sciences.) Such arrangements comply with the spirit and intention of a federated system. Saint-Paul University could thus have had the power of availing itself of a certain right of vigilance not only over the Faculty of Philosophy, but over all the Faculties and Schools of the University of Ottawa, and this in its capacity of the founding University, taking the initiative to establish a new university Corporation.[60]

This concise statement demonstrated the Faculty of Philosophy's opinion of itself as a legitimate bridge between the new and old institutions. It was also a narrow interpretation of The University of Ottawa Act. The Faculty argued that Saint Paul, as the founding corporation, could have sought the right to nominate the officers of each Faculty, pending approval of the new corporation's Board of Governors. This kind of right typically accrued to visitors. That Saint Paul had not sought this right was an act of grace for which lay professors at the University of Ottawa should be thankful. This understanding of the old University's role ran in the face of an earlier statement to the effect that "Saint-Paul University exercises no jurisdiction over the government of the Faculty of Philosophy." While true, nomination of officers was a significant intrusion into the Board's jurisdiction and limited the pool of candidates the Board might select.

The Faculty pushed its reasoning further based on the analogy to Assumption College in Windsor. It linked the legal argument it was making to the universities' shared culture:

> The factors which appeared to have exercised a predominant role in the establishing and structuring of federated systems are the acquired rights of the first occupant, the age-long academic tradition, the very richness of the heritage transmitted by the institution which consents to enter into a contract of federation, especially when, as in the case of Assumption University and of the University of Ottawa, an institution takes the initiative of creating a new Corporation. In such a case the new Corporation will accordingly and inevitably bear to a higher degree the hall mark of the former institution as to its principles and structure.[61]

Here again, that legal space is deployed to indicate the old institution's vested interest in the new corporation's culture and mission. "Acquired rights" thus takes on an ominous meaning: the right of supervision over the new institution.

Until 1967, the University of Ottawa was financially beholden to the University of Saint Paul for its faculties. The Faculty of Philosophy noted this point by threatening to resume courses in all disciplines, which could cause Ottawa's debt to become due. The Faculty's opinion threatened defederation by asserting that the old University could always reclaim its powers:

> It agreed to renounce to a part of its property, to the control of all the Faculties teaching secular subjects, but on certain conditions by which Saint-Paul University intended to exercise an active presence in the line of its tradition and in response to the needs of a sociological milieu. It is after all proper that it should not let a new Corporation be formed from its own accomplishments without requiring guarantees that its fundamental orientation will be assured.[62]

That fundamental orientation was a Christian one, and the Faculty of Philosophy was dominated by Oblates intent upon their religious mission: the Faculty was composed of seven Oblates in Council, and a lay member, Jean-Louis Allard, who later became President of the Senate Committee appointed to study the Duff-Berdahl report.[63] To these nine were added members of the Department of Philosophy when matters debated in Council affected the Department. The names appearing for the Department were almost entirely lay, save the Oblate Father Francis G. Morrisey, who would become one of the Catholic Church's leading canon law scholars. Morrisey did, however, have an association with the Faculty of Philosophy: he was secretary for the ecclesiastical faculties in the old University, and was the Registrar of Saint Paul from 1965 to 1971.

This tit-for-tat exchange of inexpert legal opinions about the federation agreement maintained the stalemate, and the University as yet did not interfere. It allowed the Department's frustrations to play out on a grander stage. The little Department made itself heard across campus by involving the Association of Professors of the University of Ottawa (APUO), which attacked the University by alleging breaches of its charter. While the faculty held the ear of both

Oblate rectors, the Department looked to sway lay professors' opinion by arguing that their academic freedom was being eroded. The APUO's attacks were further facilitated by the federation agreement's first circulation to Senate on January 27, 1966, following a virulent public attack against the University by one of the Department's professors, Andrew Robinson.[64]

The public nature of Robinson's comments alienated the APUO. Though his charge in the press resembled the APUO's inquiry, the scale and relative lack of tact could not be condoned. The *Ottawa Citizen* published Robinson's allegation on January 19, 1966, with the University's reply. The professor claimed continued religious control through the Oblate rector, the federation agreement, and the Board of Governors. The University countered that Robinson was confused in his reading of the Act and the Board's actions in June and July 1965. *Le Droit* picked up the thread a day later to repeat Robinson's and the University's affirmations.

Donat Pharand and Edward O. Dodson, directors of the APUO, proposed a motion the next day, January 21, 1966, to the Association's Board of Directors disassociating the Association from Robinson's public comments. It passed, but was controversial, and it was reviewed on March 17, 1966. The outcome of the review is unclear. Pharand and Dodson, however, justified their position with a factum to the March assembly. In it, Pharand commented on a request for clarification on the points Robinson raised from the Board of Governors:

> The main reason for this second motion, as explained by Dr. Dodson [the motion's mover], was that the matter in question was of an internal management nature and could be best settled internally. It was, therefore, felt that all efforts should be made to obtain an explanation and, if necessary, remedial action, without going to the Press. Indeed, the chances of obtaining such action were deemed better by not going to the Press.[65]

The APUO agreed in principle with some of Robinson's allegations, namely the argument against Saint Paul nominating the dean of the Faculty of Philosophy. It took a more tactful approach to save face. This was, ironically, the approach the University ought to have taken with the government of Ontario in 1965.

This second motion caused Roger Guindon to argue that Robinson's allegations had no merit and that the University was operating within its powers. His letter to Richard Lebrun, President of the APUO, on March 14, 1966, was characteristically diplomatic. He emphasized the charter's stipulations while valuing the APUO's concerns:

> Your concern with the autonomy of the University is legitimate and the members of the Executive Committee of the Board of Governors, as you can well imagine, are rather jealous of their prerogative as well as of that of the Senate. The Act is very clear on this point.[66]

The APUO's thrust was parried with a cool assertion of legal realities. Guindon was correct to invoke the Act: the contract did not derogate from it. Rather, it modified the Board's proceedings under the Act by mandating that it take notice of Saint Paul's desires regarding a lay faculty essential to Saint Paul's mission. Guindon communicated the extent of the Board's commitment. The accusation of Oblate control, not the first time Guindon fielded the question in the years after reform, was answered in customary fashion: the Oblates held a minority in the Board of Governors due to their involvement with Saint Paul. The Lieutenant-Governor in Council and Alumni Association held similar minorities. No one group controlled the University.

These legal realities, however, were not of the complainants' focus. The principles animating the debate were the Department's and the APUO's concern with academic freedom over all else. Secular faculty assumed that the new university was non-denominational, with a federated religious institution attached. The other corporation did not have standing in the larger university's affairs. Guindon's parry simply denied the existence of trouble by respecting the letter of the law. He did nothing to constructively address the substantive issue, that the university was not respecting the spirit of its charter and, thus, was not respecting the letter of the law as the governed foresaw it. Guindon supplied Dean Croteau's administrative argument for folding the department into a faculty:

> It was felt that the reorganized University of Ottawa had to have a Faculty of Philosophy and that the existing Faculty at the "former" University of Ottawa had built such a reputation of academic excellence that it would have taken many years before the reorganized University could have recruited the teaching

staff and built a similar reputation. On the other hand, it was felt that two distinct Faculties of Philosophy would have competed unnecessarily for both staff and students.[67]

There was no reason to complicate administrative processes by having two academic units completing the same function in civil and ecclesiastical jurisdictions. The cost, however, of adopting such an approach, or perhaps the optics of the approach, was an Oblate rector giving power to a faculty run by an Oblate dean, whose preoccupation remained Oblate and ecclesiastical.

These kinds of responses were grist to Robinson's mill. He did not putter out in the press, nor was he silenced by the APUO. He complained to the Attorney General of Ontario on June 5, 1966. He addressed those two familiar points: the appointment of officers for the Faculty of Philosophy, in which the Oblate corporation was invested by the federation agreement, and the powers of expropriation. Both contravened section 8 of The University of Ottawa Act, 1965, which proscribed denominational influence. He argued, much like the APUO, that both these clauses were outside of the University's powers. In Robinson's opinion, the clauses in question represented attacks against the Legislature's authority to constitute the University. Robinson appended a statement by his departmental colleagues agreeing with his position.[68]

Robinson used the government's utilitarian language. He viewed the University as a "public trust." He wrote the attorney general to complain of an abuse of that trust, which (again, indirectly), raised the spectre of government visitation. The University was under the direct supervision of government, which was itself acting in trust: "[T]here is, above the vested interests of any particular group or any set of institutional administrators, the twin principles of public welfare and citizen's rights that take precedence." The citizen's right referred to expropriation. Public welfare was a utilitarian allusion to the role of the university as a social reformer.[69] No longer concerned with the development of individuals, Robinson viewed university education as a societal good. Public monies were invested; public good was sought; the public, through its ministers, had supervisory rights. This view interpreted the University's authorities as an intermediary subject to direct intervention from the government when it exceeded its mandate. Hence Robinson's appeal. Robinson viewed the Oblates making a concerted effort to maintain religious control over the University.

Roger Guindon's private response to news of Robinson's fresh complaint does not contradict the professor's underlying allegation. Guindon discussed the complaint with J. R. McCarthy, the Deputy Minister of University Affairs, several times before it came to the government's Committee on University Affairs on July 25, 1966: McCarthy

> was directed to write [...] to ask if it is a fact that an agreement along the lines mentioned [i.e., the substance of Robinson's complaint] has been consummated and, if so, if a copy might be made available to the Committee [...]
>
> The Committee was of the opinion that if the two particular clauses were actually included in the agreement, they would be a cause of considerable concern on the part of the Committee.[70]

Relations with this committee were cooling through 1966 over the negotiations for Saint Paul's money. Ontario threatened financial punishment if the University attempted to maintain its religious character. Guindon understood the threat and wrote confidentially to his counterpart at Saint Paul on August 11:

> Nous sommes ici sur un terrain délicat et je suis d'avis que nous devons faire tout en notre pouvoir pour éviter que l'affaire ne soit jugée par ces messieurs comme illégale. Même l'opinion légale de notre propre aviseur peut être renversée par les législateurs. À mon avis, si les choses en venaient là, nous serions dans une position très embarrassante.

Guindon requested permission from Saint Paul to modify article five of the federation agreement to strategically appease the Committee on University Affairs. One year later, in August 1967, the article was duly modified to coincide with the further agreement between Saint Paul and Ottawa on the value of assets transferred in 1965.[71] The government seized upon Andrew Robinson's letter to force the issue.

Robinson's complaint, and the APUO's involvement, foretold the Oblate saga's century-long end at the University of Ottawa. Their effort to preserve some religious control was valiant, but (for all the good it might have done) retrograde. The overwhelming majority of lay professors joined with the government's suspicion of Catholic religious institutions. Private and public sentiment worked against the Oblates.

IV

The Faculty of Philosophy's claim to supervisory jurisdiction was checked by the government's involvement in negotiations. The fine distinction on which the government acted made it akin to a visitor, yet without the visitor's traditional mandate. The visitor's office was taken up based on a historic transfer of property. The first donor was considered the founder. Saint Paul could, then, claim the founder's role. It could not, however, provide continuing support that the University needed. The Faculty of Philosophy consequently failed to make good their claim. The government checked their discourse by withholding funds to pay for the new university's faculties. This roadblock forced the University of Ottawa's Board of Governors to become brokers in a multi-million dollar deal between Saint Paul and government, which perverted the Board's legal position as a contracting party. Relatively straightforward amicable negotiations were replaced with two years of back-and-forth between government, the University of Ottawa, and Saint Paul. Negotiations only ended in 1967 when the government was satisfied with the entire transaction.

The government's conduct, primarily through the Committee on University Affairs was designed to bleed Saint Paul and the Oblates until they came to terms. This kind of conduct patently fulfilled requirements for bad faith even if it is viewed as a response to Andrew Robinson's letter. Government's involvement interfered with economic relations and discriminated against Oblates by withholding funds because they were a charitable organization. The problematic nature of the government's conduct would, moreover, have been known to the government's agents. The Committee was chaired by Chief Justice Dana Porter, onetime Attorney General of Ontario elevated to the Ontario Court of Appeal; Leslie Frost and John Robarts were both lawyers by trade.

The University's chairman of the Board, Justice Fauteux (a puisne justice of the Supreme Court), engaged Justice Porter on roughly equal terms to negotiate the University of Ottawa's payment to Saint Paul. Porter's Committee attended at the University in May 1966. Leslie Frost led the delegation. He discussed the transfer of property and its financial ramifications with Fauteux and General Jean-Victor Allard. An example of the little love lost between Frost himself and the University, Frost insisted on more concessions from Saint Paul before payment issued. Frost was concerned about giving government funds to a religious organization, even if those funds were exchanged for real property.[72] Fauteux was the unfortunate delegate to Saint Paul, whose campus was located a twenty-minute walk from the University of Ottawa, on Main Street by the Oblate house. His attempts to toe the government line were fruitless in the face of Oblate opposition, as his July 6 letter to Porter indicates. Before making his report Fauteux allowed some frustration to seep in:

> On the 1st of July, 1965, — the effective date of The University of Ottawa Act, 1965, — the government of the new University of Ottawa was assumed by the Governors named in the Act and, on Government's assurance, previously given, that Saint-Paul University would be paid the fair value of its assets, the new University was given, by the latter, possession and control of all the assets of the Sandy Hill campus of what was, up to then, the former Université d'Ottawa, as well as of all its Faculties (except Theology and Canon Law), and all related administrative personnel and services.[73] (Original emphasis)

The government had broken its tacit agreement with the Oblates prior to the transfer to offer fair value for the faculties. Roger Guindon makes this point more explicitly in his October 25 report of a discussion with Minister of University Affairs William Davis. He qualified the University's assumption of the government's good faith as a "gentleman's agreement."[74] It was quite clearly broken in the months after the government accomplished its purpose. Instead of treating the University of Ottawa as an independent organization, Frost and the Committee on University Affairs instead prejudged the University's administration on religious grounds (thus filling in the old University's charge to the McCruer Commission). The religious nature of the Committee's concerns was nowhere more manifest than when it asked A. K. Gilmore, the new lay first vice-rector, "depuis quand il s'était converti au catholicisme" and "combien d'Oblats enseignaient à l'Université."[75] These questions betrayed an unusual and detailed interest in the University of Ottawa's personnel, one that can only be explained by a desire (born of suspicion) to further curb Oblate influence.

The government's intervention was untimely and unexpected. After the federation agreement was ratified, the Board of Governors established a negotiating committee on July 5, 1965. The Committee was composed of Board members: General Allard as chair, Lawrence Freiman, James P. Gilmore, and J. Barry O'Brien. These men worked with Saint Paul to establish a fair market value for the transferred property. They reported the number to be $21,000,000. By March 25, 1966, the Board of Governors had unanimously approved the figure. The report came to Porter's Committee, which countered with $15,000,000 as a fair figure. Fauteux rejected the government's number outright—a $6,000,000 devaluation of assets (equivalent to approximately $46,000,000 in 2019 terms—nearly 30 percent of the University's valuation) was outrageous. The Oblates were willing to accept their quoted sum—$21,000,000—disbursed over three years.[76]

Fauteux cautioned against the Committee's seemingly arbitrary desire to withhold required funds. He used the government's language:

> It is now one year since we have the possession, use and enjoyment of these assets, as well as of all the Faculties and administrative services transferred to us. Our negotiations with Saint-Paul University to determine the fair and reasonable value of these assets were conducted by us with a sense of responsibility attending trusteeship of public moneys. The report of General Allard's committee, subsequently presented to your Committee, has previously received the unanimous approval of the Board of Governors. The fact that Government authorities have not as yet given their approval to this report, is likely to create—if it has not already created—in the mind of the governors named in the Act, the frustrating impression, to say the least, that doubts as to the correctness and soundness of the report may be entertained.[77]

Fauteux echoed Roger Guindon's timely warning at convocation in October 1965 by referring to the University's "trusteeship of public moneys." The Judge implied that the obligations upon the University as a trust imposed reciprocal obligations upon government. So long as the University discharged its responsibilities with due diligence, the government was to support the University financially. Given the depth of Justice Porter's understanding of the provincial government's operations, and the Executive Committee's personalities under John Robarts's Progressive Conservative government, Fauteux's legal language reads as a shot across the government's bow. An apparent intransigence existed toward the disbursement of funds to Saint Paul. Money was power, and money from the public purse was a politically sensitive topic, and even more so when it was diverted to a Catholic institution. The University understood this politics. The use of legal language recalls the University's legal obligation in the transfer of property. The judges could not have overlooked the point.

The government's dollar diplomacy pressured the Oblates to settle for less than fair value. It was also a message to Roger Guindon and his Board of Governors: power had inexorably shifted from Oblates to the government in 1965. The government had crimped continuing Catholic control beyond repair. The power to withhold funds to the civil corporation hamstrung the University's ability to negotiate effectively, or in good faith. The new need to bring the government into alignment with the University's priorities and legal obligations added a layer of bureaucracy and popular politics that suspended the University's independence.

As tensions escalated between the Board and the Committee, Roger Guindon met with William Davis, the Minister of University Affairs, on October 25, 1966. Pauline Vanier, the University's new chancellor, mediated the exchange at Rideau Hall. The setting was no doubt meant to intimidate the minister, but Guindon's account shows only that he was suspicious of the government's discomfort with the University's French and Catholic character. Indeed, Justice Fauteux was likely the best candidate to deal with the government. His use of the government's language made for a more amicable exchange. Guindon's experience as an Oblate tainted his view: Ontario was betraying the Oblates and, through them, the minority francophone population it represented.

The meeting arose out of the mistrust engendered by government micromanagement, especially the hostile environment that met the University's delegation to the Committee on University Affairs on October 3, 1966. Ignoring their agenda, Guindon and Davis instead opted to engage in a mutually hostile line of inquiry into the University's internal politics:

> J'ai été très franc avec lui, exposant ce qui me semblait être un changement d'attitude à Toronto, surtout au Comité des Affaires Universitaires et même au ministère. Au désir de nous aider qui était si manifeste lors des discussions en vue de la réorganisation de l'Université, avait succédé, depuis 6 ou 8 mois une

espèce d'attitude soupçonneuse qui était vivement ressentie par tous ceux de l'Université qui avaient eu à faire avec le Comité ou le ministère.[78]

The Committee's members doubted the goodwill under which the University operated and had operated. The Committee members' conduct had left a deep mark on the University's representatives, not now just Oblates, but businessmen, generals, and judges. It appeared incensed by its own dark speculation against the University for having a continued religious agenda. This impression was an obvious manifestation of a pattern of discrimination that, Guindon asserted, was developing over the course of negotiations between the Universities of Ottawa and Saint Paul.

Guindon proceeded somewhat disingenuously. The University, both before and after passing the *Act*, worked under the assumption that it could trust the government and vice versa. The University acted on this assumption and did not require writing from the government. Oblates' faith in an entity other than their own Christian faith was misplaced. Guindon now personally and politically found himself at the impasse of needing funds to defray legitimate obligations to a body not under government control and having to engage the politics inherent in elected government to receive it. These politics contained a discriminatory bias that affected the University of Ottawa's ability to operate:

> Depuis février que nous attendons. Depuis ce temps que nous ne pouvons entreprendre aucun projet de construction, car on met tout en cause et on nous assure que rien ne peut se faire tant que cela ne sera pas réglé. Cela, pour nous, est réglé. Tout le fatras qu'on nous a fait, à Toronto, le 3 octobre, concernant l'indécision du gouvernement à envisager le développement du campus de l'Université là où elle est depuis un siècle, nous a bouleversés. Ceci, incontestablement, est une guerre de nerfs ou un "change of horse in mid-stream."

This was a game of chicken that Ontario had already successfully played against the Oblates to force consent for reform to a non-denominational university. Government funding was necessary to continue the enterprise. The game a year on, however, was different for the Oblates and Ontario. While the government was suspicious of the Catholic charity, and its members at the head of Saint Paul, this same charity required payment for its assets.[79]

The Oblates held the legal high ground. Roger Guindon echoed Justice Fauteux's description of Leslie Frost's request of the University:

> Soudain, M. Frost affirme que les O.M.I. devraient transférer les biens à rabais puisqu'ils étaient des religieux et qu'ils voulaient le bien de l'Université. J'ai immédiatement répliqué que l'Université Saint-Paul seule était le juge des dons qu'elle voulait faire et à qui elle voulait les faire.[80]

If any doubt existed about the government's intentions, Leslie Frost's gauche comment puts them beyond the pale. The government starved the Oblates into relinquishing their assets for less than fair consideration because they viewed the religious corporation as not capable of receiving these funds, or as less than capable of receiving them. The insulting caricature of Oblate charity, moreover, assumed that the Oblates were charitable to a fault. Frost might have been bargaining hard, but his tactics only ensured further Oblate resistance.

General Allard's correspondence with Leslie Frost and William Davis after he became chair of the Board of Governors in 1966 continued the University's trouble with government. The government handily undid the Oblates' legal high ground through the end of the year. All it had to do was continue to offer money that fell short of the agreement between the University of Ottawa and Saint Paul. By thus financially starving both the University of Ottawa and the Oblates, the government ensured that it would bring both to heel.

William Davis offered a package to the universities on February 27, 1967, that became the basis of final negotiations between the government and universities. The challenge was to amend the government's even poorer offer of $13,500,000 up to what the Board and Saint Paul could accept: $17,451,000. Davis's offer granted the lowest sum in real funds, while granting credits to the University "through the Ontario Universities Capital Aid Corporation" totalling $3,950,000. In total, Davis offered the University slightly more than the University had wanted, but he did not offer the entire sum to Saint Paul.[81] Leslie Frost rejoined the Minister the day after with a personal note for General Allard:

> I may say that I am delighted beyond expression that our efforts in the Ottawa University matter have been successful. It is a delight

indeed that all parties are satisfied and that things are now going along smoothly and that the great University of Ottawa will attain its place in buildings, equipment, etc. in keeping with the importance of the great institution.[82]

Frost's tone is condescending. Unless General Allard, or perhaps Roger Guindon, in whose archive this letter wound up, placed a call to the Minister or Deputy Minister accepting their proposal, there was no reason to assume its success. The Board was still required to formalize the decision by vote, and Saint Paul had to be consulted. In fact, the Board was only informed of the Minister's letter on March 13, and unanimously accepted the terms so long as Saint Paul assented.[83]

Roger Guindon grumpily communicated the Board's decision to his counterpart, Jacques Gervais, on March 14. He specified the terms to which Ottawa's Board had agreed, and the Board's disapproval of the government's reference to "Oblate Order" rather than Saint Paul University as the recipient of the proceeds. The news, for Saint Paul, was not good and represented a significant financial loss from the $21,000,000 both parties had agreed to in 1965. Saint Paul would not recover the $7,500,000 difference, although the University of Ottawa would have its capital building expenses defrayed. This loss was a further charity demanded of the Oblates, and it was one that Guindon had railed against in his convocation speeches the past two years. Saint Paul nevertheless agreed on March 22.[84]

The Board's and Saint Paul's acceptance and stipulations were communicated to the Minister thereafter, and the tensions which had grown between government and University manifested in this final episode. The government added to Leslie Frost's condescension by referring four times to Saint Paul's administration as the "Oblate Order," which Roger Guindon, on behalf of the Board of Governors, went to lengths to correct in an unsent letter to William Davis dated March 27. He was angered by the government's bias against the Oblates and rebuked Davis:

> We respectfully submit that this must be a clerical error since the only official name of that corporation has been the Université d'Ottawa [...] The assets owned by the former Université d'Ottawa, now Saint Paul University, are not and never were owned by the Oblate Order. We therefore respectfully urge that

this be rectified for the record, as all negotiations have always taken place between the two universities.⁸⁵

Guindon's restrained his passion but made his point. The Oblate Order administered the University, but Saint Paul maintained separate funds and a separate corporate identity. This minor detail was a parting shot after two years of haggling that, for Guindon, in part represented the future of his brothers at Saint Paul and in Canada.

Alongside the frustration in this unsent letter, a *Globe and Mail* article entitled "Province urged to provide 100% of capital costs for universities" appeared on March 22, 1967. The article summarized statements made by Dr. Douglas T. Wright, the new Chairman of the Committee on University Affairs, before the Legislature's Standing Committee on Education and University Affairs. Wright suggested a radical policy shift from the split financing of university buildings in Ontario to complete government funding of basic facilities.⁸⁶ This change further complicated the University of Ottawa's perception of the government's offer. Whether a serious proposal or not, Wright's suggestion came a week after Saint Paul had accepted a humiliating defeat. This defeat was only palatable because the University of Ottawa was granted special funding through the Ontario Universities Capital Aid Corporation. Wright's proposal potentially altered the structure of capital aid to growing universities, which would have changed the funding agreement between the University of Ottawa and the government.

These concerns played themselves out in Guindon's unsent letter to Minister Davis, which carried a clue as to why it was not sent. It bears a manuscript annotation "pas envoyée," and additional markings: "[N]ous ne voulons pas être réduits à 'O' : no endowment, no sinking fund, no money for scholarship." Guindon might have finally been listening to Bill Boss. The University did not wish to antagonize the government out of fear that payment to Saint Paul or even its own operating funds would suffer. That fear shows just how much influence, if not outright control, the government accrued. Its dollar diplomacy forced the universities to exchange that control for their continued operation.

The University plainly considered the threat serious. The Board of Governors' executive committee held an extraordinary meeting on Saturday, March 25, to discuss the government's apparent change of plan. The Board sought to understand the "effect this [policy] would have to the agreement they had accepted with the understanding that a credit of $3,950,000 would be established in the name of the University of Ottawa."[87] The Committee could not see through the government's game, so it altered the Board's previous decision. If it was going to accept the funding scheme, that acceptance was now conditional pending clarification from government.

Guindon's handwritten notes from this executive committee lends further credence to the hypothesis that government controlled the university's affairs. Suspicions circulated through the rector and the Committee. "Gentleman's agreements" no longer applied: "[A]re we to propose 2 letters? /do it quietly/go with memorandum for clarification/say it was accepted/but too many queries from members of the Board."[88] The politics were delicate, for the government had the potential to be embarrassed, and the University had a recent history (when it was Catholic) of attacking the government in public, notably during the Commissions on Bilingualism and on Human Rights. A member of the Committee reviewed the timeline showing the University's agreement, Saint Paul's acquiescence and the subsequent policy shift. The proximity of these events was patently on members' minds, and the government's intent was not favourably construed.

Whatever action was taken, the deal was maintained, but the trust over two years between the University and its sponsor had broken. In a letter to Jacques Gervais, Guindon indicated *post scriptum* that "[u]ne nouvelle publiée par le Globe and Mail de Toronto le 22 mars 1967 vient changer le contexte et je rencontrerai en fin de semaine plusieurs membres du Bureau à ce sujet. Je retiens pour le moment toute correspondance avec Toronto," which suggested a shrewd political move in the works.[89] In follow-up correspondence on April 19, Guindon indicated to the rector of Saint Paul's that an agreement with the government was reached on the original terms proposed by the Minister.[90]

These exchanges between university and government over payment to Saint Paul broke the remaining bonds of trust between university and government. The palpable suspicion of university officials rankled; more critically, the government proved willing to interfere in the University's business even though the University of Ottawa was ostensibly independent. The government and its agents were fully aware of their financial influence and exerted it with ease. University administrators' and governors' response to this influence was to wholly cave to government control. Little choice remained, for the University had no alternate source of funding. Roger Guindon's speeches throughout the negotiations pushed against this view, but to little avail.

V

The Oblates expected the two universities to come together in a happy union of mother and child, which was the first step in a wider attempt to continue Oblate influence after reform. The government of Ontario treated the universities shabbily, but not without reason. The Oblates unduly exerted their influence over the new corporation in an attempt to maintain the status quo through different means. Roger Guindon's speeches point to Oblate values being projected throughout the University of Ottawa even after reform. The federation agreement, which gave Saint Paul influence over the Faculty of Philosophy, allowed that Faculty to claim a supervisory jurisdiction for Saint Paul. Such a claim was, and remains, weighty. It was a powerful testament to Oblate sentiment; it now disrupts government's claim to jurisdiction over the University of Ottawa. The short form of this observation is that Saint Paul won a potentially lasting claim against the government of Ontario. The University of Ottawa was significantly indebted to the Oblate university, a debt only cleared by Ontario for a substantially reduced price. Oblate consent to that reduction became its own charity—one not only recognized by Ontario's agents: it was encouraged in those terms. The reduction affected the quality of the Oblate's gift. They had not sold all of their faculties. They had instead gifted a large portion of the fair value sale price to the University of Ottawa. The Oblates formally continued their foundation, and their stubborn resistance may prove decisive in some future legal contest.

The internal dispute over the Faculty of Philosophy, though not determinative of the issue, changed relations between the University and government during these negotiations. Roger Guindon and members of the Board of Governors were already irritated by Ontario's cavalier attitude toward negotiations. The government held the financial high cards. With Andrew Robinson's complaint to the attorney general, the field shifted further to the government's side. Evidence of the Oblates maintaining soft power while the government assumed formal control through the power of the purse exacerbated the mistrust between proponents of religion and supports of the non-denominational university. By so openly telegraphing Oblate plans, the universities invited government scrutiny. The stubbornness of the Oblate Order may have by this time become legend in the Department of University Affairs. All that Ontario had been missing was the invitation to stamp Oblate influence out.

Andrew Robinson's complaint was precisely that invitation. The APUO's rhetoric, however, points to wider sentiment among professors. Though it is likely that many of these professors were Catholic, the concerns of lay Catholics likely resembled non-Catholic professors' concerns for their personal freedoms and intellectual inquiries. These were no new feelings. Professors, like Robert Keyserlingk in early 1965, had complained to Guindon about morale and the administration's conduct from different corners of the University. The Department of Philosophy was a lightning rod for these frustrations. Once the battle was joined, Robinson's comments to the attorney general were enough to tip the scales of Oblate fortunes. Saint Paul lost $7,000,000; the University of Ottawa was embarrassed before its new masters; the federation agreement was amended to appease government, not the Department. The Department nevertheless fell willingly after these changes to the Faculty of Philosophy.

The University of Ottawa would become non-denominational as the Oblates puttered into oblivion, their numbers and their finances shrinking in Canada. Ontario strongly asserted its power of the purse to show the way forward. The Oblate focus on hearts and minds could not keep up with this impetus.

Epilogue:
Settling the Religious Character

> Ye are all the children of light, and the children of the day: we are not of the night, nor of darkness.
>
> Therefore let us not sleep, as do others; but let us watch and be sober.
>
> For they that sleep sleep in the night; and they that be drunken are drunken in the night.
>
> But let us, who are of the day, be sober, putting on the breastplate of faith and love; and for an helmet, the hope of salvation.
>
> — Thessalonians 5:5–8

The costly debate over the Department of Philosophy sparked a discussion about the University of Ottawa's future as a Christian institution. These discussions ran through 1967–1969 and attest to the waning influence of Oblate fathers. Even Roger Guindon, who would remain rector until 1984, lost ground to lay concerns. At issue was Ontario's latest snub, where the University's autonomous Christian character was virtually ignored immediately after the reform. The government instead forced the University to conform to a rigid non-denominational framework that betrayed Oblate aspirations and, it seems, Oblate trust.

Lessening of Oblate influence was growing increasingly apparent as the decade of the 1960s wore on. The Oblates gave up control of their university with the plan to retain Christian influence through grandfathered teaching and administrative staff. These holdovers coupled with the federation agreement with Saint Paul, which preserved a substantial, though not controlling, amount of religious influence, especially in the Faculty of Philosophy. Lay professors, however, contributed toward undoing these plans. The government pushed back against religious influence in the Faculty of Philosophy and again against any perceived generous payment to Saint Paul for the fair value of its faculties. The University of Ottawa, now dependent on the government's dime, buckled across the board. Saint Paul received a lesser sum after two years of negotiations, and ecclesiastical influence, such as there was, was shown to be greatly reduced.

The government's tack unwittingly ushered in a new era at the University of Ottawa, which may be representative of some aspects of other universities' transformations from religious or denominational institutions to non-denominational ones. This transformation at Ottawa removed religious laws and culture and instituted a regime that theoretically better responded to the needs of communities. That regime in fact might better be compared (especially in more recent times) to the structure of school boards in Ontario.[1] School boards are politically responsible to their communities (hence their election by ratepayers); they are operationally responsible to the Minister of Education.[2] In similar wise, the present review of a critical point in the University of Ottawa's history demonstrates that its Board of Governors, though politically independent from the Crown and its agents, had that political independence quickly wrested from its grasp. The University and its Board became responsible to the Minister of Training, Colleges and Universities.

Roger Guindon would not, however, take this lying down. True to stubborn Oblate form, the University Senate appointed a committee to study the University's Christian character in 1967. The University was back in the ring just as the dust settled from Robinson's complaint and from the negotiations over Saint Paul's funding. This time, the Senate was interpreting its home statute,[3] which commanded the University to further, in accordance with Christian principles, the intellectual, spiritual, moral, physical and social development of, as well as a community spirit among, its undergraduates, graduates and teaching staff, and to promote the betterment of society.[4]

Section 8 rejoined these objects and purposes:

> The management, discipline and control of the University shall be free from the restrictions and control of any outside body, whether lay or religious, and no religious test shall be required of any member of the Board, but such management, discipline and control shall be based upon Christian principles.

The University was to be governed with "Christian principles" in mind, but this enigmatic phrase was broad enough to mean nothing. Such was the lesson handed out by government when it shorted the sale of Saint Paul's faculties; the Oblates at the University of Ottawa read the words with more heart.

The Senate's quest was at first confined to reconciling the courses offered by the Department of Religious Studies to those offered by the Faculty of Theology.[5] The issue mirrored recent discord over the Department of Philosophy. The Senate had to reconcile the existence of two similar academic units. Unlike the Faculty and Department of Philosophy, the goal was simply to delineate areas of responsibility. With the Robinson letter to the attorney general, however, the Committee quickly changed focus from the academic question to the greater question of principle that underlay Robinson's claims. Was the University of Ottawa still at all beholden to Christian teaching or doctrine? The question was especially pressing because the University had to respond to Ontario's threatening posture. Rallying the academic community behind a single interpretation of the University's mission would accomplish Roger Guindon's desire for unity, which, by 1967, he had been preaching for two years.

The committee first met on January 26, 1967. It agreed to invite the authorities responsible for preparing The University of Ottawa Act, 1965, and the federation agreement between the Universities to testify.[6] A legal opinion on the exact meaning the Legislature assigned to "Christian principles" was also sought, from the Justice George Addy, a member of the Board of Governors and a bencher of Ontario's High Court of Justice. These initial steps set the pace for thorough work that lasted until February 1969. Over this time, the committee submitted an interim and a final report that fleshed out the University's Christian history and that culture's inclusion in University life moving forward. This process formalized cultural links with Saint Paul, which allowed the committee to cut off Oblate appeals to history. It defined an official history between the two universities.

The committee worked through two phases to produce reports. The first phase of information gathering preceded the interim report. Commentary was received from witnesses and memoranda. George Addy's legal opinion also came in, but not without criticism from surprising corners. This document and the opinions of University members created the interim document that sparked discussion in the second phase. Debate here focused on the substance of Andrew Robinson's complaint. The APUO, this time more militant after the government's successful intervention on the Department of Philosophy's behalf, pushed the University to recognize the legislator's intention: the University of Ottawa was now non-denominational and the Oblates had a limited place in the new Order. The students also spoke up by launching a challenge to the legality of the Committee's work. The final report thus came to Senate on February 3, 1969, after much contention. It recommended that every undergraduate program offers the option of religious study. This formal victory for the Oblates rang hollow after the concerted opposition that was brought to bear from the APUO and also the students' federation.

The Committee operated under the quaint presumption that it was crafting private law for an eleemosynary corporation. This assumption explains the presence of Saint Paul's faculty on the Committee—Saint Paul was represented on the University's Senate; its members had a vested interest in crafting this policy. Saint Paul's claim to supervision over the University of Ottawa played in these appointments. Members were brought in from the former University of Ottawa, which ignored legal divisions between federated corporations. Though the old University had sacrificed its controlling stake on the understanding that Christian teaching would continue unimpeded, its members' participation defining the University's Christian character was supervision by other means. Saint Paul's legacy depended in large measure on the meaning of these two words.

The committee polled the University community on what it thought about religious influence at the University. A first survey interrogated faculty on their thoughts concerning the *Act* and the contract. The second asked for faculty's view of the practical implications of each legal instrument.[7] The Committee's wide-ranging surveys addressed professors' concerns about Oblate insouciance. Asking the University's members strengthened the Committee's conclusions: the Committee was defining the operation of legislation on specific territory; only the members of that territory could properly comment. This democratic impulse attempted to fold lay professors into a conversation about the University's essential values, which could, perhaps, diffuse the tension created by Robinson's complaint and the schism between Faculty and Department of Philosophy.

The rector's testimony, however, figured prominently in the Committee's eyes. He was, after all, a theologian. His appearance with Jacques Croteau on February 27 rehashed the message Guindon had been expressing since 1965. He began with an appeal to the University's history. Oblate control was at issue in the government's reform, not the University's Christianity. As such, the *Act* explicitly enabled the University to continue its mission with the phrase "Christian principles." Croteau, Dean of the Faculty of Philosophy, echoed Guindon's view by adding an interpretation of federation that accorded with his Council's opinion:

> La fédération est un contrat conclu soit entre deux universités soit entre une université et d'autres universités par lequel les parties contractantes s'engagent, moyennant certaines conditions et dispositions notamment la mise en veilleuse partielle de la charte de l'une des parties ou des deux, à collaborer à une œuvre universitaire commune et à satisfaire par là aux aspirations diverses d'une population diversifiée sans devoir occasionner pour autant des dépenses coûteuses qu'entraînerait nécessairement la multiplication de centres complets universitaires.[8]

Croteau argued efficiency. He addressed the Committee's first mandate by depicting the Department of Religious Studies' position in the organization as against the Faculty of Theology's. His comments also touched on his Faculty's recent growth. The federation created a joint goal that brought part of Saint Paul's religious mission into the University of Ottawa's non-denominational government via "Christian principles." Saint Paul's existence enriched the University of Ottawa's religious character such that it need not create fresh religious academic units.[9]

The rector's and the dean's statements were fraught with religious bias. Professor Colin Wells, of the Faculty of Arts, warped that bias by noting the rector's nod toward a more expansive understanding of the University. He argued that implicit in the rector's statement was an acknowledgment that the University should be free from "religion and philosophy" (Guindon's and Croteau's respective home disciplines), and instead tied to "academic standards." Such reasoning was especially necessary in light of "new financial arrangements with Toronto." In short, religion and religiosity were the causes of financial woe; Wells did not acknowledge any wider principle being at stake. His sole focus was the University's competition with other public, secular, institutions for funding.[10] Wells' commentary echoed Edgar Scully's 1966 letter to Dean Quirion: another Faculty of Arts professor was suspicious of the "authoritarian control" exerted by religious authorities in the new corporation.[11] Professor Lawrence T. Dayhaw, a Committee member from Social Sciences and hired one year after Roger Guidon, agreed with Wells's suspicion, but he came to the rector's defence when he counselled against ascribing "causality on one thing, v.g. religion, if something else goes wrong, v.g. Competence [sic]."[12] While Guindon and Croteau were Oblates, they were not so biased as to be incapable. Targeting religion in the wake of the rector's presentation was nevertheless palpable resistance against an old yoke.

The Committee adopted this suspicion in part and sought further information about Croteau's idea of federation. It needed to substantiate Croteau's claims about federation's effects, and Andrew Robinson's failed legal challenge heightened the need for such clarity. Yet another member, Robert Choquette (himself a historian of the Canadian Catholic church), requested copies of the acts incorporating the universities of Laurentian, Windsor, and Toronto—all universities affiliated with Catholic universities or colleges—from Maurice Chagnon, the Vice-Rector, Academic. These acts would elucidate the legal idea of federation in Ontario, which would allow the Committee to better understand the University of Ottawa's federation. Chagnon obliged. He indicated that the rector's office held a book with all the acts incorporating Ontarian universities, and that Choquette could obtain it by writing to that office. Information necessary for legal comparison was to hand, and not just for the Committee's members.[13]

As the Committee interviewed administrators in February and March, several professors responded in writing to the Committee's questionnaires. Some approved the Christian yoke; others violently disagreed. Both sides placed the administration's discourse in relief. The Dean of Law, Thomas Feeney, sent a letter to the Committee on February 24, 1967. The letter recalls Feeney's brief to the McCruer Commission on Human Rights:

> Universities are now recognized by government as charged by society with settling the problems of mankind. This I regard as implicit recognition of the fact that the world outside of university has failed to solve most of the serious problems of humanity. It has failed, I believe, for having no coherent philosophy. It therefore behooves our universities to formulate collectively and individually a clear code of ethical and social values. The Christian ethics in the pluralistic society is, of course, apparent in most of our universities but only in a few. The University of Ottawa has been one of the few. In the *University of Ottawa Act, 1965*, the Province of Ontario is to my mind charging this University with continuing its Christian tradition.[14]

Feeney reiterated unity of purpose in a human rights context. Catholic views of university education responded to a legislative mandate, one designed to unify at least some segment of Ontario's population around a core of similar beliefs. The government's wider policy of supporting strictly non-denominational institutions was accounted for by Saint Paul's minority representation on the Ottawa Board. Such an imposition created a duty, perhaps even a public duty, that the University could not shirk. It had to embody its "Christian tradition." In this argument, however, lay the rub—the dangerous precedent—of denominational control through the old University and through religious executives. It was this kind of argument that the provincial government was suspicious of, and it was this kind of suspicion that prompted Andrew Robinson's complaint. A reasonably well-informed observer could impute an attempt by the Oblates to retain control of the jewel in their crown.

George Addy echoed Dean Feeney's opinion as a member of the Board of Governors, and as the University's former counsel, now as a sitting high court justice. He delivered his views on March 9, 1967. The committee considered it alongside Feeney's letter, but the text was kept mum until the committee had made its interim report to Senate on January 8 and 15, 1968, to which it was appended. Addy submitted three legal questions:

1. Does the expression "Christian principles" in the present context have any definite legal meaning?
2. If not, who is to determine the meaning and how?
3. Assuming either a definite legal meaning or a meaning determined by proper authority, how does one reconcile the maintenance of Christian principles with the proscription of any religious test?[15]

The heart of these questions goes to who or what constitutes the "proper authority." Addy located that authority in the University, but it was owed to the Legislature. The grant was plain in his response to the first question: "There exists an irrebuttable presumption against legislative pleonasm." That is, the Provincial Parliament never used extra words. Addy created his own legal definition using an analogy from a 1917 House of Lords case that considered Christianity "the law of the land," defining it as "belief in the Trinity" without specifying a particular denomination. It was an admittedly tenuous analogy, better suited in Addy's opinion to "ascertaining the meaning of Christian principles."[16] This general tenet only showed that the Legislature acknowledged the University as a Christian institution.

Addy did not quite answer question two. He considered the authority capable of defining the term in the absence of legislative or judicial interpretation. He submitted that it was the Senate, responsible for supervising the University's mission, that had statutory authority to define the phrase. It was also obligated under the *Act* to enforce the proscription of religious tests and the application of Christian principles.

The Committee's interim report, submitted to the Senate on November 6, 1967, with debate held over until January 1968, broadly upheld the administration's opinion as it was expressed in Addy's brief. It also mimicked the Faculty of Philosophy's earlier interpretation of the federation agreement and The University of Ottawa Act. The Committee interpreted the Act as an almost purely administrative shift to make the University eligible for Ontario grants. It affirmed the University's Christian, Catholic, tradition. Any other interpretation would, in the Committee's view, require express legislative amendment to include a full non-denominational clause in the charter. Federation publicly manifested this continuity.[17] The report reprised arguments made over and over again after 1965. The University may be non-denominational, but its administration carried Catholic culture forward.

The APUO predictably disagreed with Addy's opinion and the Committee's interim report, just as they had disagreed in 1966 with the Faculty of Philosophy's opinion. Professor George Ling of the Faculty of Medicine, President in 1967–1968, engaged the Committee.[18] It was, however, his replacement and Vice-President, Gordin Kaplan, who would bother the University most with his outspoken dislike of "Christian principles."[19] Like Robinson, Kaplan sought a wider audience. He forwarded a copy of Addy's opinion to the Canadian Association of University Teachers (CAUT).[20] CAUT's Associate Executive Secretary, Edward J. Monahan,[21] a graduate of Saint Michael's College and a historian of Ontario universities, in turn consulted the Dean of the Faculty of Law at Windsor, Mark Rudolph MacGuigan,[22] and the Honourable Chief Justice Bora Laskin of the Court of Appeal for Ontario, later fourteenth Chief Justice of the Supreme Court of Canada. The justice was recently of Osgoode Hall law school, holding a Master of Laws and a professor at University of Toronto (1940–1965) and Osgoode Hall (1945–1949). Laskin's interest in universities was a personal one, which he carried into his time on the bench.[23] Monahan consulted these two academics in varying capacities: MacGuigan generated a countervailing opinion anonymously submitted through CAUT to the Association of Professors. Laskin gave a scant appraisal of Addy's opinion. Both men's names were not associated with CAUT when the information was passed to the APUO; their association after the fact shows the lengths to which CAUT was willing to go against the University's efforts to maintain its Christian character.

Edward Monahan was seized with the opinion early in the process, before the University of Ottawa's Senate debate the Committee's report. He solicited Chief Justice Laskin's opinion on December 29, 1967:

> I was especially intrigued ("appalled" might be a more accurate term) by the contents of the legal opinion. Though you may not wish to comment on it, particularly in view of its source, I should be interested in having any reaction you care to voice.[24]

Both Monahan and the Chief Justice were aware of the delicacy of his action, for Addy had become a member of Ontario's Superior Court. Laskin's reply spelled out the problem:

Dear Ed:

Thank you for the material attached to your letter of December 29th, 1967. I have read the legal opinion with more than the usual interest, because the writer is now a member of the High Court of Justice. I must say, with the caution that one should exercise in the circumstances, that "intriguing" is an apt characterization of the opinion. Perhaps I may have a chance to talk to you or Percy about it after I have read it with more care than was involved in the short perusal that I have so far given it.

With best wishes for the New Year, and warm personal regards to both Percy and to you.

Yours sincerely,

[Signed]
Bora Laskin[25]

The legal value of the opinion was debatable, to say the least. It was certainly produced by a biased councillor, who had no business, as a member of the bench, giving a legal opinion of any sort. Laskin's familiar note bears an ominous tone: "more than the usual interest" being paid to a fresh justice on the bench did not bode well for Addy, although nothing seems to have come of it. Laskin's position foreshadowed Dean MacGuingan's comments on March 8 after the New Year.

In the intervening period, the APUO took note of the politics in Addy's opinion. They openly aligned themselves against it at the Senate meeting of January 8 and 15, 1968, where the interim report was publicly approved, but the text remained confidential. Jean-Louis Allard spoke on the Committee's behalf to make four recommendations:

> 1. Que le Sénat reconnaisse que la description du caractère chrétien de l'Université d'Ottawa présentée dans l'essai de synthèse soumis au Sénat le 6 novembre 1967 (p. 9 à 11, en excluant la définition du contenu des principes chrétiens) est conforme, en substance, à la situation de droit et de fait de l'Université d'Ottawa.
> 2. Que le Comité prépare un texte final sur cette question en tenant compte des remarques, suggestions et propositions qui lui seront faites par les membres du Sénat. Ce texte devra évidemment être soumis à l'approbation du Sénat.
> 3. Que le recteur exprime aux membres du corps professoral, dans le plus bref délai possible et de manière qu'il jugera la plus

pratique, le sens du caractère chrétien de l'Université d'Ottawa, compte tenu des transformations survenues en 1965 et en conformité de la décision du sénat sur cette question.

4. Que le rapport final du Comité, dûment approuvé par le Sénat, soit distribué en temps et lieu à tous les membres du personnel enseignant de l'Université.[26]

Paul Robson, on behalf of the Faculty of Science, moved a motion to distribute the report to all affected professors before the report was approved. If adopted, the motion would provoke a much wider discussion on the definition of "Christian character." The Chair, Roger Guindon, intervened with "un commentaire explicatif" that quickly undid the motion. The Senate instead resolved to distribute the report to faculty councils and to the University's schools before its adoption. This compromise gave the Faculty of Science some of what it wanted. The Senate adopted the committee's recommendations, as amended.[27]

Insidious power politics in the Senate and at the committee studying the Christian character raised the APUO's ire. The Association had submitted its views to the rector before the meeting. Its members were on the Senate, and the formality of its communication could have been avoided. Alas, as debate on adopting the Committee's report was ending, the rector presented an APUO communication endorsing the Faculty of Science's defeated motion. The Chair's timing rendered the APUO's intervention moot.[28] Guindon's parliamentary tactic allowed him to ensure the result. The APUO was dismissed even as it submitted legitimate commentary. The rector provoked the APUO to further resistance.

The Students' Union of the University of Ottawa rejoined the APUO's displeasure at the University's selective distribution of information a month later, on February 7, 1968. Its President, Alphonse Morissette, communicated the Union's long disapproval of the University's denominational character. He requested all documentation pertinent to understanding the work of the Senate's committee. He then addressed the questions put to the University community:

> Je me réfère au document précité pour mettre en question le mandat même qui a été accordé à ce comité. En effet, on y pose la question suivante : "En quel sens, compte tenu de la loi de l'Université d'Ottawa 1965 et du contrat de fédération entre l'Université d'Ottawa et l'Université St-Paul, l'Université d'Ottawa est-elle

chrétienne ?" Cette question porte en elle-même une contradiction d'ordre légal. Comment pourrait-on interpréter le texte d'une loi passée par le gouvernement ontarien en se servant des termes d'un contrat privé survenu entre l'Université d'Ottawa et l'Université St-Paul ?[29]

Morissette communicated the prevailing opinion on The University of Ottawa Act, 1965. Morissette's view, however, ignored the Committee's mandate. He reasoned that, because the Committee's interpretation of the University's charter relied upon the text of a contract, it made a critical error. Only the legislator's text mattered, and the Committee, in adopting George Addy's brief and Jacques Croteau's comments, read too much into the Act.[30] This view was flawed because it did not address how the federation agreement might be seen to carry the phrase "Christian character" into effect under the powers granted in the new charter.

The University was obfuscatory toward Morissette's concerns. Maurice Chagnon advised the rector on his response: "La lettre contient plusieurs imprécisions et erreurs d'interprétation. Je ne crois pas que nous devrions engager la discussion à ce point." Chagnon proposed a brief statement rehearsing Addy's legal opinion, and finally advised that the students' concerns be referred to the Committee. Whether the Committee actually met with the students, as it did with the professors, is unclear, but it likely did not, for the students subsequently complained to the government's Committee on University Affairs on much the same legal basis as Andrew Robinson complained to the attorney general.[31] The students felt disenfranchised, so they referred their complaints to the body that had exercised the visitor's powers in Robinson's case. They no doubt did so unwittingly, but the recourse's use early in the University's reformed era again suggested that government had more direct control over the University than we currently recognize.

The APUO rejoined the fray with Dean MacGuigan's legal opinion in hand. MacGuigan replied to Monahan's request on March 8, but insisted his name be disassociated from the product.[32] While he remained anonymous, it is ironic that the dean of law at Windsor, a university once owned by the Catholic Basilian Fathers, and federated to a Catholic college, would convincingly agree with the APUO's and CAUT's secular position. His letter made its way to Gordin Kaplan at the University around March 28.[33] MacGuigan's opinion then went around to members of the APUO Board in a memorandum. It also made its way to the Committee as follow up to a tense meeting with the APUO's Board of Directors on February 26, 1968.

In this meeting, the APUO rejected the University's Christian character as a divisive issue over which the Senate did not have jurisdiction or competence. Gordin Kaplan was explicit, and undiplomatic, on this point:

> Referring to the words "sans opposition" which are found in the conclusion of the interim report, Dr. Kaplan advises the Committee that it now has opposition from the A.P.U.O. It would be naïve for the Committee not to expect opposition if and when it tries to prepare administrative policies which would follow from the conclusions of the interim report.
>
> The Committee has wrongly concluded from the words "in accordance with Christian principles" that the University of Ottawa is Christian. Just as it is possible for an individual to base his life on Christian principles without being a Christian in any sense it is possible for a university to base its educational philosophy on those principles without being defined as a Christian institution.[34]

The Committee was struck by Kaplan's suggestion that it had no competence to conduct its study. It reported to the Senate on March 4 that it had met with the APUO, but it did not capture the APUO's demeanour. The Senate's small size, and the Committee's relatively extensive membership, ensured that nothing, including Addy's legal opinion, remained secret for long. The Committee's feeble response to a jurisdictional question asserted its ability to define the University's Christian character on March 25. It further claimed the right to report to the Senate, if only because its terms of reference were from the Senate.[35]

Dean MacGuigan concurred with Kaplan's view of the committee in more neutral terms. Citing Addy's opinion, he suggested that the University of Ottawa's duty to impose "Christian principles" did not exist because:

> In nominally Christian countries without an established Church, the expression ["Christian principles"] seems to have tended to lose any credal significance and to imply only that which is ethically praiseworthy or socially customary.[36]

MacGuigan used Addy's case, the 1917 House of Lords decision in *Bowman v. Secular Society Ltd.*, as a straw man. An established state Church had to legally exist for the expression "Christian principles" to have intrinsic legal value. It was no wonder Chief Justice Laskin was interested in Addy's biased opinion: it misrepresented law in Ontario, for the province had no official Church.[37]

While McGuigan's logic was sound, the Committee did not accept the APUO's countervailing opinion. It pressed on with its work in the face of the APUO's formal opposition, and CAUT's besides. Such obstinacy caused a frustrated Kaplan to send a circular letter on May 17, 1968, which stated in no uncertain terms his personal disagreement with the Committee's proceedings. It is unclear to whom the letter was addressed. Roger Guindon, unimpressed by Kaplan's hostility, read his response to the Senate on July 8, which indicates that at least senators were aware of the letter. He adopted parliamentary terms and addressed Kaplan directly:

> As chairman of the Senate, I feel obligated to take objection to your statement concerning the action of the Senate: "the quixotic, not to say foolish, attempts to define 'Christian principles'."
>
> You may have personal convictions and opinions on this matter. It is your acknowledged privilege. But neither you nor any one else in the University has the right to ridicule anyone else's opinion, especially if it is a decision rightfully taken by a responsible body of the University like the Senate [sic].[38]

Guindon defended freedom of speech in the University, but more specifically in deliberative bodies. His defence, however, smacked of that same power politics he brought to bear against the APUO in January 1968. Kaplan's frustrated opinion was again curbed using parliamentary procedure. Members of the Senate could express themselves during meetings; they were not free to speak against the body once a decision had been made. While the terms he deployed to express himself were inappropriate, the substance of his comments was dismissed along with his expression. Though Kaplan leaves the scene at this point, his opposition and that of the APUO's foretold of times to come. The University's ability to sweep critical voices under the rug was less and less effective if it was going to fly in the face of prevailing lay opinion.

The Committee's saga ended on February 3, 1969, when the Senate discharged its mandate by adopting the Committee's tame final report. The Committee's final recommendations said little about the new charter. The report recommended that, despite students' questioning the legality of the Committee's proceedings and the APUO's protests, undergraduate education in every program offer the option of religious studies, but that no graduate program be obliged to offer such an option. The Department of Religious Studies would teach these courses.[39] The Committee imposed no obligation upon a student to take a course in religious studies. It imposed an obligation upon the administration to leave that option open to any student who wished to pursue such a course.

The fuss over the Committee was, in the end, over little more than a principle, but it against focused attention on dwindling Oblate control. The strain between the University's administration and its community during and immediately after the reform became focused on these Oblate efforts to impose religious discipline at the new university. Opposition intensified with this latest committee. Though little information exists to show Roger Guindon's or other Oblates' strain, these repeated challenges increasingly exposed the University to criticism within and without—the APUO inadvertently brought in a dean of law and Justice Laskin to dispute George Addy's legal reasoning. Andrew Robinson had brought public exposure to the University's conduct.

These incidents reflected another incident of ill-contained hostility that again spilled over into the public. The University was, however, on such a course for years. Before reform, its dire financial straits prevented investment in additional facilities and competitive salaries. Lack of funds strained the relationship between administration and professors. It also created tension within the Oblate community. That disunity undermined the Oblates' response to increasing government pressure. That pressure, however, might not have abated unless the Oblates had, in the end, come to terms.

The way in which the Oblates gave up control was cautious, with extreme regard for the Order's legacy. Administrators attempted to maintain Catholic influence at the University by appealing to its history. These historical claims allowed the priests to argue for a share of the decision-making power in the new corporation. A powerful moral argument, but one not contemplated by the legal instrument that made the change. The Oblates received their eight representatives on the new University's Board. That minority, appointed by the University of Saint Paul, was the only legislative acknowledgment of the Oblates' past. The Oblates would, perhaps, argue that they were interpreting their own creation with the Senate's committee to study the University's Christian character. They had, after all, drafted the Act. That kind of reasoning, however, ignored the legal reality of statutory corporations. The Oblates lost control over their creation the minute the Lieutenant Governor of Ontario signed the bill into law. Courts and politicians would interpret The University of Ottawa Act, 1965, not the Oblates.

The lay faculty, including the Association of Professors, assumed as much. Though Roger Guindon remained rector, and thus some Catholic rhetoric was bound to slip into the University's discourse, an expectation existed that he would leave his Oblate affiliation out of his administrative duties. The rector used up his goodwill with his convocation speeches. The federation agreement created an arrangement that deferred to Saint Paul for appointments to the Faculty of Philosophy. This agreement was not immediately reported to the wider academic community (and still is not too widely circulated in its current form). It instead came to light a year later after Andrew Robinson publicly criticized the University's proposal to merge the faculty and department together. Even here, the administration only circulated the agreement to Senate, although circulation to Senate effectively publicized the document. The administration's lack of transparency complicated matters to the point where Robinson felt the need to address his concerns directly to the government of Ontario.

Secrecy was characteristic of the Oblates, but they likely viewed it as tact or discretion. Their Order governed itself beyond public view and the University was similarly governed in the years leading to reform: The Council of Administration was exclusively Oblate, and these brothers lived and worked together. Public discussion was not deemed necessary in this political environment, yet lack of wider debate on university affairs excluded lay members. Exclusion hindered faculty's comprehension of the administration's aims and rationale. That lack of communication before the reform drove the criticism that appeared once the University was supposedly non-denominational.

Once the federation agreement was more or less publicly available, criticism came from more quarters. The Professors' Association used the agreement as a wedge issue after the Robinson affair before the committee on Christian character. Here, the Oblate claim to historic influence won out, but again the government of Ontario was brought into the mix.

The government's continued involvement in the University's affairs was characteristic of the time. Its pushes to turn the University non-denominational and again to ensure that it held reasonably close to that non-denominational spirit were both conducted with instrumental precision and force. The Oblates were no match for Ontario's larger organization and means. The priests consistently backed down when faced with this impersonal force.

They remained, however, to fight a guerrilla campaign. The Oblates could no longer accomplish their educational end by fiat; the Church was also struggling as it went into Vatican II. The reform that coincided at the University of Ottawa and around the world opened the Church to a more supple doctrine. The Oblates had to be as a city on a hill: the struggle was for individual minds, not institutional spaces. Though a university was important for educating the next generation of Catholics, the Oblates could now instead rely on the purity of their message. Roger Guindon showed some of that wisdom in his convocation speeches. The Committee on Christian character again showed some of that desire to teach a spiritual way.

Implicit in that desire, and what we might most take note of now, is the time scales on which Oblates and governments operated. Both looked forward to a certain degree, but Oblates were on the whole more conscious of their historical place. Theirs was a charity rooted in morality, derived from faith, and carried out with hope. The Oblates and religion more generally focused on a salvific mission: each soul had value in Christ's world. That humanist mission was timeless, yet it stood on millennia of intellectual and institutional history. A Catholic university education transmitted this content into waiting souls, thus giving them a view of the sublimity in God's work. The University of Ottawa's part in this tradition predated Ottawa's municipal government. Bishop Guigues' college served his community's economic interest by training a francophone elite. The college also, as it expanded, accomplished the Oblate apostolic mission of spreading Mary's grace: lifting those less fortunate up toward God by folding them into the humanist tradition. Students inherited a worldview into which the individual's narrative could be inserted.

The government of Ontario, in the post-war student boom, instead wanted to spur Ontario's and Canada's economies. This wide view is often mistaken for charitable investment in citizens' lives. It might be better characterized as an imposition only capable of cognizing system-wide views. A vibrant economy drove the post-War welfare state. That state, a redistributive ideal, relied on centralization and rationalization. These forces could not cognize the individual's salvation, and the importance of that focus was forgotten in the social movement away from religion. Reformed universities were left dependent on government financial assistance yet divorced from their somewhat pastoral function. Students did not feel the effects then, but we see some of these effects now as the governments further instrumentalize universities. Professors in the 1960s could feel the pinch. Many were staunchly against religious control and religion in education; faculty also bayed for funds.

Roger Guindon was prescient. He foresaw some of this threat, though he expressed it primarily as a loss of faithful and as a loss of united purpose. Other Oblates expressed themselves in similar terms. The government perhaps saw the reform at the University of Ottawa as yet another step toward achieving purposes similar to what we see in elementary and secondary schools policy, "to provide students with the opportunity to realize their potential and develop into highly skilled, knowledgeable, caring citizens who contribute to their society."[40] The Oblates would invert the phrase: caring citizens come first, with knowledge mediating between that compassion and resulting skills. As an albeit rabid Protestant, John Milton said, in his appraisal of education, something which may have resonated with that patient Oblate view of caring first and foremost, not just for others, but of the self as well:

> The end then of learning is to repair the ruins of our first parents by regaining to know God aright, and out of that knowledge to love him, to imitate him, to be like him, as we may the nearest by possessing our souls of true vertue; which being united to the heavenly grace of faith makes up the highest perfection. But because our understanding cannot in this body found itself but on sensible things, not arrive so cleerly to the knowledge of God and things invisible, as by orderly coming over the visible and inferior creature, the same method is necessarily to be follow'd in all discreet teaching.[41]

Appendix A: The Charters, including the Oblate Charter

1849	An Act to incorporate Les Révérends Pères Oblats de l'Immaculée Conception de Marie, in the Province of Canada	200
1849	An Act to incorporate the College of Bytown, Canada	204
1861	An Act to change the name of the College of Bytown, and to amend the Act incorporating the same	207
1866	An Act to amend the Acts incorporating "The College of Ottawa," and to grant certain privileges to the Said College	209
1885	An Act to amend the Acts incorporating the College of Ottawa	213
1891	An Act to amend the Acts incorporating the College of Ottawa	216
1933	An Act respecting the College of Ottawa	217
1941	An Act respecting the County of Carleton and the University of Ottawa	229
1959	An Act respecting Université d'Ottawa	231
1960–1961	An Act respecting Université d'Ottawa	240
1964	An Act respecting Université d'Ottawa	241
1965	An Act respecting Université d'Ottawa	244

ANNO DUODECIMO
VICTORIÆ REGINÆ.

CAP. CXLIII.

An Act to incorporate Les Révérends Pères Oblats de l'Immaculée Conception de Marie, in the Province of Canada.

[30th May, 1849]

WHEREAS an Association of Ecclesiastics hath existed for several years in the Province of Canada, under the name of *Les Révérends Oblats de l'Immaculée Conception de Marie*, having for its object the establishing of missions, procuring Instruction and Education, erecting and conducting Hospitals for indigent sick persons; And whereas the Said *Révérends Pères Oblats*, have by the Petition presented in their name by the Reverend Father Jean Claude Léonard, one of their Body, prayed that the said Association may be incorporated; And whereas, in consideration of the great benefits which must arise from the Institution, it is expedient to grant their prayer: Be it therefore enacted by the Queen's Most Excellent Majesty, by and with the advice and consent of the Legislative Council and of the Legislative Assembly of the Province of Canada, constituted and assembled by virtue of and under the authority of an Act passed in the Parliament of the United Kingdom of Great Britain and Ireland, and intituled, *An Act to Reunite the Provinces of Upper and Lower Canada, and for the Government of Canada*, and it is hereby enacted by the authority of the same, That the Reverend Fathers Joseph Eugène, Bishop of Bytown, the said Jean Claude Léonard, Damase Dandurand, John Ryan, M. Molloy, and such other persons being natural born or naturalized subjects of Her Majesty as may be now or may hereafter become under the provisions of this Act, Members of the said Institution, shall be and are hereby declared to be a Body Politic and Corporate in deed and in name by the name of Les Révérends Pères Oblats de l'Immaculée Conception de Marie, and by that name shall have perpetual succession and a Common Seal, with power to change, alter, break or renew the same when and as often as they may think proper, and shall by the same name, at all times hereafter be able and capable to purchase, acquire, hold possess and enjoy, and to have, take, and receive to them and their Successors, to and for the uses and purposes of the said Corporation under any legal title whatsoever, and without any further authorization or letters of Mortmain, any lands, tenements and hereditaments, moveable and immoveable property situate, lying and being within this Province, not exceeding in yearly value the sum of two thousand pounds currency of this Province, and the same to sell alienate and dispose of, and to purchase acquire and possess others in their stead for the said purposes; and by the same name shall and may be able and capable in law, to sue and be sued, implead and be impleaded, answer and be answered unto in all Courts of Law and places whatsoever, in as large, ample and beneficial a manner as any other Body Politic or Corporate, or as any persons able or capable in law may or can sue and be sued, implead and be impleaded, answer and be answered unto, in any manner whatsoever, and the service of any summons or process made at the domicile of any one of the said Members of the Corporation in any one of their establishments wherein two or more of the said Members may reside, shall be a valid service thereof, upon the said Corporation; and the said Corporation shall have full power and authority to make and establish such Bylaws, Rules, Orders and Regulations, not being contrary to this Act nor to the Laws in force in this Province, as shall be deemed useful and necessary for the interests of the said Corporation and for the management thereof, and of the affairs and property of the said Corporation, and for their qualification and for all other purposes having for their object the promotion of the welfare and interests of the said Corporation, and from time to time to amend, alter or repeal the said Bylaws, Orders and Regulations or any of them, in such manner as the said Corporation may deem meet and expedient.

II. And be it enacted, That the said Corporation shall also have power to appoint, if they think fit, one or more Attorneys for the purpose of conducting the affairs of the said Corporation, and shall, generally, enjoy all the rights and privileges enjoyed by other legally Incorporated Bodies in this Province.

III. And be it enacted, That the rents, revenues, issues and profits of all property, real or personal, moveable or immoveable, held by the said Corporation, shall be appropriated and applied solely to the maintenance of the Members of the said Corporation, the construction and repair of the buildings requisite for the purposes of the said Corporation, and the payment of the expenses incurred for objects legitimately connected with or depending on the purposes aforesaid.

IV. And be it enacted, That if the said Corporation, shall from any cause whatsoever be dissolved, the moveable property which shall then be *en nature*, and the immoveable property and *rentes constituées* which shall have been given, devised or bequeathed to the said Corporation, or the immoveable property received in exchange for or purchased by means of the sale of the property so given, devised or bequeathed, and which shall be in possession of the said Corporation at the time of its dissolution, shall return to and belong to the legal Heirs of the person or persons respectively who shall have given, devised or bequeathed, such property to the said Corporation.

V. And be it enacted, That in case of such dissolution of the said Corporation, the real property by them purchased and acquired and paid for out of their revenues, and not by the sale or exchange of any property given, devised or bequeathed to them as well as all other property then belonging to the said Corporation, and not liable to be claimed by and revert to the Heirs of any Donor or Testator under the provisions of the next preceding section of this Act, shall be at the disposal of the Provincial Parliament for the purpose of being applied to the maintenance of some Charitable Institution, or to the Education of the Poor, in the Parish or Township in which such property shall be situate.

VI. And be it enacted, That no Deed of Sale or Conveyance by which the said Corporation shall purchase or acquire any real or immoveable property or annual rents (*rentes constituées*) shall be valid or effectual to any intent or purpose whatsoever, unless in such Deed it be stated and set forth that such purchase or acquisition is made with the funds of the said Corporation itself, or with funds arising from the sale or alienation of such and such property, describing the same, given, devised or bequeathed to the said Corporation by such and such person or persons, designating the same by name, or otherwise, as the case may be.

VII. And be in enacted, That it shall be the duty of the said Corporation at all times when they may be called upon to do by the governors of this Province, to render an account in writing of their property and affairs, in which shall be set forth in particular the income by them derived from property held under this Act and the means by which the same has been acquired.

VIII. And be it enacted, That no Member of the said Corporation shall be individually liable or accountable for the debts, contracts or securities of the said Corporation.

IX. And be it enacted, That nothing herein contained shall affect or be construed to affect in any manner or way, the Rights of Her Majesty, Her Heirs and Successors, or of any Body Politic or Corporate, such only excepted as are hereinbefore mentioned and provided for.

X. And be it enacted, That this Act shall be deemed a Public Act, and shall be publicly taken notice of as such by all Judges, Justices of the Peace, and other persons whomsoever, without being specially pleaded.

Montréeal: Printed by Stewart Derbishire & George Desbarats,
Law Printer to the Queen's Most Excellent Majesty.

An Act to incorporate the College of Bytown, Canada, 1849
(30th May, 1849)

WHEREAS His Lordship, Joseph Eugène, Roman Catholic Bishop of Bytown, hath by his Petition to the Legislature represented that a College hath been established at Bytown for the education of youth, and hath prayed that corporate powers be conferred on the said College, and in consideration of the great advantages to be derived from the said Institution, it is expedient to grant the prayer of the said Petition: Be it therefore enacted by the Queen's Most Excellent Majesty, by and with the advice and consent of the Legislative Council and of the Legislative Assembly of the Province of Canada, constituted and assembled by virtue of and under the authority of an Act passed in the Parliament of the United Kingdom of Great Britain and Ireland, and intituled, "An Act to Reunite the Provinces of Upper and Lower Canada, and for the Government of Canada," and it is hereby enacted by the authority of the same, That the said College, the Professors of Philosophy and Belles Lettres, and the Bursar of the said College, together with all such other necessary officers as may be hereafter appointed under the provisions of this Act, and their several and respective successors,—shall be and is hereby constituted a Body Politic and Corporate in deed and in name, by and under the name of The College of Bytown, and by that name shall have perpetual succession and a common seal, and shall have power, from time to time, to alter, renew, or change such common seal at their pleasure, and shall, by the same name, from time to time and at all times hereafter, be able and capable to purchase, acquire, hold, possess and enjoy, and to have, take, and receive, to them and their successors, to and for the uses and purposes of the said Corporation, any lands, tenements, and hereditaments, and real or immoveable property and estate, situate, lying and being within this Province, not exceeding in yearly value the sum of Two thousand Pounds currency, and the same to sell, alienate and dispose of, and to purchase others in their stead for the same purposes; and by the said name shall and may be able and capable in law to sue and be sued, implead and be impleaded, answer and be answered unto in all courts of law and places whatsoever, in as large, ample and beneficial a manner as any other body politic or corporate, or as any persons able or capable in law may or can sue and be sued, implead and be impleaded, answer and be answered unto in any manner whatsoever; and any majority of the members of the Corporation for the time being, shall have power and authority to make and establish such Bylaws, Rules, Orders and Regulations, not being contrary to this Act, nor to the laws in force in this Province, as shall be deemed useful or necessary for the interests of the said Corporation, and for the management thereof, and for the admission of Members into the said Corporation, and from time to time to alter, repeal and change the said Bylaws, Rules, Orders and Regulations or any of them, or those of the said Institution in force at the time of the passing of this Act; and shall and may do, execute and perform all and singular other the matters and things relating to the said Corporation and the management thereof, or which shall or may appertain thereto; subject, nevertheless, to the rules, regulations, stipulations and provisions hereinafter prescribed and established.

II. Provided always, and be it enacted, That the rents, revenues, issues and profits of all property, real or personal, held by the said Corporation, shall be appropriated and applied solely to the maintenance of the Members of the Corporation, the construction and repair of the buildings requisite for the purposes of the said Corporation, and to the advancement of education by the instruction of youth, and the payment of the expenses to be incurred for objects legitimately connected with or depending on the purposes aforesaid.

III. And be it enacted, That all and every the estate and property real and personal belonging to or hereafter to be acquired by the Members of the said Institution as such, and all debts, claims and rights whatsoever due to them in that quality, shall be and are hereby vested in the Corporation hereby established; and the Bylaws, Rules, Orders and Regulation now made for the management of the said Institution, shall be and continue to be the Bylaws, Rules, Orders and Regulations of the said Corporation until altered or repealed in the manner herein provided.

IV. And be it enacted, That the Members of the said Corporation for the time being, or a majority of them, shall have power to appoint such Attorney or Attorneys, Administrator or Administrators of the property of the Corporation, and such Officer and Teachers and Servants of the said Corporation as shall be necessary for the well conducting of the business and affairs thereof, and to allow to them such compensation for their services respectively as shall be reasonable and proper; and all Officers so appointed shall be capable of exercising such other powers and authority for the well governing and ordering of the affairs of the said Corporation, as shall be prescribed by the Bylaws, Rules, Orders and Regulations of the said Corporation.

V. And be it enacted, That nothing herein contained shall have the effect or be construed to have the effect, of rendering all or any of the Members of the said Corporation, or any person whatsoever individually liable or accountable for or by reason of any debt, contract or security incurred or entered into for or by reason of the Corporation, or for or on account or in respect of any matter or thing whatsoever relating to the said Corporation.

VI. And be it enacted, That it shall be the duty of the said Corporation to lay before each branch of the Provincial Legislature within fifteen days after beginning of each Session, a detailed Statement of the number of Members of the said Corporation, the number of Teachers employed in the various branches of instruction, the number of Scholars under instruction, and the course of instruction pursued, and of the real or immoveable property or estate held by virtue of the present Act, and of the revenue arising therefrom.

VII. And be it enacted, That nothing herein shall affect, or be construed to affect in any manner or way, the rights of Her Majesty, Her Heirs or Successors, or of any person or persons, or of any body politic or corporate, such only excepted as are hereinbefore mentioned and provided for.

VIII. And be it enacted, That this Act shall be deemed to be a Public Act, and shall be judicially taken notice of as such by all Judges, Justices of the Peace and other persons whatsoever, without being specially pleaded.

CAP. CVIII.

An Act to change the name of the College of Bytown, and to amend the Act incorporating the same.

[Assented to 18th May, 1861]

WHEREAS the Roman Catholic Bishop of Bytown, President of the College of Bytown, the Superior of the said College, the Curé of the Parish of Bytown, the Direction of the said College, the Professor of Philosophy and *Belles Lettres*, and the Bursar of the said College, constituting a body corporate, under the name of "The College of Bytown," under the Act passed in the twelfth year of Her Majesty's Reign, intituled: *An Act to incorporate the College of Bytown*, have petitioned, that the corporate name of the said Corportation may be changed, and that the Act incorporating it may be amended, in manner hereinafter mentioned, and it is expedient to grant the prayer of the said petition: Therefore, Her Majesty, by and with the advice and consent of the Legislative Council and Assembly of Canada, enacts of follows:

1. From and after the passing of this Act, the Corporation incorporated by the Act of the Parliament of this Province, passed in the Session of Parliament held in the twelfth year of Her Majesty's Reign, intituled: *An Act to incorporate the College of Bytown*, by the name of "The College of Bytown," shall be called and known by the name of "The College of Ottawa."

2. From and after the passing of this Act, the said, "College of Ottawa," shall be composed of the Superior of the said College as President thereof, the Director of the said College, the Professor of Philosophy and *Belles-Lettres*, and the Bursar of the said College, together with such other necessary officers as have been or may hereafter be appointed, under the provisions of the said Act, and their several and respective successors.

3. Neither the Roman Catholic Bishop of Bytown, nor the Curé of the Parish of Bytown, nor their respective successors, shall hereafter by members of the said Corporation; Provided always, that such change of name, and such change in the Members composing the said Corporation, shall not be construed to make the said Corporation a

new Corporation, or to impair or alter the effect of any Act relating to the said Corporation, or of any instrument or proceeding to or in which the said Corporation, by its former name, may be or may have been a party, or in anywise concerned or interested, but the same shall have full force and effect, and shall apply to and be continued with respect to the said Corporation, by the name and style hereby assigned to it.

4. This Act shall be deemed to be a Public Act.

No. 140.) (1866
An Act to amend the Acts incorporating "The College of Ottawa,"
and to grant certain privileges to the said college

Canada, Cap. 135. (Assented to 15th August, 1866.)

(As amended by the Standing Committee on Miscellaneous Private Bills.)

WHEREAS the corporation of the College of Ottawa have, by their petition, set forth that the said institution was incorporated by Act of Parliament of this Province in the year 1849, and hath since that time continued in full and successful operation; that in the opinion of the petitioners the time has arrived when the usefulness of the said institution might be more widely extended by conferring on the said institution the status and powers of an university; and whereas it is desirable to grant the same: Therefore, Her Majesty, by and with the advice and consent of the Legislative Council and Assembly of Canada, enacts as follows:

1. For and notwithstanding anything contained in Act of the Parliament of Canada, passed in the twelfth year of Her Majesty's reign, chapter one hundred and seven, the said corporation shall have power to hold, possess and enjoy real property and estate not exceeding in yearly value the sum of four thousand pounds, currency, and may from time to time, as may be deemed advisable for the interest, progress and success of the said college, mortgage the real estate which the said corporation owns, or which at any time or times hereafter it may acquire.

2. For the purposes hereinafter mentioned, the President of the said college, the Bursar of the said college, the Professor of Divinity of the said college, the Professor of Philosophy of the said college, the Professor of Rhetoric of the said college, the Professor of Belles Lettres of the said college, and the Prefect of Studies of the said college, together with the *ex-officio* members hereinafter named, shall constitute the "College Senate."

3. The Roman Catholic Bishop of Ottawa shall be *ex-officio* a Member of the "College Senate."

4. "The College Senate" shall have power and authority, after proper examination, to confer the several Degrees of Batchelor of Arts, Master of Arts, Batchelor of Laws, Doctor of Laws, Barchelor of Medicine, and to examine for Medical Degrees in the four branches of Medicine, Surgery, Midwifery, and Pharmacy; and such reasonable fees shall be charged to the candidates for examination for degrees as the "College Senate" shall, by statute or order in that behalf, from time to time determine, and such fees shall be paid into the general fund of the said corporation.

5. Once, at least, in every year, at a time or times to be fixed by the "College Senate," the College Senate shall cause to be held an Examination of the Candidates for Degrees, Scholarships, or Prizes, and at any such examination the candidates shall be examined by examiners appointed for the purpose by the College Senate, and at every such examination the candidate shall be examined orally or in writing or otherwise, and in as many branches of general knowledge as the College Senate shall consider the most fitting subjects for such examination; and special examinations may be held for honors, and such examinations shall be open and public. But the first examination of candidates for degrees shall not be held until proper arrangements are made for carrying out the provisions of this Act: and the College Senate shall, so soon as such arrangements are made, appoint, by resolution, the time for the first examination to be held.

6. The Statutes of the Senate, with respect to the Literacy and Scientific attainments of persons obtaining degrees or certificates of honor, and their examination, shall, in so far as circumstances will, in the opinion of the Senate, permit, by similar to those at present in force for like purposes in the University of London, to the end that the standard of qualification in the University of Ottawa may not be inferior to that at present adopted for a like degree of Certificate of Honor in the University of London; Provided always that any Statute passed for the purposes mentioned in this section shall be deposited with the Provincial Secretary within ten days after the passing thereof, to be laid before the visitor, and such Statute shall have interim force and effect, and shall have full force and effect unless such Statute be dissallowed by the visitor, and such disallowance signified through the Provincial Secretary within three months after such deposit as aforesaid.

7. All such Statutes shall be reduced into writing, and the common seal of the University shall be annexed thereto, and they shall be binding upon all members or officers of the University, and upon all candidates for degrees, scholarships, prizes or certificates of honor, to be conferred by the said University, and upon all others whom it may concern.

8. The College Senate shall have power to appoint, by Statute or resolution, and from time to time, as there shall be occasion, to remove in like manner, all examiners of the said college.

9. The examiners may be required to make the following declaration before the president of the said college: I solemnly declare that "I will perform my duty of examiner, without fear, love, or affection, or partiality towards any candidate, and that I will not knowingly, allow to any candidate any advantage which is not allowed to all."

10. The College Senate may grant scholarships, prizes and honors to persons who shall distinguish themselves at their examinations: and all such scholarships, prizes and rewards shall be granted according to regulations previously made and published.

11. The College Senate shall meet at the College Buildings, in Ottawa, from time to time, and at such times as they shall by Statute appoint, and for carrying the provisions of this Act fully into effect, shall have power and authority to make and pass such Statutes, rules, orders and regulations as may be deemed advisable, and to alter, vary and change the same.

12. The President of the Corporation of the said College of Ottawa shall be Chairman of the College Senate, or, in his absence, a chairman shall be chosen by the members present, or a majority of them; and no question shall be decided at any meeting unless a majority of the Senate are present at the time of such decisions, nor shall any meeting be legal unless held at the time or convened in the manner provided for by Statute to be passed as aforesaid.

13. All questions which shall come up before the College Senate shall be decided by the majority of the members present; but in case of equality of votes, the maxim *præsumitur pro negante* shall prevail.

14. The Governor shall, on behalf of Her Majesty, be visitor of the said University.

15. The College Senate of the University shall report to the Governor, at such time as he may appoint, on the general state, progress and prospects of the University, and upon all matters touching the same, with such suggestions as they think proper to make; and the Senate shall also at all times, when thereunto required by the Governor, inquire into, examine and report upon any subject or matter connected with the University; and copied of such annual or other reports shall be laid before both Houses of the Provincial Parliament at the next Session thereof.

16. This Act shall be deemed a public Act.

No. 31) (1885
An Act to amend the Acts incorporating the College of Ottawa

ONTARIO, 1885, C. 91.   (Assented to 30th March, 1885.)

WHEREAS the corporation of the College of Ottawa have by their petition, represented that the institution was incorporated under the name of "The College of Bytown" by an Act of the Parliament of the Province of Canada passed in the year one thousand eight hundred and forty-nine, that in the in the year one thousand eight hundred and sixty-one, the Act of Incorporation was amended, and the name changed to "The College of Ottawa," and that in the year one thousand eight hundred and sixty-six the Parliament of the Province of Canada passed an Act conferring on the college the powers and status of a university; and whereas the corporation have represented that certain amendments are required for more clearly defining the members who shall compose the college senate, for enlarging the powers of the senate in the granting of degrees, and also for enabling the corporation to make certain other minor changes in the government of the institution, and it is expedient to grant the prayer of the petition;

Therefore Her Majesty, by & with the advice & consent of the Legislative Assembly of the Province of Ontario, enacts as follows:—

1. Section two of the Act passed in the twenty-ninth & thirtieth years of Her Majesty's reign, chapter one hundred & thirty-five, intituled "An Act to amend the Acts incorporation The College of Ottawa, and to grant certain privileges to the said College" is hereby repealed, and the following enacted in lieu thereof:—The College Senate shall consist of the President and the Bursar of the college and of the persons, for the time being, filling the following positions in the college, namely:—the professors of Divinity, the prefect of studies, the professors of metaphysics, of ethics, of higher mathematics, the first professor of natural science, the first professor of Greek, the first professor of Latin, the first professor of English, the first professor of French, the professors of mechanical sciences, and the deans of the faculty of law and of medicine, together with the ex-officio members named in the last mentioned Act.

2. Section four of the last mentioned Act is hereby repealed, and the following enacted in lieu thereof:—The college senate shall have power to examine for, and after examination to confer, in such mode, and on compliance by the candidate with such conditions, as they shall, from time to time determine, the several degrees of bachelor & masters of arts, bachelor & doctor in laws, in science & in music, and also the degree of civil engineer, of mining engineer, & of mechanical engineer, and the senate shall also have power to examine for the medical degrees in the four branches of medicine, surgery, midwifery, & pharmacy, and after examination, to confer the several degrees of bachelor of medicine, doctor of medicine & master in surgery, and such reasonable fees shall be charged to the candidates for examination for degrees as the college senate shall, by statute or order in that behalf from time to time determine, and such fees shall be paid into the general fund of the said corporation.

3. The President and members of the college senate shall also have power to confer any of the said degrees as *ad eundem* degrees.

4. The college senate may, by statute in that behalf, prescribe that any college, seminary or other institution established in any province of Canada, other than Ontario, for the promotion of literature, science or art, or for instruction in law, medicine or mechanical science in any province of Canada may, upon application, affiliate to and connect with the University of the College of Ottawa, for the purpose of admitting therefrom as candidates, at any of the respective examinations, for standing or for scholarships, honors, degrees & certificates, which the senate are authorized to confer, such persons as may have respectively completed in such college, seminary or other institution whilst affiliated with the University of the College of Ottawa, such course of instruction preliminary to any of the said respective examinations, for standing or for scholarships, honors, degrees or certificates as the senate shall form time to time, by regulations in that behalf, determine.

5. Section thirteen of the last mentioned Act, is hereby repealed and the following enacted in lieu thereof:—All questions which shall come up before the senate shall be decided by the majority of votes of the members present, including the vote of the president of the senate, or other presiding members of the senate, and in case of an equal

division of such votes, the president or the presiding member at such meeting shall have an additional or casting vote.

6. The Lieutenant-Governor of Ontario shall be a visitor of the said university.

7. The college senate shall report to the Lieutenant-Governor at such time as he may appoint, on the general state, progress and prospects of the university, and upon all matters touching the same, with such suggestions as they think proper to make, and the senate shall also at all times when thereunto required by the Lieutenant-Governor, inquire into, examine and report upon any subject or matter connected with the university, and copies of such annual or other reports shall be laid before the Legislative Assembly of the Province of Ontario, at the then next session thereof.

No. 31.) (1891
An Act to amend the Acts incorporating the College of Ottawa

ONTARIO, 1891, CAP. 104.   (Assented to 4th May, 1891.)

WHEREAS the corporation of the College of Ottawa have by their petition prayed that an Act may be passed to enable, subject as hereinafter provided, any college, seminary or other institution established in Ontario for the promotion of literature, science or art, or for instruction in law, medicine or mechanical science, upon application to affiliate & connect with the University of the College of Ottawa; and whereas it is expedient to grant the prayer of the said portion; therefore Her Majesty, by & with the advice & consent of the Legislative Assembly of the Province of Ontario, enacts as follows:—

1. Section 4 of the Act, passed in the 48th year of Her Majesty's reign, chaptered 91, intituled "An act to amend the Acts incorporating the College of Ottawa," is hereby amended by striking out the words "other than Ontario" in the third line of said section, and adding thereto the following:

Provided always that no college, seminary or other institution of learning in the Province of Ontario now in affiliation with the University of Toronto, and no university of the Province of Ontario shall affiliate to or connect with the said university of the College of Ottawa.

No. 34

4th Session, 18th Legislature, Ontario
23 George V. 1933

BILL

An Act respecting the College of Ottawa.

Mr. Cote

(Private Bill)

No. 34   1933

Bill

An Act respecting the College of Ottawa

WHEREAS the College of Ottawa has by its petition represented that it was incorporated by an Act of the Parliament of the late Province of Canada, passed in the twelfth year of the reign of Her Majesty Queen Victoria, chapter 107, and entitled *An Act to incorporate The College of Bytown*, which Act of incorporation has been amended and added to by the various Acts referred to in schedule A hereto, and has by its petition sought further powers and amendments, and whereas it is expedient to grant the prayer of the said petition;

Therefore, His Majesty, by and with the advice and consent of the Legislative Assembly of the Province of Ontario, enacts as follows:

1. This Act may be cited as *The University of Ottawa Act, 1933*.

2. The Acts set out in schedule "A" hereto are repealed and the provisions of this Act are substituted therefor.

3. The corporation of "The College of Bytown" of which corporation that name was changed to "The College of Ottawa" is hereby continued under the name of "Université d'Ottawa," hereinafter referred to as the University, and, subject to the provisions of this Act, shall have, hold, possess and enjoy all the property, rights, powers and privileges which it may now have, hold possess or enjoy.

4. The University shall be a body corporate and politic in deed and in name.

5. The University shall be constituted of the following members: The Rector, The First Vice-Rector, The Second Vice-Rector, The Secretary, The Bursar, The First Councillor and the Second Councillor of the said University now in office, and their several and respective successors together with such other members as the Council of Administration may admit pursuant to its bylaws.

6. The University shall have power to purchase or otherwise take or receive, hold and enjoy any estate whatsoever, real or personal, and

to alienate, sell, convey, lease or otherwise dispose of the same or any part thereof from time to time and as occasion may require, and to acquire other estate, real and personal, in addition to or in place thereof to and for the uses and purposes of the said university.

7. If and when authorized by bylaws duly passed by the council of administration, the University shall have power to,—

>   (a) Borrow money on its credit in such amount, on such terms and from such persons, firms of corporations, including chartered banks, as may be determined by the said council;
>
>   (b) Make, draw and endorse promissory notes or bills of exchange;
>
>   (c) Hypothecate, pledge or charge any or all the personal and real property of the University to secure any money so borrowed or the fulfilment of the obligation incurred by it under any promissory note or bill of exchange signed, made, drawn or endorsed by it;
>
>   (d) Issue bonds, debentures and obligations on such terms and conditions as the council may decide, and pledge or sell such bonds, debentures and obligations for such sums and at such prices as the council may decide and may mortgage, charge, hypothecate or pledge all or any part of the real or personal property of the University to secure any such bonds, debentures and obligations.

8. The rents, revenues, issue and profits of all property, real and personal, held by the said University and all other income of the University shall be appropriated and applied solely to the maintenance of the members of the University, the construction and repair of the building requisite for the purposes of the University, and to the attainment of the objects for which the University is constituted and to the payment of expenses to be incurred for objects legitimately connected with or depending on the purposes aforesaid.

9. All and every estate and property, real and personal, belonging to or hereafter to be acquired by the officers or members of the University as such and all debts, claims and rights whatsoever due to them in that quality shall be and are hereby vested in the University.

10. Nothing herein contained shall have the effect or be construed to have the effect of rendering all or any of the members or officers of the said University, or any person whatsoever individually liable or accountable for or by reason of any debt, contract or security incurred or entered into for or by reason of the University or for or on account or in respect of any matter or thing whatsoever relating to the University.

11. The real property of the University shall not be liable to be entered upon, used or taken by any municipal or other corporation or by any person possessing the right of taking land compulsorily for any purpose; and no power to expropriate real property hereafter conferred shall extend to such real property unless in the Act conferring the power it is made in express terms to apply thereto.

12. The property, real and personal, vested in the University shall not be liable to taxation for municipal or school purposes, and shall be exempt form every description of such taxation; but the interest of every lessee and occupant (who is not a member of the University or a member of the teaching staff or a servant or a student of the University) of real property vested in the University shall be liable to taxation.

13. Nothing in this Act shall affect any right of His Majesty, his heirs or successors, or of any party or persons whomsoever; such rights only excepted as are herein expressly mentioned or affected.

14.—(1) The Lieutenant-Governor of Ontario shall be a visitor of the said University.

(2) The council of administration of the University shall report to the Lieutenant-Governor at such time or times as he may appoint, on the general state, progress and prospects of the University, and upon all matters touching the same, with such suggestions as they think proper to make; and the Council shall also at all times, when thereunto required by the Lieutenant-Governor, inquire into, examine and report upon any subject or matter connected with the University, and copies of the annual report of the University and of such other reports as may be by the Lieutenant-Governor required shall be laid before the Legislative Assembly of the Province of Ontario, at the next session thereof.

15. The objects of the University are hereby declared to be:

> (a) to promote art, science, instruction in law, medicine, engineering, agriculture, pharmacy and every other useful branch of learning;
>
> (b) to promote the intellectual, moral and physical welfare of its undergraduates, graduates and teaching staff.

16.—(1) Subject to the provisions in this Act contained the status and powers of the University as a university are hereby continued and shall be deemed to have subsisted as from the 15th day of August, 1866.

(2) The University shall have power and authority after proper examinations to confer in all branches of learning any and all degrees which may properly by conferred by a university.

(3) The University shall also have power and authority to confer any of the said degrees as *ad honorem* degrees.

17. The governing and managing persons of and bodies of the University shall be the chancellor, the rector, the council of administration, the senate and the faculties, which bodies shall be constituted as hereinafter provided and which persons and bodies shall enjoy and possess the power and authority respectively hereinafter conferred upon each one of them.

18.—(1) The chancellor of the University is and shall be the Roman Catholic Archbishop of Ottawa for the time being.

(2) The chancellor shall be the titular head of the University, and be accorded the place of honour at commencement exercises and other functions; he shall preside at examinations if he is present, and shall, at his option, as of right first sign all diplomas to degrees.

(3) During the vacancy of the said archepiscopal seat the prelate who shall assume the temporary administration thereof shall also assume the duties and enjoy the rights of the chancellor.

19.—(1) The council of administration shall consist of the following members: The Rector, the First Vice-Rector, the Second Vice-Rector, the

Secretary, the Bursar, the First Councillor and the Second Councillor together with such other officers as the council may by bylaws provide for, and shall be designated under that name.

(2) The members of the council now in office shall continue in office until their respective and several successors are appointed.

20.—(1) The council of administration, subject only to the powers which are by this Act expressly and exclusively conferred upon the chancellor, the rector, the senate, the faculties and the officers of the council respectively, shall have the control and management of all the affairs and business of the University, and for greater certainty but not so as to limit the generality of the foregoing, it is declared that the council shall have power to

> (a) pass bylaws providing for the term of office and mode of appointment of the members of the council and for filling any vacancy which may occur in the council by death, resignation or otherwise;
>
> (b) pass bylaws providing rules and regulations pertaining to the meetings of the council and its transactions and for fixing the quorum of the council;
>
> (c) appoint such officers, professors, lecturers, teachers and servants of the said University as shall be necessary for the good government of the affairs of the University and to allow to them and to the examiners such compensation for their services as to the council may be deemed reasonable and proper and define and limit the duties of all such officers, lecturers, teachers and servants;
>
> (d) subject to the limitations imposed by any trust as to the same, invest all such money as shall come to the hands of the council in such manner as to the council may seem meet;
>
> (e) upon the advice and report of the senate and pursuant to the terms of such report, establish in the University such faculties, special schools, departments, chairs and courses of instruction as to the council may seem meet;

(f) subject to the provisions of this Act, provide for the affiliation with the University of any college, seminary or other institution of learning;

(g) upon the advice and report of the senate to cancel, recall and suspend any degree whether heretofore or hereafter granted or conferred of any graduate of the University heretofore or hereafter convicted in Ontario or elsewhere of an offence which if committed in Canada would be an indictable offence, or heretofore or hereafter guilty of any infamous or disgraceful conduct or of conduct unbecoming a graduate of the University, to erase the name of such graduate from the roll or register of graduates and to require the surrender for cancellation of the diplomas, certificate or other instrument evidencing the right of such graduate to a degree of which he shall have been deprived under the authority of any bylaws passed by the council under this subsection.

(2) Notwithstanding anything in this Act contained, the council of administration shall have the power and the right, for reasons affecting the general welfare of the University of which reasons the council shall be the sole judge, to veto any act or decision of the senate or of the councils of the faculties, excepting the exercise by the senate of its right to allow and grant degrees.

21.—(1) The rector, subject to the bylaws of the council of administration shall be the manager of the affairs of the University and in all cases not provided for by this Act or by the bylaws of the council shall have power and authority to act on behalf of the University; he shall, subject only to the bylaws of the council as to the place and notice of meetings, have the right to call any meeting of the council, of the Senate and of the councils of the faculties and preside, if he is present, at all meetings of the council, of the senate and of the councils of the faculties whether called by him or not and vote thereat; he shall in the absence of the chancellor preside, if he is present, at examinations and shall first sign all University diplomas or degrees unless the chancellor chooses to do so, in which event he shall sign immediately after the chancellor and shall have such other powers as the council may by bylaws provide.

22. The secretary shall maintain and keep the register or roll of graduates of the University and of those persons who have or shall receive *ad honorem* degrees; he shall be the secretary of the council of administration and of the senate; he shall sign all University diplomas after the rector and he shall perform such other duties as may assigned to him by the rector, by the council of administration and by the senate.

23. The first vice-rector and the other officers of the council of administration shall have such rights and perform such duties as may from time to time be assigned to them by bylaws of the council of administration.

24. The senate of the University, in this Act referred to as "the senate," shall consist of the following members:

   (a) The chancellor for the time being;

   (b) The rector;

   (c) The other officers of the council of administration, namely, the first vice-rector, the second vice-rector, the secretary, the bursar, the first councillor and the second councillor of the University;

   (d) The persons for the time being holding the following positions in the University:

   (I) The dean, the vice-dean, and the secretary of each of the faculties of the University;

   (II) The directors of the special schools operated by the University, but not conducted by any of its organized faculties;

   (III) Such professors of the faculty of divinity, not exceeding seven, as may be chosen by the council of administration;

   (IV) Four professors of the faculty of arts, to be chosen by the council of the said faculty;

(V) One member from each of the institutions affiliated with the University, in all cases where the conditions of the agreement of affiliation entitle such affiliated institution to appoint a representative.

25.—(1) At all meetings of the senate, the rector, or, in his absence, the first vice-rector, or in the absence of both, the second vice-rector, shall preside.

(2) All questions which shall come up before the senate shall be decided by a majority of votes of the members present, including the vote of the rector, or other presiding member of the senate, and in case of an equal division of such votes the rector or in his absence the presiding member at such meeting shall have an additional or casting vote.

(3) A majority of all the members of the senate shall constitute a quorum for the transaction of business.

(4) The senate shall meet at the University Building in Ottawa form time to time when convened by the rector, and at such times as the members of the senate shall by bylaws appoint.

26. The senate shall have the power and authority to control the system and course of education pursued in the University and all matters pertaining thereto; to determine the courses of study and the qualifications for admission into any and all of the said courses of study and the qualifications for degrees; and to confer any and all degrees which may be conferred by the University, provided the courses of study prescribed for matriculation into the University shall in an essential sense be equivalent to those prescribed for matriculation into the University of Toronto and in respect to any degree which the said senate has power to confer the courses of instruction and the scope of examinations for such degree shall also be equivalent to the courses and examinations for a corresponding degree in the University of Toronto, to the end that the standard and qualifications for admission and degrees in the University may be not inferior to, although not necessarily identical with those adopted in the University of Toronto.

27.—(1) The senate shall receive the reports from the councils of the faculties and from the special schools, departments, chairs and courses of instruction as to the examinations passed by the students, and shall grant academic promotion to those who, in the opinion of the senate, shall be worthy of promotion.

(2) The senate may either refuse or confer *ad honorem* degree to persons recommended by the council of administration.

(3) After proper examinations the senate shall have the power and authority to confer degrees upon payment of such reasonable fees as the council of administration shall by bylaws from time to time determine, such fees to be paid to the general fund of the University.

(4) The senate shall advise and report to the council of administration as to the establishing, including the constitution thereof in the University of such faculties, special schools, departments, chairs and courses of instruction, as to the senate may seem meet.

28.—(1) Every faculty established by the University shall be governed by a council which shall consist of the dean, the vice-dean, the secretary and of the members of the teaching staff.

(2) The dean, vice-dean and the secretary of each faculty shall be elected by the members of the teaching staff, but their election must be confirmed by the council administration.

(3) The lecturers and instructors whose appointments are temporary shall not for the purposes of this section be deemed to be members of the teaching staff.

(4) The councils of the faculties shall have power and authority to appoint examiners, and to make bylaws for the good and efficient management of the affairs of the faculty, provided, however, that no such bylaws shall be valid until and unless the same shall be approved by the senate with regard to matters of a purely academic nature, and by the council of administration with regard to all other matters.

29. Once at least in every year at a time or times to be fixed by the senate, the senate shall cause to be held an examination of the candidates for degrees, certificates of proficiency, scholarships and prizes, and at any such examination the candidates shall be examined by examiners

appointed for the purpose by the councils of the faculties and by the directors of special schools, departments, chairs and courses of instruction and at every such examination the candidates shall be examined orally or in writing or otherwise.

30. The examiners may be required to make in writing the declaration which appears in schedule "B" hereto.

31. The senate may grant such scholarships and prizes as to the senate may seem meet, provided, however, the council of administration has previously approved of the granting of such scholarships and prizes.

32. — (1) The University may by bylaws passed by the senate and confirmed by the council of administration, provide that any college, seminary or other institution established in any province of Canada may become affiliated to and connected with the University for the purposes of admitting therefrom as candidates at examinations for the degrees which the University is authorized to confer, such persons as may have successfully completed in such college, seminary or other institution whilst affiliated with the University, such course of instruction, preliminary to any of the said respective examinations for standing or for scholarships, honours, degrees or certificates as the University shall from time to time by regulations in that behalf determine; provided always that no college, seminary or other institution of learning in the province of Ontario now in affiliation with the University of Toronto and no university in the province of Ontario shall affiliate to or connect with the said Université d'Ottawa.

(2) The agreement of affiliation entered into between the University and the affiliated college, seminary or other institution shall contain provisions setting out the conditions upon which the said affiliated institutions shall be entitled to representation in the senate of the University.

(3) The said agreement of affiliation shall also contain provisions stipulating that the qualifications for admission into any such affiliated institution and the courses of study therein shall not be inferior to those by this Act prescribed for the said University.

33. This Act shall come into force on the day upon which it receives the Royal Assent.

SCHEDULE "A"

(Referred to in Section 2)

1. An Act of the Legislature of the late Province of Canada, passed in the twelfth year of the reign of Her Majesty Queen Victoria, chapter 107, and entitled *An Act to incorporate the College of Bytown*.

2. An Act of the Legislature of the late Province of Canada, passed in the twenty-fourth year of the reign of Her Majesty Queen Victoria, chapter 108, and entitled *An Act to change the name of the College of Bytown, and to amend the Act incorporating the same.*

3. An Act of the Legislature of the late Province of Canada, passed in the twenty-ninth year of the reign of Her Majesty Queen Victoria, chapter 135, and entitled *An Act to amend the Acts incorporating the College of Ottawa, and to grant certain privileges to the said College.*

4. An Act of the Legislature of the Province of Ontario, passed in the forty-eighth year of the reign of Her Majesty Queen Victoria, chapter 91, and entitled *An Act to amend the Acts incorporating the College of Ottawa.*

5. An Act of the Legislature of the Province of Ontario, passed in the fifty-fourth year of the reign of Her Majesty Queen Victoria, chapter 104, and entitled *An Act to amend the Acts incorporating the College of Ottawa.*

SCHEDULE "B"

form of declaration
examiners

I, ..., solemnly declare that I will perform my duty of examiner without fear, love or affection or partiality towards any candidate, and that I will not knowingly allow to any candidate any advantage which is not equally allowed to all.

CHAPTER 83

An Act respecting the Country of Carleton
and the University of Ottawa
Assented to April 9th, 1941.
Session Prorogued April 9, 1941.

WHEREAS the Corporation of the County of Carleton has by its petition prayed for special legislation amending *The University of Ottawa Act, 1933*, in respect of the exemption from taxation of the real property of the University; and whereas it is expedient to grant the prayer of the said petition:

Therefore, His Majesty, by and with the advice and consent of the Legislative Assembly of the Province of Ontario, enacts as follows:

1. Section 12 of *The University of Ottawa Act, 1933*, is amended by adding thereto the following subsections:

(2) The exemption from taxation provided by subsection 1 shall not apply to any real property vested in the University, or otherwise held for the University, situate within the limits of the County of Carleton, other than the City of Ottawa.

(3) Notwithstanding anything to the contrary in *The Assessment Act*, all real property vested in the University, or otherwise held for the University situate within the County of Carleton, other than the City of Ottawa, shall be liable to taxation, except the following which shall not be liable to taxation for municipal or school purposes and shall be exempt from every description of such taxation. —

> (a) the buildings and grounds, not exceeding in the whole one parcel of fifty acres; provided such buildings and grounds are solely and *bona fide* used and occupied by the University for farming or agricultural pursuits, or in connections with instruction in agriculture; and provided further the same are not worked on shares with any other person, or the annual or other crops or livestock or produce therefrom, or any part thereof, are not sold, or distributed; but *bona fide* distribution to charity or the sale or exchange of livestock for the purpose

of controlling the quality thereof or the sale of surplus certified seed shall not be deemed sale or distribution within the meaning of this clause;

(b) the buildings and grounds, except buildings and grounds used for farming or agricultural pursuits or in connection with instruction in agriculture; provided such buildings and grounds shall be exempt only while actually used and occupied by the University and not if otherwise occupied; and provided further that such exemption shall be limited to parcels not exceeding three acres each.

2. This Act shall come into force on the day upon which it receives the Royal Assent and shall have effect from and after the 1st day of January, 1940.

3. This Act may be cited as *The University of Ottawa Amendment Act, 1941*.

No. Pr17

5th Session, 25th Legislature, Ontario
7-8 Elizabeth II, 1959

BILL

An Act respecting Université d'Ottawa

Mr. Dunbar

Toronto
Printed and Published by Baptist Johnston
Printer to the Queen's Most Excellent Majesty

No. Pr17   1959
BILL

An Act respecting Université d'Ottawa

WHEREAS Université d'Ottawa, herein called the University, by its petition has represented that it was incorporated by *An Act to incorporate The College of Bytown*, being chapter 107 of the Provincial Statutes of Canada, 1849, that its powers were extended and amended and its name changed by subsequent enactments, that its present powers and name were granted by *The University of Ottawa Act, 1933*, as amended by *The University of Ottawa Amendment Act, 1941*, and that the purposes of the University would be further promoted if the directors of the university were granted the power to expropriate certain lands and to hold the lands so expropriated; and whereas the petitioner has prayed for special legislation in respect of the matter hereinafter set forth; and whereas it is expedient to grant the prayer of the petition;

Therefore, Her Majesty, by and with the advice and consent of the Legislative Assembly of the Province of Ontario enacts as follows:

1. Université d'Ottawa, also known as The University of Ottawa, shall have the power to enter upon, take, use and expropriate the interest of the owner or of any other person, other than a municipal corporation, without the consent of the owner or of any other person, other than a municipal corporation, without the consent of such owner or other person, in any and all of the lands and premises described in Schedule A hereto as the University may deem advisable for the use of or for the future use and expansion of the University, making due compensation for any such real property to the owners and occupiers thereof, and all persons having any interest therein, and the provisions of *The Municipal Act* as to taking land compulsorily and making compensation therefor and as to the manner of determining and paying the compensation shall, *mutatis mutandis*, apply to the University and to the exercise by it of the powers conferred by this section, and, where any act is by any of such provisions required to be done by the council of administration of the University and, where any act is by any such provisions required to be done by the clerk of a municipality or at the office of such clerk, the like act shall be done by or at the office of the Treasurer of the University or by or at the office of such officer of the University exercising the office of treasurer, as the case may be.

2. Notwithstanding section 1, the power to expropriate lands under this Act shall apply only for a period of five years form the date this Act comes into force with respect to the lands mentioned in Schedule B hereto.

3. Notwithstanding any special Act, the University of Ottawa shall be liable for water service rates and sewer service rates imposed by the City of Ottawa.

4. This Act comes into force on the day it receives Royal Assent.

5. This Act may be cited as *The University of Ottawa Act, 1959*.

Schedule A

All and Singular those certain parcels or tracts of lands and premises situate, lying and being in the City of Ottawa, in the County of Carleton and Province of Ontario, and being composed of:

STEWART STREET

Lot 3 and the west half of Lot 4 on the south side of Stewart Street, Registered Plan No. 6.

WILBROD STREET

Lot 2 on the north side of Wilbrod Street, Registered Plan No. 6.

LAURIER STREET

Lot "A" on the south side of Laurier Avenue, Registered Plan No. 4324. The easterly 50 feet of Lot "C" on the south side of Laurier Avenue, Registered Plan No. 25270. Lots 1 and 2 on the south side of Laurier Avenue, Registered Plan No. 14141.

OSGOODE STREET

Lot 1 and the westerly 40 feet and the northerly 30 feet of Lot 2 and the whole of Lots 4, 5, 6 and 7 on the north side of Osgoode Street, Registered Plan No. 15632. Lots 6 and 9 on the south side of Osgoode Street, Registered Plan No. 33841. Street Lot lying between Lots 6 and 7 on the south side of Osgoode Street, Registered Plan No. 33841. Lot 7 on the south side of Osgoode Street, Registered Plan No. 15632. The northerly 45 feet of Lots 9 and 10 on the south side of Osgoode Street, Registered Plan No. 15632. The southerly 50 feet of Lot 11, and the whole of Lots 12, 13, 14, 15, 16, 17 and 18 on the south side of Osgoode Street, Registered Plan No. 25223.

MacDOUGAL STREET

The westerly 30 feet of Lot 1, and the east half of Lot 2 on the north side of MacDougal Street, Registered Plan No 40654. Lots 9 and 11 on the south side of MacDougal Street, Registered Plan No 40654.

NICHOLAS STREET

The north half of Lot 11 and the whole of Lot 13 on the east side of Nicholas Street, Registered Plan No. 3922. Lots 20 and 21 and the northerly 95 feet of Lot 22 on the east side of Nicholas Street, Registered Plan No. 3350. The easterly 50 feet of Lots 3 and 4 on the east side of Nicholas Street, Registered Plan No. 3613. Part of Lot "E", Concession "D", Rideau Front (Nepean) now in Ottawa and more particularly described as follows:

Commencing at a point on the westerly limit of that part of the said Lot described in a Deed of Sale from Mary Ann McGovern to the Artificial Ice Company dated 4th April, 1913 and registered in the Registry Office as No. 118741, distant 35.7 feet measured southerly and along the said westerly limit from the north west angle thereof; thence south 38 degrees 23 minutes west, and along the north westerly boundary of the lands as present owned by the Ottawa Artificial Ice Company, 273 feet more or less, to a point distant 200 feet from the water's edge of the Rideau Canal; thence in a south easterly direction on a course parallel with the water's edge of the Rideau Canal and following the south westerly boundary of the lands of the said Ottawa Artificial Ice Company, 113 feet more or less, to the south easterly boundary of the lands of the said Ottawa Artificial Ice Company; thence easterly and following the south easterly boundary of the said lands, 253 feet 3 inches more or less, to the southerly boundary of the said lands; thence easterly and following the southerly boundary of the lands of the said Ottawa Artificial Ice Company, to the easterly boundary of the said lands; thence northerly and following the easterly boundary of the said lands, 100 feet to the northerly boundary of the said lands; thence westerly and following the northerly boundary of the said lands, 100 feet to the westerly boundary thereof; thence southerly and following the westerly boundary of the said lands, 35.7 feet to the point of commencement.

WALLER STREET

Lot "C", the westerly 30 feet of Lot "D" and the whole of Lot "E" on the west side of Waller Street, Registered Plan No. 4323.

HASTEY AVENUE

Lot 5 and the north halves of Lots 6 and 8 on the west side of Hastey Avenue, Registered Plan No. 25270. Lots 7, 8 and 9 on the east side of Hastey Avenue, Registered Plan No. 25270.

CUMBERLAND STREET

The south half of Lot 6 and the whole of Lots 7, 8 and 9 on the west side of Cumberland Street, Registered Plan No. 25270. The easterly 63 feet of Lots 1 and 2 on the west side of Cumberland Street, Registered Plan No. 33841. Lots 15, 16, 18, 20 and 21 on the west side of Cumberland Street, Registered Plan No. 40654. Lot 11 and the south half of Lot 12; Lot 13 and the north half of Lot 14; the south half of Lot 15; the northerly 50 feet of Lot 16 and the whole of Lots 17 and 18 on the east side of Cumberland Street, Registered Plan No. 15632.

COLLEGE AVENUE

Lot 1; the north half of Lot 2; the south half of Lot 3 and the whole of Lots 4, 5, 6 and 7 on the west side of College Avenue, Registered Plan No. 14141. Lots 11 and 12; the south half of Lot 13; Lots 14 and 15; the north half of Lot 16, and the south half of Lot 17 on the west side of College Avenue, Registered Plan No 15632. Lots 1, 5, 8 and 9 and the northerly 15 feet of Lot 10 on the east side of College Avenue, Registered Plan No. 14141. The north halves of Lots 12 and 13 and the whole of Lots 14, 15, 16, 17, 18, 19 and 20 on the east side of College Avenue, Registered Plan No. 25223.

KING EDWARD STREET

Lots 1, 2, 3 and 4; the north half of Lot 5; the south half of Lot 6; the south half of Lot 7, and the whole of Lots 8, 9 and 11 on the west side of King Edward Avenue, Registered Plan No. 15632. Lot 12; the south half of Lot 13 and Lots 15, 17 and 19 on the west side of King Edward Avenue, Registered Plan No. 25223.

Save and Except thereout and therefrom any interest in any portion of the above-mentioned lands which might be vested in the Crown or in any Corporation representing or acting on behalf of the Crown, in the Corporation of the City of Ottawa, in the Ottawa Public School Board, or in the Ottawa Separate School Board, and Save and Except any present church properties.

SCHEDULE B

All and Singular those certain parcels or tracts of lands and premises situate, lying and being in the City of Ottawa, in the County of Carleton and Province of Ontario, and being composed of:

1. Lots 7, 8, 9 and 10 on the south side of Osgoode Street, Lots 11, 12, 13, 14, 15, 16, 17 and 18 on the west side of College Avenue, and Lots 11, 12, 13, 14, 15, 16, 17 and 18 on the east side of Cumberland Street, all as shown on Registered Plan No. 15632; also Lots 11, 12, 13 and 14 on the south side of Osgoode Street, Lots 12, 13, 14, 15, 16, 17, 18, 19 and 20 on the west side of King Edward Avenue, and Lots 12, 13, 14, 15, 16, 17, 18, 19 and 20 on the east side of College Avenue, all as shown on Registered Plan No. 25223.

2. Part of Lot "E", Concession "D", Rideau Front (Nepean) now in Ottawa and more particularly described as follows:

Commencing at a point on the westerly limit of that part of the said Lot described in a Deed of Sale from Mary Ann McGovern to the Artificial Ice Company dated 4th April, 1913 and registered in the Registry Office as No. 118741, distant 35.7 feet measured southerly and along the said westerly limit from the north west angle thereof; thence south 38 degrees 23 minutes west, and along the north westerly boundary of the lands as present owned by the Ottawa Artificial Ice Company, 273 feet more or less, to a point distant 200 feet from the water's edge of the Rideau Canal; thence in a south easterly direction on a course parallel with the water's edge of the Rideau Canal and following the south westerly boundary of the lands of the said Ottawa Artificial Ice Company, 113 feet more or less, to the south easterly boundary of the lands of the said Ottawa Artificial Ice Company; thence easterly and following the south easterly boundary of the said lands, 253 feet 3 inches more or less, to the southerly boundary of the said lands; thence easterly and following the southerly boundary of the lands of the said Ottawa Artificial Ice Company, to the easterly boundary of the said lands; thence northerly and following the easterly boundary of the said lands, 100 feet to the northerly boundary of the said lands; thence westerly and following the northerly boundary of the said lands, 100 feet to the westerly boundary thereof; thence southerly and following the westerly boundary of the said lands, 35.7 feet to the point of commencement.

N.B.

1st Reading
February 12th, 1959

2nd Reading
March 4th, 1959

3rd Reading
March 16th, 1959

CHAPTER 138

An Act respecting Université d'Ottawa

Assented to March 29th, 1961
Session Prorogued, March 29th, 1961

WHEREAS Université d'Ottawa herein called the University, by its petition has represented that it was incorporated by *An Act to incorporate The College of Bytown,* being chapter 107 of the Statutes of the Province of Canada, 1849, that its powers were extended and amended and its name changed by subsequent enactments, that its present powers and name were granted by *The University of Ottawa Act, 1933,* as amended by *The University of Ottawa Amendment Act, 1941,* and that the purposes of the University would be further promoted if the officers of the council of each faculty were appointed by the council of administration; and whereas the petitioner has prayed for special legislation in respect of the matter hereinafter set forth; and whereas it is expedient to grant the prayer of the petition;

Therefore, Her Majesty, by and with the advice and consent of the Legislative Assembly of the Province of Ontario, enacts as follows:

1. Subsection 2 of section 28 of *The University of Ottawa Act, 1933* is repealed and the following substituted therefor:
   (2) The dean, vice-dean and the secretary of each faculty shall be appointed by the council of administration.

2. This Act comes into force on the day it receives Royal Assent.

3. This Act may be cited as *The University of Ottawa Act, 1960–61.*

CHAPTER 148

An Act respecting Université d'Ottawa
Assented to March 25th, 1964
Session Prorogued May 8th, 1964

WHEREAS Université d'Ottawa, herein called the University, by its petition has represented that it was originally incorporated by *An Act to incorporate The College of Bytown,* being chapter 107 of the Statutes of the Province of Canada, 1849; that its powers were further extended and amended and its name changed by *An Act to change the name of the College of Bytown, and to amend the Act incorporating the same,* being chapter 108 of the Statutes of the Province of Canada, 1861, *An Act to amend the Acts incorporating "The College of Ottawa," and to grant certain privileges to the said College,* being chapter 135 of the Statutes of the Province of Canada, 1866, *An Act to amend the Acts incorporating the College of Ottawa,* being chapter 91 of the Statutes of Ontario, 1885, *An Act to amend the Acts incorporating the College of Ottawa,* being chapter 104 of the Statutes of Ontario, 1891, and *The University of Ottawa Act, 1911,* as amended by *The University of Ottawa Amendment Act, 1941* and *The University of Ottawa Act, 1960–61,* and that certain powers of expropriation were granted to the University by *The University of Ottawa Act, 1959,* which powers of expropriation as to the lands described in Schedule B thereto are due to expire; and whereas the petitioner has prayed that its powers of expropriation as to such lands be made permanent and that its powers of expropriation be extended to cover certain other lands, and has further represented that the purposes of the University would be further promoted if the University were granted the power to expropriate and hold such certain other lands; and whereas the petitioner has further prayed for special legislation in respect of the matters hereinafter set forth; and whereas it is expedient to grant the prayer of the petition;

Therefore, Her Majesty, be and with the advice and consent of the Legislative Assembly of the Province of Ontario, enacts as follows:

1.—(1) Université d'Ottawa, also known as The University of Ottawa, shall have the power to enter upon, take, use and expropriate in the interest of the owner or of any other person, other than a municipal corporation, without the consent of such owner or other person, in any and all of the lands and premises described in the Schedule hereto, as the University may deem advisable for the use of, or for the future use and expansion of, the University.

(2) *The Expropriation Procedures Act, 1962–63* applies to the expropriation of lands and premises under this Act.

2.—(1) Section 2 of *The University of Ottawa Act, 1959* is repealed.

(2) Schedule B to *The University of Ottawa Act, 1959* is repealed.

3. This Act comes into force on the day it receives Royal Assent.

4. This Act may be cited as *The University of Ottawa Act, 1964*.

SCHEDULE

ALL AND SINGULAR those certain parcels of tracts of land and premises situate, lying and being in the City of Ottawa, in the County of Carleton and Province of Ontario, and being composed of:

HENDERSON AVENUE

West Side

Lots 1 to 10 inclusive, Registered Plan No. 15632. Lots 11 to 19 inclusive, Registered Plan No. 25223. Lots 22 to 31 inclusive, Registered Plan No. 37219.

KING EDWARD AVENUE

East Side:

Lots 1 to 10 inclusive, Registered Plan No. 15632. Lots 11, 12, 13 and 14; the South half of Lot 15 and the whole of Lots 16, 17, 18 and 19, Registered Plan No. 25223. Lots 19 to 21 inclusive, Registered Plan No. 31694. Lots 22 to 31 inclusive, Registered Plan No. 37219.

West Side:

Lot 12; The South half of Lot 13 and the whole of Lots 15, 17 and 19 on Registered Plan No. 25223.

OSGOODE STREET

South Side:

Lot 7 and the Northerly 45 feet of Lots 9 and 10, Registered Plan No. 15632; the Southerly 50 feet of Lot 11, and the whole of Lots 12, 13 and 14, Registered Plan No. 25223.

CUMBERLAND STREET

East Side:

South half of Lot 11 and the South half of Lot 12; the Southerly 30 feet of Lot 13 and the North half of Lot 14; the South half of Lot 15; the Northerly 50 feet of Lot 16 and the whole of Lot 17 and the South half of Lot 18, Registered Plan No. 15632.

COLLEGE AVENUE

West Side:

Lots 11 and 12; the South half of Lot 13; Lots 14 and 15; the North half of Lot 16 and the South half of Lot 17, Registered Plan No. 15632.

East Side:

The North half of Lot 13 and the whole of Lots 14, 15, 16, 17, 18, 19 and 20, on the Registered Plan No. 25223.

SAVE AND EXCEPT thereout and therefrom any interest in any portion of the above-mentioned lands which might be vested in the Crown or in any Corporation representing or acting on behalf of the Crown, in the Corporation of the City of Ottawa, in the Ottawa Public School Board, or in the Ottawa Separate School Board, and Save and Except any present church properties.

CHAPTER 137

An Act respecting Université d'Ottawa

Assented to June 22nd, 1965
Session Prorogued June 22nd, 1965

HER MAJESTY, by and with the advice and consent of the Legislative Assembly of the Province of Ontario, enacts as follows:

PART I

1.— (1) The corporation of "The College of Bytown", which corporation had its name changed to "The College of Ottawa" and further changed to "Université d'Ottawa", is hereby continued under the name of "Université Saint Paul" in the French language and "Saint Paul University" in the English language and, subject to the provisions of this Act, shall have, hold, possess and enjoy all the property, rights, powers and privileges which it may now have, hold, possess and enjoy.

(2) Where before the passing of this Act the name "University of Ottawa" or "The University of Ottawa" or "Ottawa University" was used by Université d'Ottawa, such name shall for all purposes be taken to have meant Université d'Ottawa.

(3) Saint Paul University, formerly Université d'Ottawa, has and shall be deemed always to have had, in addition to the powers, rights and privileges mentioned in section 26 of *The Interpretation Act*, power to purchase or otherwise acquire, take or receive by gift, bequest or devise and to hold and enjoy without licence in mortmain and without limitation as to the period of holding any estate or property whatsoever, whether real or personal, and to sell, grant, convey, mortgage, lease or otherwise dispose of the same or any part thereof from time to time and as occasion may require and to acquire other estate or property in addition thereto or in place thereof.

PART II

2. In this Part,
    (*a*) "Board" means the Board of Governors of the University of Ottawa;
    (*b*) "Chancellor" means the Chancellor of the University;

(c) "property" includes real and personal property;
(d) "real property" includes messuages, lands, tenements and hereditaments, whether corporeal or incorporeal, and any undivided share thereof and any estate or interest therein;
(e) "Rector" means the Rector of the University;
(f) "Senate" means the Senate of the University;
(g) "teaching staff" includes the professors and associate professors, the assistant professors, lecturers, associates, instructors, demonstrators and all others engaged in the work of teaching or giving instruction or in research;
(h) "University" means the University of Ottawa.

3. The persons named in section 9, and such other persons who may hereafter become members of the Board, are hereby created a body corporate with perpetual succession and a common seal to be known in the French language under the name of "Université d'Ottawa" and in the English language under the name of "University of Ottawa".

4. The objects and purposes of the University are,
(a) to promote the advancement of learning and the dissemination of knowledge;
(b) to further, in accordance with Christian principles, the intellectual, spiritual, moral, physical and social development of, as well as a community spirit among, its undergraduates, graduates and teaching staff, and to promote the betterment of society;
(c) to further bilingualism and biculturalism and to preserve and develop French culture in Ontario.

5. No religious test shall be required of any professor, lecturer, teacher, officer, servant or student of the University, nor shall any religious observances according to the regulations of any particular denomination or sect be imposed upon them.

6. The University may establish and maintain faculties, schools, institutes, departments, chairs and courses.

7. The University may grant in all branches of learning any and all university degrees, honorary degrees, diplomas and certificates.

8. The management, discipline and control of the University shall be free from the restrictions and control of any outside body, whether lay or religious, and no religious test shall be required of any member of the Board, but such management, discipline and control shall be based upon Christian principles.

9. There shall be a board of governors of the University of not more than thirty-two members, consisting of,
    (*a*) The Rector;
    (*b*) the following twelve persons:
        Georgy A. Addy,
        Jean-Victor Allard,
        Paul Desmarais,
        Louis-Paul Dugal,
        Mr. Justice Gérald Fauteux,
        Lawrence Freiman,
        James P. Gilmore,
        Aurèle Gratton,
        Ascanio J. Major,
        Leo McCarthy,
        J. Barry O'Brien,
        Marcel Vincent;
    (*c*) four persons appointed by the Lieutenant Governor in Council who, in the first instance, shall be,
        John J. Deutsch,
        Roger Duhamel,
        Cecil Morrison,
        Roger Séguin;
    (*d*) two persons appointed by the Senate from among those of its members elected under clause *d* of sub-section 1 of section 15;
    (*e*) two persons appointed by the Alumni Association from among its own members;
    (*f*) eight persons appointed by the Council of Administration of Saint Paul University who, in the first instance, shall be,
        Jules Bélanger, O.M.I.,
        Arthur Caron, O.M.I.,
        Gerald Cousineau, O.M.I.,
        Sylvio Ducharme, O.M.I.,
        Jean-Charles Laframboise, O.M.I.,
        René Lavigne, O.M.I.,

Rodrigue Normandin, O.M.I.,
Léo-Paul Pigeon, O.M.I.;
  (*g*) such other persons appointed by the Board for such terms as the Board may determine by bylaws.

10.—(1) No members of the Board, except the Rector, shall be appointed for terms exceeding three years, and all members mentioned in clauses *b* and *g* of section 9 shall be appointed in rotation in such manner as the Board may determine by bylaws.

(2) The Baord shall be bylaws prescribe the terms of office and the method of retirement of the persons named in clause *b* of section 9, and the terms of office and the method of appointment, replacement and retirement of their successors, and of the persons provided for in clause *g* of section 9.

(3) All members of the Baord are eligible for re-appointment.

(4) After thirty days' notice to any member, the Board, by a resolution passed at a meeting at which at least two-thirds of the members of the Board are present, may declare vacant the seat of such member.

(5) Where a vacancy on the Board occurs before the term of office for which a member has been appointed or elected has expired, the vacancy shall be filled in the same manner and by the same authority as the member whose membership is vacant was appointed or elected, as the case may be, and the member so appointed or elected shall hold office for the remainder of the term of office of the member whose membership is vacant.

(6) Fourteen members of the Board constitute a quorum.

(7) The Board shall elect from among its members a chairman and vice-chairman.

11. Except in such matters as are assigned by this Act to the Senate and the boards of federated and affiliated colleges and universities, the government, conduct, management and control of the Universty and of its property, revenues, business and affairs are vested in the Board, and the Board has all the powers necessary or convenient to perform its duties and achieve the objects and purposes of the University, including, without limiting the generality of the foregoing, power,
  (*a*) to appoint and remove the Rector and the Vice-Rectors;
  (*b*) to appoint, promote and remove the heads of all faculties and schools, all officers of the University and of the faculties, the teaching staff of the University and all such other officers,

clerks, employees, agents and servants as the Board deems necessary or expedient for the purposes of the University, but no person shall be appointed, promoted or removed as head of a faculty or school, as a senior administrative officer or as a member of the teaching staff of the University except on the recommendation of the Rector;

(c) to fix the number, duties, salaries and other emoluments of officers, members of the teaching staff, agents and servants of the University;

(d) to appoint an executive committee and such other committees of the Board as it deems advisable, and to delegate to any such committee any of its powers;

(e) to borrow money on the credit of the University in such amount, on such terms and from such persons, firms or corporations, including chartered banks, as may be determined by the Board;

(f) to make, draw and endorse promissory notes or bills of exchange;

(g) to hypothecate, pledge or charge any or all the property of the University to secure any money so borrowed or the fulfilment of the obligation incurred by it under any promissory note or bill of exchange signed, made, drawn or endorsed by it;

(h) to issue bonds, debentures and obligations on such terms and conditions as the Board may decide, and pledge or sell such bonds, debentures and obligations for such sums and at such prices as the Board may decide, and mortgage, charge, hypothecate or pledge all or any part of the property of the University to secure any such bonds, debentures and obligations;

(i) to provide for the appointment and establishment of such advisory, deliberative or administrative persons, offices and bodies of the University, including a joint committee of the Senate and the Board to discuss matters of mutual concern, as the Board deems advisable, and to fix their respective memberships, powers and duties;

(j) to make bylaws, rules and regulations in respect of all such matters as may seem necessary or advisable for the government, management, conduct and control of the University.

12.— (1) There shall be a Chancellor of the University who shall be appointed by the Board with the concurrence of the Senate and who shall hold office for four years and is eligible for re-appointment.

(2) The Chancellor shall be the titular head of the University and be accorded the place of honour at commencement exercises and other functions, and, if present, he shall preside at examinations.

(3) The Rector is Vice-Chancellor of the University and, in the absence of or vacancy in the office of the Chancellor, shall perform the functions of the Chancellor.

(4) In the absence of the Chancellor and the Vice-Chancellor, the Senate shall appoint one of its number to confer degrees.

13.— (1) There shall be a Rector of the University who shall be appointed by the Board and who, unless otherwise provided by the Board, shall hold office during the pleasure of the Board.

(2) The Board shall appoint at least two Vice-Rectors and may appoint any other officers who shall have such powers and duties as may be conferred on them by the Board on the recommendation of the Rector, and one Vice-Rector shall act as Rector when the Rector is absent or if there is a vacancy in the office of Rector and, while so acting, he has all the rights, privileges, powers and duties of the Rector.

(3) The Rector is the chief executive officer of the University and chairman of the Senate and has supervision over and direction of the academic work and general administration of the University, the teaching staff, officers, servants and students thereof, and has such other powers and duties as from time to time may be conferred upon or assigned to him by the Board.

14. The Secretary shall,
   (a) be the Secretary of the Board and of the Senate;
   (b) maintain and keep the register or roll of graduates of the University and of those persons who receive honorary degrees;
   (c) sign all University diplomas after the Rector; and
   (d) perform such other duties as may be assigned to him by the Rector or by the Board.

15.— (1) There shall be a Senate of the University composed of,
   (a) the Chancellor;
   (b) the Rector, the Vice-Rectors and the Secretary;

(c) the dean and the secretary of each faculty, including those of the federated universities, or, in the absence of the dean, the vice-dean;

(d) one professor or associate professor on the teaching staff of each faculty, including those of the federated universities, elected by the council of each faculty for a term of three years;

(e) the director of each special school operated by the University but not conducted by any of its organized faculties;

(f) the head of each federated college and university;

(g) subject to clause *b* of subsection 1 of section 29 being implemented, the head and the Dean of Studies of St. Patrick's College of the University of Ottawa;

(h) such other members as the Senate may determine by bylaws.

(2) All elected or appointed members of the Senate are eligible for re-election or re-appointment.

16.— (1) The Rector or, in his absence, the first Vice-Rector or, in the absence of both, the second Vice-Rector shall preside at all meetings of the Senate.

(2) All questions before the Senate shall be decided by a majority of the votes of the members present, including the vote of the Rector or other presiding member of the Senate, and, in the case of an equal division of such votes, the Rector or, in his absence, the presiding member at such meeting has an additional or casting vote.

(3) A majority of all the members of the Senate constitutes a quorum.

(4) The Senate shall meet from time to time, when convened by the Rector, and at such other times as the members of the Senate appoint and at such place in the City of Ottawa as the Rector may choose.

17. The Senate is responsible for the educational policy of the University and, subject to the approval of the Board in so far as the expenditure of funds is concerned, may create, maintain and discontinue such faculties, departments, schools or institutes or establish such chairs as it may determine, may enact bylaws and regulations for the conduct of its affairs, and, without limiting the generality of the foregoing, has power,

(a) to control, regulate and determine the educational policy of the University according to Christian principles and its bilingual tradition and character;

(b) to determine the courses of study and standards of admissions to the University and continued membership therein, and qualifications for degrees and diplomas;

(c) to deal with all matters arising in connection with the awarding of fellowships, scholarships, bursaries, medals, prizes and other awards;

(d) to confer the degrees of Bachelor, Master and Doctor, and all other degrees and diplomas in all branches of learning that may appropriately be conferred by a university;

(e) to confer honorary degrees in any branch of higher learning with the concurrence of the Board;

(f) to create committees to exercise its powers.

18.— (1) Every faculty established by the University shall be governed by a council, which shall consist of the Dean, the Associate Dean, if any, the Vice-Dean, the Secretary and such other members as may be determined by the Senate.

(2) The councils of the faculties may appoint examiners and make bylaws for the good and efficient management of the affairs of the faculty, provided that no such bylaws is valid until approved by the Senate with regard to matters of a purely academic nature and by the Board with regard to all other matters.

19. The Board may by bylaws, confirmed by the Senate, provide that any college, seminary or university may become federated or affiliated with the University on such terms and for such periods of time as the Senate and the Board may determine.

20. The University has, in addition to the powers, rights and privileges mentioned in section 26 of *The Interpretation Act*, power to purchase or otherwise acquire, take or receive by gift, bequest or devise and to hold and enjoy without licence in mortmain and without limitation as to the period of holding any estate or property whatsoever, whether real or personal, and to sell, grant, convey, mortgage, lease or otherwise dispose of the same or any part thereof from time to time and as occasion may require and to acquire other estate or property in addition thereto or in place thereof.

21. The property vested in the University and any lands and premises leased to and occupied by the University are not liable to taxation for provincial, municipal or school purposes, and are exempt from every description of taxation so long as the same are actually used and occupied for the purposes of the University.

22. Real property vested in the University is not liable to be entered upon, used or taken by any corporation, except a municipal corporation, or by any person possessing the right of taking real property compulsorily for any purpose, and no power to expropriate real property hereafter conferred shall extend to such property unless in the Act conferring the power it is made in express terms to apply thereto.

23. All property vested in the University shall, as far as the application thereto of any statute of limitations is concerned, be deemed to have been and to be real property vested in the Crown for the public uses of Ontario.

24. The property and the income, revenues, issues and profits of all property of the University shall be applied solely to achieving the objects and purposes of the University.

25. The funds of the University not immediately required for its purposes and the proceeds of all property that come to the hands of the Board, subject to any trust or trusts affecting the same, may be invested and re-invested in such investments as the Board deems meet.

26. The accounts of the Board shall be audited at least once a year.

27. Upon the request of the Lieutenant Governor in Council, the Board shall submit to him its annual report and shall submit such other reports as he may request from time to time.

PART III

28. Saint Paul University, upon the coming into force of this Act, shall become federated with the University of Ottawa, subject to such terms and conditions as may be agreed upon by the two corporations.

29.— (1) St. Patrick's College, upon the coming into force of this Act, has the option of,
    (a) becoming either federated or affiliated with the University

of Ottawa, subject to such terms and conditions as may be agreed upon by the institutions concerned; or

(b) becoming an integral part of the University of Ottawa, to be known as St. Patrick's College of the University of Ottawa, upon such terms and conditions as may be mutually agreed upon between the University of Ottawa and the administrators of St. Patrick's College as it presently exists, which terms and conditions shall be incorporated in the bylaws of the University of Ottawa with the specific object of ensuring the preservation and development on the present campus of St. Patrick's College of the presently established sections of the Faculty of Arts and of the School of Social Welfare.

(2) Nothing in clause *b* of subsection 1 shall be construed to imply that the University of Ottawa is prevented from undertaking any other academic activities on the campus of St. Patrick's College of the University of Ottawa, provided such other activities are not inconsistent with the terms and conditions mentioned in subsection 1 as incorporated in the bylaws of the University of Ottawa.

30. Any other college or institution affiliated with Saint Paul University upon the coming into force of this Act has the right under this Act of continuing its affiliation with the University of Ottawa through Saint Paul University or of negotiating separate affiliation or federation agreements with the University of Ottawa, or both, as in its discretion it deems meet.

31. The University of Ottawa shall grant to all students past and present of Saint Paul University full recognition towards their respective university degrees for all credits and marks awarded by Saint Paul University before this Act came into force, and shall grant degrees in its own name to all of those students who are recommended for degrees by Saint Paul University during the fall convocation for the year 1965.

32. The University of Ottawa and Saint Paul University, in order to give effect to the intent and purpose of this Act, may make and accept as between themselves such transfers of property upon such terms and for such consideration, including nominal consideration, and subject to such conditions and security for payment, as may be mutually agreed upon.

33. Until the University of Ottawa has organized its Senate, the Senate of Saint Paul University has power to carry out in the name of and on behalf of the Senate of the University of Ottawa its duties, functions and powers as mentioned in section 17, but such power shall not in any event be exercised by the Senate of Saint Paul University after the 31st day of October, 1965.

PART IV

34. This Act comes into force on the 1st day of July 1965.

35. This Act may be cited as *The University of Ottawa Act, 1965*.

Notes

NB: Over the course of this research, the University of Saint Paul archives agreed to allow the University of Ottawa to begin administering its collection. The collection was transferred to the University of Ottawa, where the library's shelfmark system that is still used to identify documents here was replaced. The University of Ottawa instead created a new Fonds, Fonds 315. The archives are able to give equivalencies for the shelfmarks used here.

Introduction

1. Sir William Blackstone, "Chap. XVIII 'Of Corporations,'" in *Commentaries on the Laws of England*, vol. 1, Making of Modern Law (London: J. Bell, 1813), 467; David Bebbington, "The Secularization of British Universities since the Mid-Nineteeth Century," in *The Secularization of the Academy*, ed. George M. Marsden and Bradley J. Longfield (Oxford: Oxford University Press, 1992), 264–266, 270–271; R. D. Anderson, *European Universities from the Enlightenment to 1914* (Oxford: Oxford University Press, 2004), 194.
2. A. B. McKillop, *Matters of Mind: The University in Ontario, 1791–1951* (Toronto: University of Toronto Press, 1994), 566; Paul Axelrod, "Business Aid to Canadian Universities — 1957–1965," *Interchange* 11 (1980): 25–38; Paul Axelrod, "Businessmen and the Building of Canadian Universities: A Case Study," *Canadian Historical Review*, 63, no. 2 (1982): 202–222; Paul Axelrod, *Scholars and Dollars: Politics, Economics and the Universities of Ontario, 1945–1980* (Toronto: University of Toronto Press, 1982).
3. Gary R. Miedma, *For Canada's Sake: Public Religion, Centennial Celebrations, the Re-Making of Canada in the 1960s* (Montréal: McGill-Queen's University Press, 2005), 34.
4. Kathleen A. Mahoney, *Catholic Higher Education in Protestant America: The Jesuits and Harvard in the Age of the University* (Baltimore: Johns Hopkins University Press, 2003), 10.
5. Roberto Perin, *Rome in Canada: The Vatican and Canadian Affairs in the Late Victorian Age* (Toronto: University of Toronto Press, 1990), 7.

6. An Act to Repeal so Much of the Act of Parliament of Great Britain Passed in the Thirty-First Year of the Reign of King George the Third, and Chaptered Thirty-One, as Relates to Rectories, and the Presentation of Incumbents to the Same, and for Other Purposes Connected with Such Rectories, 1851 S Prov Can (14–15 Vict.), c 175 § (n.d.); Religious Freedom Act, RSO 1990, c. R. 22 § (n.d.); Freedom of Worship Act (n.d.).
7. For a general statement of the legal evolution of the state's relationship with religion in the present day, see Benjamin Berger, "Faith in Sovereignty: Religion and Secularism in the Politics of Canadian Federalism," *Istituzioni del federalismo* 4 (2014): 939–961, esp. 944.
8. Stephen J. Ball, "Performativity, Commodification and Commitment: An I-Spy Guide to the Neoliberal University," *British Journal of Educational Studies* 60 (2012): 17.
9. Statute of Westminster, (UK), 22 & 23 Geo V, c. 4 § (1931); whereas Canada only received full control of its government when the amendment formula was repatriated with the Constitution Act, 1982, being Schedule B to the Canada Act 1982 (UK), 1982, c. 11 § (n.d.), pt. 5, being Schedule B to the Canada Act 1982 (UK), 1982, c. 11.
10. Annic Coupal et al., "La contribution de l'Université d'Ottawa au patrimoine de la capitale nationale" (Monograph, Ottawa, 1991), Fonds 315, FH 47 .H67R, uOttawa Archives; Pierre H. Gosselin, "L'université d'Ottawa" (Monograph, Ottawa, 1984), NB-1670, uOttawa Archives.
11. McKillop, *Matters of Mind*, 566.
12. Axelrod, *Scholars and Dollars*, 12.
13. Edward J. Monahan, *Collective Autonomy: A History of the Council of Ontario Universities 1962–2000* (Waterloo: Wilfrid Laurier University Press, 2004); Howard C. Clark, *Growth and Governance of Canadian Universities: An Insider's View* (Vancouver: UBC Press, 2003); Edward Emslie Stewart, "The Role of the Provincial Government in the Development of the Universities of Ontario 1791–1964" (PhD diss., University of Toronto, 1970).
14. Walter Ruëgg, ed., *Universities in the Nineteenth and Early Twentieth Centuries*, vol. 3 of *A History of the University in Europe* (Cambridge: Cambridge University Press, 2004), 5, 9, 165, 167, 175; Walter Ruëgg, ed., *Universities since 1945*, vol. 4 of *A History of the University in Europe* (Cambridge: Cambridge University Press, 2011), 27, 372.
15. Eamon Duffy, *Saints & Sinners: A History of the Popes* (New Haven: Yale University Press, 2006), 297–298.
16. Vincent J. McNally, *The Lord's Distant Vineyard: A History of the Oblates and the Catholic Community in British Columbia* (Edmonton: University of Alberta Press, 2000), xxi–xxv.
17. *Études Oblates*, vol. 10 (Montréal: Maison Provinciale, 1951), 129–130.
18. Vincent J. McNally, *The Lord's Distant Vineyard: A History of the Oblates and the Catholic Community in British Columbia* (Edmonton: University of Alberta Press, 2000), xxii.
19. McNally, *The Lord's Distant Vineyard*, xxi–xxv.
20. Jeffrey von Aex, *Varieties of Ultramontanism* (Washington, DC: Catholic University of America Press, 1998), 39–40.
21. Martha McCarthy, *From the Great River to the Ends of the Earth: Oblate Missions to the Dene, 1847–1921* (Edmonton: University of Alberta Press, 1995), xvii–xviii.
22. See, e.g., Truth and Reconciliation Commission of Canada, "What We Have Learned: Principles of Truth and Reconciliation," Final Report (Ottawa, 2015), 119–120; C. (R.) v. McDougall, 2008 CarswellBC 2041 (n.d.); McLean v Canada, 2019 FC 1074 (n.d.).

23. Thomas Hobbes, *Leviathan: The English and Latin Texts (ii)*, ed. Noel Malcolm, vol. 5 (Oxford: Clarendon Press, 2012), 850.
24. Mark McGowan, "Rendering Unto Caesar: Catholics, the State, and the Idea of a Christian Canada," *Canadian Society of Church History: Historical Papers*, 2011, 80.
25. Richard Risk and Robert C. Vipond, "Rights Talk in Canada in the Late Nineteenth Century: The Good Sense and Right Feeling of the People," *Law and History Review* 14 (1996): 1–32.
26. Mark A. Noll, *A History of Christianity in the United States and Canada* (Grand Rapids, MI: Eerdmans Pub. Co., 1992), 161; Hugh McLeod, *The Religious Crisis of the 1960s* (Oxford: Oxford University Press, 2007), 220–221.
27. *Études Oblates*, vol. 16 (Montréal: Maison Provinciale, 1957), 133.
28. Cf. *Études Oblates*, vol. 14 (Montréal: Maison Provinciale, 1955), 126.
29. "Munificentissimus Deus," A.A.S. XXXXII § (1950), 770: dum « materialismi » commenta et quæ inde oritus morum corruptio [Vatican translation].
30. *Études Oblates*, vol. 9 (Montréal: Maison Provinciale, 1950), 173.
31. *Études Oblates*, vol. 17 (Montréal: Maison Provinciale, 1958), 81–82.
32. Laurence K. Shook, *Catholic Post-Secondary Education in English-Speaking Canada: A History* (Toronto: University of Toronto press, 1971), 239.
33. Monica Gattinger and Diane St. Pierre, "The 'Neoliberal Turn' in Provincial Cultural Policy and Administration in Québec and Ontario: The Emergence of 'Quasi-Neoliberal' Approaches," *Canadian Journal of Communication* 35 (2010): 291.
34. Religious Corporations Act, CQLR c C-71 § (n.d.), sec. 9(2).
35. UAlberta Pro-Life v Governors of the University of Alberta, 2020 ABCA 1 (n.d.). (Emphasis in original)
36. See Mckinney v. University of Guelph, 3 SCR 229 (1990).
37. Canadian Federation of Students v. Ontario, 2019 ONSC 6658 (n.d.).
38. Terence J. Fay, *A History of Canadian Catholics: Gallicanism, Romanism, and Canadianism* (Montréal: McGill-Queen's University Press, 2002), 79.
39. For a synopsis of the linguistic tensions playing between the Diocese of Ottawa and its southern counterparts, see Fay, 158.
40. The most notable incident of Leo XIII's intervention in Canadian affairs is *Affari Vos*, where the Pope enjoined bishops to form a united front to press the federal government for remedial legislation; Pope Leo XIII, *Epipstola encyclica Sanctissimi Domini Nostri Leonis Papae XIII ad Ordina- rios phoederatarum civitatum Canadensium quoad puerorum scholas*, Acta Sanctae Sedis, XXX: 356–362 § (1897).
41. Fay, *A History of Canadian Catholics*, 256.
42. John C. Barry, "Law in the Post-Conciliar Church," *Studia Canonica* 5, no. 2 (1971): 259–278, discusses this movement in his presentation to Canadian Canon Law Society in Montréal.
43. Ramsay Cook, *The Regenerators: Social Criticism in Late Victorian English Canada* (Toronto: University of Toronto Press, 2016), 4–5.
44. Fay, *A History of Canadian Catholics*, 272.
45. David B. Marshall, *Secularizing the Faith: Canadian Protestant Clergy and the Crisis of Belief, 1950–1940* (Toronto: University of Toronto Press, 1992), 249–256.
46. Marshall, 53–59, 70–71; 21–22.
47. J. George Hodgins, *Documentary History of Education in Upper Canada*, vol. 20 (Toronto: Warwick Bros. & Rutter, 1907), 158–160; J. George Hodgins, *Documentary History of Education in Upper Canada*, vol. 21 (Toronto: Warwick Bros. & Rutter, 1907), 34–52.
48. John Webster Grant, *A Profusion of Spires: Religion in Nineteenth-Century Ontario* (Toronto: University of Toronto Press, 1988), 140–143.
49. McKillop, *Matters of Mind*, 179–187, 200, 203.

50. McKillop, 334.
51. Mark G McGowan, "Rethinking Catholic-Protestant Relations in Canada: The Episcopal Reports of 1900–1901," *CCHA Historical Studies* 59 (1992): 11–32.
52. Robert Choquette, *Language and Religion: A History of English-French Conflict in Ontario* (Ottawa: University of Ottawa Press, 1975), 251–252.
53. This position is advanced in relation to belief and the state in Berger, "Faith in Sovereignty: Religion and Secularism in the Politics of Canadian Federalism."
54. Thomas Aquinas, *Summa Theologica*, trans. Father Lawrence Shapcote and Daniel J. Sullivan, vol. 1, 2 vols., vol. 17. of *Great Books of the Western World* (Chicago: University of Chicago Press, 1992), Q 79, art. 7.
55. Pierre Bourdieu, *Homo Academicus*, trans. Peter Collier (Stanford: Stanford University Press, 1988), 206–207.
56. Ruëgg, "Universities in the Nineteenth and Early Twentieth Centuries," 87–88, 119–121.
57. Bourdieu, *Homo Academicus*, 207.
58. Gilles Deleuze, *Difference and Repetition*, ed. Paul Patton (New York: Columbia University Press, 1994), 3–4, 25, 265–285.
59. *Deleuze*, 286.
60. Laframboise, Jean-Charles, "Rapport du T.R.P. Recteur année académique 1949–1950" (Typed record, Ottawa, 1950), 4, Fonds 3, Box NB-5532, File 7, uOttawa Archives.
61. Henry Giroux, "Neoliberalism, Corporate Culture, and the Promise of Higher Education: The University as a Democratic Public Sphere," *Harvard Educational Review* 72 (December 2002): 427.
62. Pridgen v. University of Calgary, 2012 CanLII 139 (n.d.), para. 109.
63. For a description of "masters" and their function, see Powlett v. University of Alberta, 1934 CarswellAlta 25 (Alberta Supreme Court, Appellate Division 1934), para. 169. Although, in fairness, Albertan universities spring from a different source than eastern/central Canadian universities. They are creatures of the state first and foremost, in the German tradition of universities rather than the English.
64. "2014–2017 Strategic Mandate Agreement: University of Ottawa," Strategic Mandate Agreements (Government of Ontario, February 22, 2017). This is a country-wide trend. See "Accountability Framework Standards Manual and Guidelines," Government (British Columbia, 2016), 5; New Brunswick is the exception. See the premier's mandate letter to the Minister of Post-Secondary Education, Brian Gallant, "To Hon. Roger Melanson," Mandate Letter, September 5, 2017, 2. Quebec's reporting framework is delineated in Act respecting Educational Institutions at the University Level, CQLR c. E-14.1 § (n.d.). Prince Edward Island's Minister Responsible for Higher Education is silent on reporting requirements, but the University Act, RSPEI 1988, c. U-4 § (n.d.), secs. 19–20, 26, grants the Crown (as visitor) power to compel the production of documents from the university; Nova Scotia has relatively decentralized government oversight (Province of Nova Scotia and Nova Scotia Universities, "Excellence Through Partnership," Memorandum of Understanding [Council of Nova Scotia University Presidents, December 20, 2011]); Newfoundland and Labrador has a decentralized oversight framework: Council on Higher Education Act, SNL 2006, c C-37.001 § (n.d.), sec. 8.
65. Maggie Berg and Barbara K. Seeber, *The Slow Professor* (Toronto: University of Toronto Press, 2016), 86–89.
66. André Guay and Jean-Charles Laframboise, "L'Université d'Ottawa statistiques 1946-7" (Typed record, December 31, 1946), Fonds 3, Box NB-5532, File 1,

uOttawa Archives; Roger Guindon, "Rapport annuel du recteur 1965-1966" (Print Report, Ottawa, 1966), Fonds 3, Box NB-5532, File 15, uOttawa Archives.
67. Guay and Laframboise., "L'Université d'Ottawa statistiques 1946–1947," 22.
68. Roger Guindon, "Transition 1966–1970" (Print Report, Ottawa, 1970), 5, Fonds 3, Box NB-5532, File 17, uOttawa Archives.
69. Henri F. Légaré, "Université d'Ottawa: rapport annuel du Recteur 1958-59" (Print Report, Ottawa, 1959), 5, Fonds 3, Box NB-5532, File 13, uOttawa Archives.
70. Henri F. Légaré, "Université d'Ottawa: rapport annuel du Recteur 1959-1960, 1960-1961" (Print Report, Ottawa, 1961), 6, Fonds 3, Box NB-5532, File 14, uOttawa Archives.
71. Donat Levasseur, "Chapitre 11 — Le gouvernement général, 1947-1985," in *Histoire des Missionaires Oblats de Marie Immaculée : Essai de synthèse (1898-1985)*, vol. 2 (Montréal: Maison Provinciale, 1985), 288–290.

Chapter 1: Overview of the University Charter (1849–1965)
1. This chapter considers the University of Ottawa's predecessor institutions, Bytown College (also known as the College of Bytown), the College of Ottawa, and Université d'Ottawa. I will switch between "College" and "University" as shorthand for our subject throughout this chapter.
2. Gaston Carrière, *L'Université d'Ottawa 1848-1861* (Ottawa: Éditions de l'Université d'Ottawa, 1960).
3. Georges Simard, *Les universités catholiques* (Ottawa: Éditions de l'Université d'Ottawa, 1939); Georges Simard, *Les États chrétiens et l'Église* (Ottawa: Éditions de l'Université d'Ottawa, 1942).
4. Justice (later Premier) John Thompson lays down the general rules for Canadian visitation in Re. Wilson, 18 NSR 180 (1885); Philips v. Bury, 90 English Reports 1294 (1694); aff'd in Canadian case law in Re Vanek and Governors of the University of Alberta, 57 D.L.R. (3d) 595 (AB CA 1975); Peregrine W. F. Whalley and Gillian R. Evans, "The University Visitor—An Unwanted Legacy of Empire or a Model of University Governance for the Future," Macarthur Law Review 2 (1998): 117–119. A more modern view of visitors that embraces the right to correct errors is found in R v Taylor, 2013 NLCA 42 (n.d.).
5. The Royal Charter of McGill University, 16 Vict. § (1852); An Act respecting the University of Western Ontario, SO 1967 c. 137 § (n.d.), sec. 41; An Act respecting the Charter of the University of Montreal, SQ 14 Geo. VI, 1950, c. 142 § (n.d.), sec. 38; An Act respecting the University of Saskatchewan, R.S.S. 1978, Cap. U-6 § (n.d.), sec. 9, accessed August 23, 2017 (since amended); University of New Brunswick Act, S.N.B. 1984, c. 40 § (1984), sec. 17 (since amended); University Act, 1901, SO 1901 c. 41 § (n.d.), sec. 4; but cf. The University Act, 1906, SO 1906 c. 55 § (n.d.), sec. 38; for the distinction between 1901 and 1906 acts, see Wong v. University of Toronto, 1990 CanLII 8102 (n.d.); see the older case that *Wong* supersedes on other grounds, Re Polten and Governing Council of the University of Toronto et al., 59 (3d) DLR 197 (ON SC [Div. Crt] 1975), for the rule that a visitor's jurisdiction, once ceded by act of the Legislature, may be resurrected by royal proclamation; see Hubert Picarda, *The Law and Practice Relating to Charities* (London: Butterworths, 1999), 403, for the rule on visitation when no visitor is expressly appointed.
6. There were two visitors in the same class at Bishop's College in Lennoxville, Quebec. The Anglican bishops of Québec and Montréal shared the jurisdiction. See Parliament of the Province of Canada, An Act to incorporate 'Bishop's College' in the Diocese of Quebec, 5 & 6 Vict. Cap. 49 § (1843); An Act to amend the Act incorporating Bishop's College, S. Prov. Can. 16 Vict. c. 60 § (1852); Royal Charter of the University of Bishop's College, 16 Vict. § (1853).

7. Private legislation is used to create an exception to normal legal rules. Universities typically petition the Legislature for an act incorporating the university, which creates an exemption from typical patterns of corporate organization.
8. James Hennesey, "The Papacy and the Universities," *Records of the American Catholic Historical Society of Philadelphia* 103 (1991): 1–11; *Sapienti Consilio*, 41 A.S.S. 462–490 § (1908), sec. 11.
9. Hennesey, "The Papacy and the Universities," 1.
10. Carrière, *L'Université d'Ottawa 1848-1861*, 5. Sandy Hill is the neighbourhood to the University's east extending to the Ottawa River, bounded on the north by Rideau Street and the south by the Queensway.
11. Shook, *Catholic Post-Secondary Education*, 242.
12. Carrière, *L'Université d'Ottawa 1848-1861*, 7–8.
13. Gosselin, "L'université d'Ottawa," 5.
14. Carrière, *L'Université d'Ottawa 1848-1861*, 21–22.
15. Pierre Hurtubise, Mark McGowan, and Pierre Savard, eds., *Planté près du cours des eaux : le diocèse d'Ottawa 1847-1997* (Ottawa: Novalis, 1998), 12.
16. Gaston Carrière, "Guigues, Joseph-Bruno," in *Dictionary of Canadian Biography* (Toronto: University of Toronto / Université de Laval, 1972).
17. Eugène de Mazenod, *Lettres aux correspondants d'Amérique : 1841-1850*, Écrits oblats, I (Rome: Postulation générale O.M.I., 1977), 77–79; Carrière, "Guigues, Joseph-Bruno."
18. Jean-Baptiste Honorat, ed., *Un ancien manuscrit des saintes règles* (Ottawa: Éditions des études oblates, 1943), 55.
19. de Mazenod, *Lettres 1841–1850*, 108–110, 126–127.
20. Earl of Durham, *Report on the Affairs of British North America* (Montréal: Morning Courier Office, 1839), 22.
21. de Mazenod, *Lettres 1841–1850*, 138, n.1.
22. de Mazenod, 83, 90–91, 93–94, 102.
23. Shook, *Catholic Post-Secondary Education*, 21–22.
24. Shook, *Catholic Post-Secondary Education*, 22.
25. J. George Hodgins, *Documentary History of Education in Upper Canada*, vol. 8 (Toronto: Warwick Bros. & Rutter, 1901), 110.
26. See An Act to amend the charter of the University established at Toronto and to provide for the more satisfactory government of the said university, and other purposes connected with the same, etcetera, S. Prov. Can. 12 Vict, c. 82 § (1849).
27. Hodgins, *Documentary History of Education in Upper Canada*, 1901, 8:111.
28. Shook, *Catholic Post-Secondary Education*, 22.
29. Carrière, *L'Université d'Ottawa 1848-1861*, 11–12.
30. Carrière, 8–10, 13–16.
31. Carrière, 19–20, 26–29, 59–71.
32. Joseph Eugène Bruno Guigues, *Mandements et circulaires de Mgr Joseph Eugène Guigues, 1er évêque d'Ottawa*, Early Canadiana Online 94445 (Ottawa, 1878), 76.
33. de Mazenod, *Lettres 1841–1850*, 82.
34. de Mazenod, 101, 103, 144–145, 152–154.
35. de Mazenod, 104.
36. de Mazenod, *Lettres 1841–1850*, 108–113, 115–117, 121–122, 125–131; for a particularly detailed recount of Canadian Oblates' rebelliousness, see p. 147 and de Mazenod's recriminations to Mgr Bourget on p. 159–161.
37. de Mazenod, 113.
38. de Mazenod, 129.
39. de Mazenod, 150.
40. de Mazenod, 151.

41. Letter of July 18, 1848 from Mgr. Guigues to Messieurs de l'Ordonnance, cited in: Carrière, *L'Université d'Ottawa 1848–1861*, 8.
42. An Act to incorporate the College of Bytown, Canada, S Prov-Can Can. 12 Vict., c 107 § (1849), preamble and s. 1.
43. Hodgins, *Documentary History of Education in Upper Canada*, 1901, 8:111–112.
44. "Eleemosynary, adj. and n.," in *Oxford English Dictionary* (Oxford: Oxford University Press, July 2018), A.1.
45. An Act to incorporate Les Révérends Pères Oblats de l'Immaculée Conception de Marie, in the Province of Canada, S. Prov. Can. 12 Vict. C. 143 § (1849).
46. Blackstone, "Chap. XVIII 'Of Corporations,'" 471, describes "eleemosynary corporations" as being "such as are constituted for the perpetual distribution of the free alms, or bounty, of the founder of them to such persons as he has directed. Of this kind are all hospitals for the maintenance of the poor, sick, and impotent; and all colleges, both in our universities and out of them: which colleges are founded for two purposes: 1. For the promotion of piety and learning by proper regulations and ordinances. 2. For imparting assistance to the members of those bodies, in order to enable them to prosecute their devotion and studies with greater ease and assiduity."
47. An Acte to Redress the Misemployment of Landes Goodes and Stockes of Money Heretofore given to Charitable Uses, 43 Eliz. 1, c. 4 § (1601): "Whereas (1) Landes Tenements Rentes Annuities Profittes Hereditamentes, Goodes Chattels Money and Stockes of Money, have been heretofore given limitted appointed and assigned, as well by the Queenes most excellent Majestie and her moste noble Prognitors, as by sondrie other well disposed persons, some for Releife of aged impotent and poore people, some for Maintenance of sicke and maymed Souldiers and Marriners, Schooles of Learninge, Free Schooles and Schollers in Universities, some for Repaire of Bridges Portes Havens Causwaises Churches Seabankes and Highewaies, some for Educacion and prefermente of Orphans, some for or towardes Reliefe Stocke or Maintenance for Howses of Correcction, some for Mariages of poore Maides, some for Supportction Ayde and Helpe of younge Tradesmen, Handiecraftesmen and persons decayed, and others for releife or remdption of Prisoners or Captives, and for aide or ease of any poore Inhabitane concerninge payment of Fifteenes, settinge out of Souldiers and other Taxes"; Maurice v. Durham (Bishop of), 32 English Reports 947 (1805), which affirms the broad definition of charities from the Statute of Uses; this practice carried into Canadian law as a benchmark for courts to determine what was charitable and what was not—see Picarda, *The Law and Practice Relating to Charities*, 10, 17.
48. See An Act to incorporate les Révérends Pères Oblats de l'Immaculée Conception de Marie, in the Province of Canada, sec. 7.
49. Blackstone, "Chap. XVIII 'Of Corporations,'" 468.
50. Re. Wilson, 18 NSR.
51. Eugène de Mazenod, *Lettres aux correspondants d'Amérique : 1851-1860*, Écrits oblats, II (Rome: Postulation générale O.M.I., 1977), 11–13.
52. de Mazenod, 20.
53. Shook, *Catholic Post-Secondary Education*, 243.
54. Émilien Lamirande, "Dandurand, Damase," in *Dictionary of Canadian Biography* (Online: University of Toronto / Université de Laval, 2005), http://www.biographi.ca/en/bio/dandurand_damase_15E.html.
55. de Mazenod, *Lettres 1851–1860*, 85.
56. de Mazenod, 86.
57. Unknown author, "Convention Guiges-de Mazenod," *Études Oblates* 15 (1956): 360–364; see also Carrière, *L'Université d'Ottawa 1848-1861*, 51–53.

58. de Mazenod, *Lettres 1851–1860*, 90–91.
59. See Bachofen, Charles Augustine, *A Commentary on the New Code of the Canon Law* Volume 6 (St. Louis: B. Herder Book Co., 1918), 426–427.
60. For a general interpretation of Catholic rules of visitation before canon law was codified in 1917, see Thomas Michael Cassidy, "The Provincial Superior Within the Missionary Oblates of Mary Immaculate as an Ordinary" (Ottawa, Saint Paul University, 1993), 7–11.
61. Carrière, *L'Université d'Ottawa 1848-1861*, 22–23.
62. de Mazenod, *Lettres 1851–1860*, 99.
63. Carrière, *L'Université d'Ottawa 1848-1861*, 53–54.
64. Unknown author, "Convention Guiges-de Mazenod."
65. Carrière, *L'Université d'Ottawa 1848-1861*, 54, n. 120.
66. de Mazenod, *Lettres 1851–1860*, 111.
67. Michel Prévost, "Histoire de la gouvernance à l'Université d'Ottawa depuis 1848," 2012, 5–6; Unknown author, "Convention Guiges-de Mazenod," secs. 2 (6–7); Congregationis missionariorum-oblatorum sanctissimæ et immaculatæ Virginis Mariæ, *Constitutiones et regulæ* (Marseille: Episcopal Typographers, 1853), Part III: VI; see also Oblats de Marie-Immaculée, *Constitutions et règles de la congrégation des Missionnaires Oblats de la Très Sainte et Immaculée Vierge Marie* (Rome: Maison générale O.M.I, 1965), sec. 529; Guigues was Oblate visitor for the Province of Canada in the nineteenth century, and the Superior-General visited the University twenty-three times between 1901 and 1964: see "Acte de Visite Canonique de La Maison de l'Université d'Ottawa Par Le R.P. Charles Tatin, O.M.I., November 1901" (Bound Manuscript, 1901), Fonds 315 University Saint Paul, NB-45273, File 63, uOttawa Archives; and see "Actes de Visite de 1905-à-1941 (Université d'Ottawa)" (Bound Manuscript, n.d.), Fonds 315 University Saint Paul, NB-45273, File 63, uOttawa Archives, accessed October 23, 2015; and see "Cahier des actes de visite de 1942- (Université d'Ottawa)" (Bound Manuscript, 1964 1942), Fonds 315 University Saint Paul, NB-45273, File 63, uOttawa Archives.
68. J. George Hodgins, *Documentary History of Education in Upper Canada*, vol. 14 (Toronto: Warwick Bros. & Rutter, 1906), 51.
69. J. George Hodgins, *Documentary History of Education in Upper Canada*, vol. 16 (Toronto: Warwick Bros. & Rutter, 1906), 229.
70. J. George Hodgins, *Documentary History of Education in Upper Canada*, vol. 17 (Toronto: Warwick Bros. & Rutter, 1907), 70.
71. Hodgins, 17:70.
72. An Act to change the name of the College of Bytown, and to amend the Act incorporating the same, S Prov Can 24 Vict., c.108 § (1861), sec. 2.
73. Carrière, *L'Université d'Ottawa 1848-1861*, 22–23.
74. Pierre Corbeil, "Dunkin, Christopher, Lawyer, Politician, and Judge," in *Dictionary of Canadian Biography* (University of Toronto / Université de Laval, 2003). Sadly, not much information pertaining to the University of Ottawa appears in Brome's archives.
75. An Act to change the name of the College of Bytown, and to amend the Act incorporating the same, sec. 2.
76. An Act to amend the Acts incorporating "The College of Ottawa," and to grant certain privileges to the said college, S Prov-Can. 29–30Vict., c. 135 § (1866), secs. 3, 2.
77. An Act to amend the Acts incorporating "The College of Ottawa," and to grant certain privileges to the said college, sec. 11.
78. An Act to amend the Acts incorporating "The College of Ottawa," and to grant certain privileges to the said college, sec. 6.

79. An Act to amend the Acts incorporating "The College of Ottawa," and to grant certain privileges to the said college, secs. 14–15, 6; n.b., the records of early Senate meetings are lost due to a fire that destroyed the repository on December 2, 1903.
80. John Fell, *The privileges of the University of Oxford, in point of visitation*, EEBO, Thomason/E.411[1] (London: Richard Royston, 1647).
81. An Act to amend the Acts incorporating the College of Ottawa, SO 1885, c. 91 § (n.d.), sec. 15.
82. Late in the game, Roger Guindon acknowledged the Crown's nominal role as visitor when he wrote to the Lieutenant-Governor of Ontario, W. Earl Rowe, to thank him for his appearance at his installation ceremony: "The University was honored by the presence of its Visitor, and, I know, joins me in the hope that the occasions will be numerous in the years ahead for the renewal of an association which we share" ("Roger Guindon to Hon. W. Earl Rowe" [Letter, November 12, 1964], NB-68, uOttawa Archives).
83. Ontario Legislative Assembly, *Sessional Papers*, vol. XVII, part VI (Toronto, 1885), no. 51.
84. Hodgins, *Documentary History of Education in Upper Canada*, 1901, 8:1–3.
85. An Act to amend the charter of the university established at Toronto and to provide for the more satisfactory government of the said university, and other purposes connected with the same, etcetera, secs. 4–5.
86. An Act to amend the charter of the university established at Toronto and to provide for the more satisfactory government of the said university, and other purposes connected with the same, etcetera, secs. 47–49. Lest someone dispute the power of a commission of visitation, see Forestell v. University of New Brunswick, 1988 CarswellNB 138 (n.d.), where a student board-of-governor member was removed by the board only to be reinstated on appeal to the Lieutenant-Governor as visitor, who commissioned Adélard M. Savoie to visit on his behalf; see also Forestell v. University of New Brunswick, 1987 CarswellNB 177 (n.d.), for the New Brunswick court's ruling requiring the dispute to be referred to the visitor.
87. J. George Hodgins, *Documentary History of Education in Upper Canada*, vol. 9 (Toronto: Warwick Bros. & Rutter, 1902), 122.
88. J. George Hodgins, *Documentary History of Education in Upper Canada*, vol. 10 (Toronto: Warwick Bros. & Rutter, 1903), 72–75.
89. An Act to amend the Laws relating to the University of Toronto, by separating its functions as a University from those assigned to it as a College, and by making better provision for the management of the property thereof and that of Upper Canada College, S Prov Can 16 Vict. c. 89 § (1853), secs. 9, 19, 27.
90. Hodgins, *Documentary History of Education in Upper Canada*, 1903, 10:157–159.
91. Hodgins, *Documentary History of Education in Upper Canada*, 1906, 16:21–22, 66–75.
92. Hodgins, 16:302–303.
93. Hodgins, 16:300–301.
94. The report in its entirety is recorded in Hodgins, *Documentary History of Education in Upper Canada*, 1907, beginning at p. 57.
95. An Act to amend the Laws relating to the University of Toronto, by separating its functions as a University from those assigned to it as a College, and by making better provision for the management of the property thereof and that of Upper Canada College.
96. All of this, from the commissioners' report cited supra.
97. Hodgins, *Documentary History of Education in Upper Canada*, 1907, 17:87.
98. Carrière, *L'Université d'Ottawa 1848-1861*, 27, n. 67; the Crown appointed both priests in a letter from Francis Hincks dated November 26, 1853 J. George

Hodgins, *Documentary History of Education in Upper Canada*, vol. 11 (Toronto: Warwick Bros. & Rutter, 1904), 5.
99. Carrière, *L'Université d'Ottawa 1848-1861*, 27.
100. The eighth Parliament of the Province of Canada sat for its fifth and last session in the newly constructed federal Parliament Buildings in Ottawa from June 8 to August 15, 1866.
101. Slightly predating the College of Bytown, the Crown and Parliament of the Province of Canada smiled upon a small college in Lennoxville, Quebec, when it granted the Anglican Bishops of Québec and Montréal joint power of visitation. See An Act to incorporate "Bishop's College" in the Diocese of Quebec; see also Royal Charter of the University of Bishop's College.
102. The power vested in the Governor General of the Province of Canada was continued at Confederation in the Lieutenant-Governor; Constitution Act, 1867, 30 & 31 Vict., c. 3 (UK) § (n.d.), sec. 65.
103. Constitution Act, 1867, sec. 92(7), but see also sec. 129.
104. An Act to amend the Acts incorporating the College of Ottawa, SO 1891, c. 104 § (n.d.), secs. 1, 6.
105. An Act to amend the Acts incorporating the College of Ottawa, sec. 7.
106. An Act to amend the Acts incorporating "The College of Ottawa," and to grant certain privileges to the said college, sec. 15; An Act to amend the Acts incorporating the College of Ottawa, n.d., sec. 7.
107. An Act to amend the Acts incorporating "The College of Ottawa," and to grant certain privileges to the said college, sec. 14; An Act to amend the Acts incorporating the College of Ottawa, n.d., sec. 6.
108. See Justice Lane's dissent in Pearlman v. University of Saskatchewan (College of Medicine), 2006 CanLII 105 (n.d.) for the historical view of visitors.
109. Leo XIII, "Papal Brief of February 5, 1889," July 29, 2014 (acquired in personal correspondence with Rector Chantal Beauvais, University of Saint Paul, July 29, 2014), sec. II.
110. Leo XIII, sec. V.
111. Bachofen, Charles Augustine, *A Commentary on the New Code of the Canon Law*, 6:426; for a statement of the modern civil power's view of judicial intervention in religious organizations, see Hart v. Roman Catholic Episcopal Corporation of the Diocese of Kingston, 2011 ONCA 728 (n.d.); this modern view is also stated in Dunnet v. Forneri, 1877 CarswellOnt 66 (n.d.).
112. Bachofen, Charles Augustine, *A Commentary on the New Code of the Canon Law*, 3:138.
113. Bachofen, Charles Augustine, 6:427.
114. Leo XIII, "Papal Brief of February 5, 1889," secs. V–VI.
115. Bachofen, Charles Augustine, *A Commentary on the New Code of the Canon Law*, can. 1382 and commentary: *Ordinarii locorum sive ipsi per se sive per alios possunt quoque scholas quaslibet, oratoria, recreatoria, patronatus, etc. in iis quam religiosam et moralem institutionem spectant, visitare*. Note the final word, "visitare," the present infinitive of "visito," which Bachofen translates as "inspect," but which may equally mean the right to visit a Catholic foundation.
116. See Canon 1519 and commentary: Bachofen, Charles Augustine.
117. An Act respecting the College of Ottawa, SO 23 Geo. V, c. 106 § (1933), sec. 14(1); An Act to amend the Acts incorporating the College of Ottawa, n.d., sec. 6.
118. An Act to amend the Acts incorporating "The College of Ottawa," and to grant certain privileges to the said college.
119. Faculté de Théologie, *La Constitution Apostolique "Deus Scientiarum Dominus": Traduction Française et Notes* (Montréal: Université de Montréal, 1960). See the

preamble at p. 4–5, where it is stated: "Nous jugeâmes de Notre devoir de préparer une loi en vertu de laquelle les instituts d'études supérieures, fondé un peu partout au nombre de plus de cent, eussent à fixer plus clairement leur but, à déterminer avec soin leur méthode d'enseignement, et à établir enfin une forme unique d'organisation, sans toutefois entraver en rien les modifications exigées par les circonstances et les lieux, de manière à pouvoir répondre entièrement aux nécessités de l'époque actuelle."

120. Pius XI, "Deus scientiarum dominus, constitutio apostolica," Acta Apostolicae Sedis vol. XXIII, no. 7 § (1931), secs. 13–18; Canon 500 of the 1917 code lays out the powers of the Ordinary. It is a diocesan jurisdiction with a general supervisory authority over the diocese. In the case of the University, the archbishop's function as ordinary allows him to enter an otherwise privileged institution, by virtue of its being under the direct control of the Holy See, to guarantee adherence to Catholic law and doctrine (Bachofen, Charles Augustine, *A Commentary on the New Code of the Canon Law*, 3:100–102.

121. "Constitutions et règles de la congrégation des Missionaires Oblats de la Très Sainte et Immaculée Vierge Marie" (Hardback Book in Octavo, Rome, 1930), sec. 153, Fonds 38, Miscellaneous Documents—BB.12, uOttawa Archives.

122. "Constitutions 1930," sec. 448.

123. "Constitutions 1930," sec. 231.

124. "Constitutions 1930," sec. 232; this kind of rule was, even in the early twentieth century, held to be unenforceable in Canadian courts. See Archer v. Society of Sacred Heart of Jesus, 9 OLR 474 (ONCA 1905).

125. Bachofen, Charles Augustine, *A Commentary on the New Code of the Canon Law*, cannons 13–14.

126. An Act respecting the University of Regiopolis, SO 21 Geo. V, c 137 § (1931).

127. Terence J. Fay, "The Jesuits and the Catholic University of Canada at Kingston," *CCHA Historical Studies* 58 (1991): 73.

128. An Act to amend the Acts respecting the College of Regiopolis, and to erect the same into an university, S Prov-Can 29–30 Vict., c. 133 § (1866).

129. Fay, "The Jesuits and the Catholic University of Canada at Kingston."

130. An Act respecting the College of Ottawa, secs. 5, 14(1), 20; It must be said, however, that the Council of Administration existed before its formal establishment in the 1933 Act. The pontifical charter of 1889 created a formal council that mirrored the body politic of the University created by the initial charter of 1849. However, the 1933 Act formalized this council as the body politic based upon the Apostolic constitution of 1931 enacted by the Holy See (Prévost, "Histoire de la gouvernance à l'Université d'Ottawa depuis 1848," 7–8).

131. An Act respecting the College of Ottawa, sec. 24.

132. Interestingly, the Senate regularly exercised "clemency:" it granted degrees even though a requirement was missing and/or partially incomplete. The minutes are not clear on this procedure; they merely indicate that it existed. Instances of clemency are moments when the Senate exercises its power in a considered way: it required some debate to grant clemency, whereas the awarding of a regular degrees was a matter of course. See "Box NB-3038" (n.d.), Fonds 2, NB-3038, uOttawa Archives, accessed June 17, 2014 for the Senate minutes of this period.

133. An Act respecting the College of Ottawa, sec. 14(2).

134. An Act respecting the College of Ottawa, secs. 5, 19, 20.

135. An Act respecting the College of Ottawa, sec. 27.

136. Cassidy, "The Provincial Superior within the Missionary Oblates of Mary Immaculate as an Ordinary," 12–13.

Chapter 2: The Road to Reform: 1959–1964

1. "CAUT and NCCUC. 'Proposal to the Ford Foundation'" (Proposal, n.d.), MG28 I 208 container 137, f. 12 — University Government — Early Memoranda, Library and Archives Canada, accessed July 22, 2014.
2. See Michel Bock, "La théologie au service du bon-ententisme à l'Université d'Ottawa : le père oblat Georges Simard (1878-1956), ou comment un groulxiste devient loyaliste," *Cahiers Charlevoix: Études franco-ontariennes* 11 (2016): 213–260, for further commentary on Simard's politics.
3. For the distinction, see "Catholic, adj. and n.," in *Oxford English Dictionary* (Oxford: Oxford University Press, 2018), A.I versus A.II; canon law also prescribes the way in which "Catholic" is to be used: see Ernest Caparros, Michel Thériault, and Jean Thorn, eds., *Code of Canon Law Annotated*, 2nd ed. (Montréal: Wilson & Lafleur Ltd., 2004), cans. 216, 300, 803, 808, cf. 312; for a consideration of how Catholics might prosecute the misuse of the word in Canadian law, see John K. Murphy, "The Governance of Church Institutions and Protection of Catholic Identity with Particular Reference to Ontario, Canada" (PhD, Rome, Pontifical Lateran University, 1995), 120–130, although this analysis needs to be pushed further if it is to persuade non-Catholic Canadian counsel.
4. Simard, *Les universités catholiques*, 19.
5. Simard, 65.
6. Simard bolsters this reading in *Les États chrétiens et l'Église*, 118–119.
7. "Academic Administration in Higher Education" (Report, 1959), iv, Fonds 197, MCF-522, uOttawa Archives.
8. See "MCF-522," n.d., Fonds 197, MCF-522, uOttawa Archives, accessed July 18, 2014, in which the report is found.
9. "Box NB-6600" (Box, n.d.), NB-6600, uOttawa Archives, accessed July 17, 2014, folder "1962–1964 Conseil d'administration-procès-verbal et documents connexes."
10. "Academic Administration in Higher Education," 1.
11. Michel Prévost, *L'Université d'Ottawa Depuis 1848* (Ottawa: Université d'Ottawa, 2008), 45–48.
12. "Academic Administration in Higher Education," 3–4.
13. "Academic Administration in Higher Education," 89–96.
14. National Education Office, "Présence catholique dans l'enseignement supérieur au Canada : Rapport d'une commission d'enquête sur quarante universités et collèges catholiques" (Windsor: Université de Windsor, 1971), 210–211.
15. This point is made just after the conclusion of the University's reform and of Vatican II in the above-mentioned report (National Education Office, 211–212), but the observations that this Catholic commission makes in 1971 ring equally true in the period leading up to Vatican II.
16. Data derived from: Roger Guindon, "Tableau comparatif des dépenses d'opération des années fiscales terminées le 30 juin" (n.d.), NB-10454.16, uOttawa Archives. I have omitted projected figures for 1966 because they are beyond the scope of this chapter.
17. Budgeted.
18. If no major construction was undertaken (cf. 1964).
19. Levasseur, "Chapitre 11 – Le gouvernement général – 1947–1985," 289–290.
20. Prévost, *L'Université d'Ottawa Depuis 1848*, 45.
21. Deschâtelets also visited the University in 1946 when he was provincial: "Cahier des actes de visite de 1942, (Université d'Ottawa)."
22. "Faculty of Philosophy Council" (Minutes of Meeting, October 7, 1965), Fonds 31, NB-5523.2, uOttawa Archives.

23. See "C.M. McDougall (Registrar, McGill) to Jean-Marie Quirion" (Letter, November 22, 1962), Fonds 197, MCF-522, uOttawa Archives; "Douglass Burns Clarke, M.A. (Vice-Principal, Sir George Williams University) to Jean-Marie Quirion" (Letter, September 17, 1963), Fonds 197, MCF-522, uOttawa Archives; "Jean-Marie Quirion to René Lavigne" (Letter, January 9, 1963), Fonds 197, MCF-522, uOttawa Archives; "Louis-Paul Dugal to Jean-Marie Quirion" (Letter, January 11, 1963), Fonds 197, MCF-522, uOttawa Archives. Each of these are inquiries relating to faculty or university statutes.
24. "Pierre Azard to Jean-Marie Quirion" (Letter, December 28, 1962), Fonds 197, MCF-522, uOttawa Archives.
25. "Projet de statut pour l'Université d'Ottawa" (Report, n.d.), sec. 21(1), Fonds 197, MCF-522, uOttawa Archives, accessed July 18, 2014.
26. "Projet de statut pour l'Université d'Ottawa."
27. "Projet de statut pour l'Université d'Ottawa," secs. 11–13. These powers are reminiscent of the visitors' powers over the University.
28. "Projet de statut pour l'Université d'Ottawa."
29. See "Constitutions 1930," for executive functions, secs. 414, 431, 486, 530, 582; for legislative functions, secs. 375–376, 564–570.
30. "Projet de statut pour l'Université d'Ottawa," sec. 13.
31. Of further interest, there is no evidence of a such an assembly having ever been called. More research on this score is required to make a definitive statement.
32. "Floyd S. Chalmers to Leslie M. Frost" (Letter, May 7, 1962), RG 32-23, barcode B354145, "University of Ottawa," Archives of Ontario.
33. "Henri Légaré to John P. Robarts" (Letter, April 30, 1963), RG 32-23, barcode B354145, "University of Ottawa," Archives of Ontario; "J. P. Robarts to Henri Légaré" (Letter, August 1, 1963), RG 32-23, barcode B354145, "University of Ottawa," Archives of Ontario; "Leslie M. Frost to J. P. Robarts" (Letter, May 29, 1963), RG 32-23, barcode B354145, "University of Ottawa," Archives of Ontario; "Leslie M. Frost to Oakley Dalgleish" (Letter, May 29, 1963), RG 32-23, barcode B354145, "University of Ottawa," Archives of Ontario.
34. "Statuta Universitatis Ottaviensis" (Statute Book, Ottawa, 1937), Fond 315, NB-45051. I am told that the Department of Philosophy continued to lecture in Latin into the 1970s, thus making these statutes still legible to a cross-section of the professoriate.
35. An Act respecting the College of Ottawa. In the legislative session of 1960–1961 (2 Sess., 26 Legislature of Ontario), Bill No. Pr42 was introduced to the Legislature and read the first time on January 25, 1961. This legislation altered section 28 (2) of the charter by eliminating the election of the dean, vice-dean, and secretary of each faculty, to replace such election with appointment by the council of administration: see S.O. 1960–1961, cap. 138.
36. An Act respecting the College of Ottawa, sec. 28(2), original phrasing.
37. An Act respecting Université d'Ottawa, S.O. 1960–1961, C. 138 § (1960).
38. "Meeting of the Committee on University Affairs" (Minutes of Meeting, December 4, 1963), Fonds 197, MCF-522, uOttawa Archives.
39. "Attributions, groupe d'étude sur les rapports entre l'Université d'Ottawa et le Gouvernement de l'Ontario" (Order, May 30, 1963), Fonds 3 Office of the Rector, Box NB-10454.10, uOttawa Archives.
40. Roger Guindon, "Re. Oblates and University Government" (Report, August 31, 1963), 2, Fonds 3 Office of the Rector, Box NB-10454.11, uOttawa Archives.
41. See, for example, Justice Campbell's comments closing out his reasons in Trinity Western University v. Nova Scotia Barristers' Society, 2015 NSSC 25 (n.d.), accessed December 30, 2017.

42. Guindon, "Oblates and University Government," 4.
43. "Université d'Ottawa : une étude sur les modifications de ses structures" (Report, December 4, 1963), AC 263. C48R 2, Saint Paul University Archives.
44. "Université d'Ottawa : une étude sur les modifications de ses structures," 4: "L'incident Pépin-Lazure, la réponse des 'autorités' de l'Université et les factions qui se sont formées depuis, pour ou contre la réponse des 'autorités', le débat de Pierre Mercier et al vs Willie Chevalier. Une lettre explosive préparée par un groupe de professeurs. La multiplication rapide de petits groupes d'études s'efforçant d'analyser les problèmes et d'offrir des solutions. La température du corps étudiant qui monte graduellement." This statement of incidents reveals unrest at the University, and is of interest for future research into the period. There are not many bald statements like this made in the archival record.
45. "Université d'Ottawa : une étude sur les modifications de ses structures," 4–7.
46. "Université d'Ottawa : une étude sur les modifications de ses structures," 8.
47. "Université d'Ottawa : une étude sur les modifications de ses structures," 12–13.
48. "Université d'Ottawa : une étude sur les modifications de ses structures," 8–9, 11; for McCarthy's speech, see "Address by Mr. J. R. McCarthy at Convocation in the Medical Auditorium, University of Ottawa, Saturday, November 16, 1963, at 3:00 p.m." (Speech, November 16, 1963), RG 32-23, barcode B354145, "University of Ottawa," Archives of Ontario; see also "Report of a Meeting Held at the General House in Rome" (Report, March 31, 1965), AC 260. C48R 9, Saint Paul University Archives; and "Leslie Frost to Henri Légaré" (Letter, January 14, 1964), AC 260. C48R 13, Saint Paul University Archives; "Henri Légaré to Leslie M. Frost" (Letter, January 7, 1964), RG 32-23, barcode B354145, "University of Ottawa," Archives of Ontario; "Henri Légaré to Leslie M. Frost" (Letter, January 30, 1964), RG 32-23, barcode B354145, "University of Ottawa," Archives of Ontario; "Henri Légaré to Leslie M. Frost" (Letter, January 31, 1964), RG 32-23, barcode B354145, "University of Ottawa," Archives of Ontario.
49. "Université d'Ottawa : une étude sur les modifications de ses structures," 12.
50. "Université d'Ottawa : une étude sur les modifications de ses structures," 12. It is unclear whether Lussier was aware of the Oblates' incorporation in 1849. His suggestion here conflates Oblate corporation and University corporation. The bonds between the two are those of ownership; they were not the same legal entity.
51. "Université d'Ottawa : une étude sur les modifications de ses structures," 12–14.
52. The rector of the University did not receive a formal seat at the Provincial Council until the council sittings of 12, 13, and 14 May, 1964: "Réunion du Conseil Provincial" (Minutes of Meeting, May 12, 1964), 3–4, AC 260. C48R 4, Saint Paul University Archives.
53. "Réunion du Conseil Provincial," 3–4.
54. Philippe J. Roy, "Marcel Bélanger : itinéraire d'un expert canadien à Vatican II," in *Vatican II. Expériences canadiennes. Canadian Experiences.*, ed. Michael Attridge, Gilles Routhier, and E. Catherine (Ottawa: Presses de l'Université d'Ottawa, 2011), 294–321.
55. Roy; "Roger Guindon to Stanislas-A. LaRochelle" (Letter, May 4, 1964), AC 260. C48R 2, Saint Paul University Archives.
56. An Oblate duly elected to the Superior-General's seat could not refuse to take office. On the compulsion to take office, see "Constitutions 1930" Part III, cap. 1, secs. 1–2.
57. Irénée Tourigny, *Le Père Léo Deschâtelets, O.M.I. (1899–1974): Supérieur Général des Missionaires Oblates de Marie Immaculée (1947–1972)*, Web (Ottawa: O.M.I. Communications, 1975), 10–11, 13, 15, 19, 42.

58. Roy, "Marcel Bélanger," 314.
59. Roy, 297–298.
60. Roy, 306.
61. "Léo Deschâtelets to Marcel Bélanger" (Letter, January 28, 1963), AC 260. C48R 14, Saint Paul University Archives.
62. "Les O.M.I. à l'Université d'Ottawa" (Report, n.d.), AC 260. C48R 14c, Saint Paul University Archives, accessed June 30, 2014.
63. "Les O.M.I. à l'Université d'Ottawa," 7; Bélanger was in good company, for this view is reminiscent of Simard's in *Les universités catholiques*, 62–63, 65.
64. This association was not formally constituted under applicable labour relations legislation until 1975, when the Labour Relations Board issued an interim certification. See A.P.U.O. v. University of Ottawa, 1975 CarswellOnt 739 (OLRB 1975). Until this certification, the APUO seems only to have representative weight, although a fuller history of the organization is required; there are no mentions of collective agreements being negotiated or enforced.
65. See "Report on the Government of the University of Ottawa Made by a Committee Appointed by the Board of Governors of the Association of Professors of the University of Ottawa" (Report, February 1965), 53–55, MG28 I 208 container 55, f. 10, University Government - Documents, Ottawa, Library and Archives Canada.
66. "Marcel Bélanger to Léo Deschâtelets" (Letter, February 10, 1963), 7, AC 260. C48R 14, Saint Paul University Archives.
67. Bachofen, Charles Augustine, *A Commentary on the New Code of the Canon Law*, can. 1382, and commentary.
68. "Deschâtelets to Bélanger, Jan. 28, 1963."
69. "Bélanger to Deschâtelets, Feb. 10, 1963."
70. "Constitutions 1930," secs. 223, 228, 231, 232.
71. "Bélanger to Deschâtelets, Feb. 10, 1963."
72. "Bélanger to Deschâtelets, Feb. 10, 1963."
73. "Léo Deschâtelets to Marcel Bélanger" (Letter, March 27, 1963), AC 260. C48R 14, Saint Paul University Archives.
74. "Marcel Bélanger to Léo Deschâtelets" (Letter, May 26, 1964), AC 260. C48R 14, Saint Paul University Archives.
75. "Entrevue avec le premier ministre de l'Ontario, l'honorable J.P. Robarts le lundi 16 décembre 1963 à 4 h 15 de l'après-midi. Le T.R. Père Recteur est accompagné du docteur J.-L. Lussier. M. Robarts est seul" (Report, December 16, 1963), Fonds 3 Office of the Rector, Box NB-10454.11, uOttawa Archives.
76. "Entrevue avec le premier ministre."
77. See An Act respecting Assumption College, SO 1953 C. 111 § (n.d.); see also Laurence K. Shook, *Catholic Post-Secondary Education in English-Speaking Canada: A History* (Toronto: University of Toronto Press, 1971), 288–289.
78. An Act to incorporate the University of Windsor, SO 1962–63 c. 194 § (n.d.), secs. 2, 5.
79. Shook, Catholic Post-Secondary Education in English-Speaking Canada: A History, 290.
80. An Act to incorporate the University of Windsor, secs. 18(3), 28.
81. An Act respecting the University of Waterloo, SO 1963, c. 193 § (n.d.), sec. 1.
82. See The Trent University Act, 1962–63, SO 1962—63 c. 192 § (n.d.).
83. See Guindon, "Oblates and University Government."
84. Roger Graham, *Old Man Ontario: Leslie M. Frost*, Ontario Historical Studies Series (Toronto: University of Toronto Press for the Ontario Historical Studies Series, 1990), 412–414; "Resume of a Meeting of the University of Ottawa Representatives and the Ontario Government's Advisory Committee on University Affairs"

85. (Report, December 18, 1963), Fonds 3 Office of the Rector, Box NB-10454.11, uOttawa Archives.
85. "Resume of a Meeting of the University of Ottawa Representatives and the Ontario Government's Advisory Committee on University Affairs"; on Windsor's non-denominational status, see An Act to incorporate the University of Windsor.
86. "Re: University of Ottawa" (Memorandum, December 18, 1963), RG 32-23, barcode B354145, "University of Ottawa," Archives of Ontario.
87. "Université d'Ottawa et octrois provinciaux : remarques et commentaires" (Report, 1963), Fonds 3 Office of the Rector, Box NB-10454.11, uOttawa Archives.
88. "Université d'Ottawa et octrois provinciaux : remarques et commentaires."
89. I do not suggest that the Government of Ontario supported the policy of limiting the independence of universities by creating standard forms of university government; the modern university possesses a standard form of government rising out of Great Britain's nineteenth-century universities. However, the government's insistence through Frost's letter appears to indicate that it desired fully non-denominational universities, and that the accommodation it was willing to make in 1963 was now removed from the equation.
90. "Frost to Légaré, Jan. 14, 1964." This draft act may be found in the University of Saint Paul Archives in the same box as Frost's letter, numbered AC 260 .C48R 14d. It is an unidentified document setting out legislative provisions, with annotations in the left margin indicating the clauses's provenance. In this document, the government's desires are clearly articulated, and thus supersede the Lussier report. The Council of Administration is maintained as the executive committee of the Board of Governors, a new body politic (p. 1, 3). Page four supplies a doubt as to provenance: the final proposed clause of the draft indicates a date as "___ day of September, 1963." It may be that this date is a typing error. It is equally possible, however, that the draft was authored at a different time. The text of the draft accords with the stipulations set out in Frost's letter, and barring the date supplied at the last page appears to be Frost making good on his offer.
91. "Frost to Légaré, Jan. 14, 1964."
92. "Frost to Légaré, Jan. 14, 1964."
93. An Act respecting Université d'Ottawa, SO 1959 c. 138 § (1959).
94. "Frost to Légaré, Jan. 14, 1964."
95. "Frost to Légaré, Jan. 14, 1964."
96. H. A. Macdougall, "Ethnicity and the Liberal Arts in Catholic Education," *CCHA Historical Studies* 49 (1982): 65.
97. H. Blair Neatby and Donald C. McEown, *Creating Carleton: The Shaping of a University* (Montréal and Jingston: McGill-Queen's University Press, 2002), 139, and see n. 30 there.
98. Bishop Lévesque's coat of arms bear the motto *In libro vitae*, "Life is in the book," which is fitting for a man of the cloth and a university founder.
99. "Lorenzo Danis to Louis Lévesque" (Letter, March 5, 1964), AC 260. C48R 14, Saint Paul University Archives.
100. "Louis Lévesque to Lorenzo Danis" (Letter, March 11, 1964), AC 260. C48R 14, Saint Paul University Archives.
101. Ontario Legislative Assembly, "Official Report – Daily Edition, April 30, 1964," in *Legislature of Ontario Debates*, Second Session of the Twenty Seventh Legislature (Toronto: The Queen's Printer, 1964), 2677.
102. Ontario Legislative Assembly, 2678.
103. Ontario Legislative Assembly, 2679.

104. Alexander Reford, "The Frustrations of Federation," *CCHA Historical Studies* 61 (1995): 172–173; Shook, *Catholic Post-Secondary Education*, 142.
105. Ontario Legislative Assembly, "Official Report – Daily Edition, April 30, 1964," 2679.
106. Roger Guindon gives us a graphic account of these chains when he goes on at length: "Ce n'est là un secret pour personne, et les administrateurs des universités le savent bien, [que] les octrois gouvernementaux calculés selon le prorata des étudiants ne suffisent jamais à financer ces deux Facultés [Medicine and Sciences] alors qu'ils suffissent abondamment pour les autres Facultés universitaires moins coûteuses" (Guindon, "Oblates and University Government," 3).
107. I wish to be clear here: I do not single out the Faculties of Medicine and Science to say that they caused the ills of the University then and now. That is entirely unfair. Rather, I am pointing out a funding scheme that created an imbalance between faculties, and indeed stigmatized the funding of humanities-related fields due to their association with the religious governors of the University. In some way, this may reflect the post-war science boom, where the training of scientists was ascendant due to a pressing economic need. This was essentially how Roger Guindon saw things: "Oblates and University Government," 3.
108. Racine expands on Guindon's analogy between universities and hospitals: "Oblates and University Government," 5.
109. Bachofen, Charles Augustine, *A Commentary on the New Code of the Canon Law*, 6:411–421, esp. the translation of canons 1372, 1373, 1377.
110. "Université d'Ottawa : une étude sur les modifications de ses structures," 8.

Chapter 3: Reforming the University Government: 1964–1965

1. See, e.g., "Constitutions 1930," secs. 298, 329, 330, 331.
2. Roger Graham, *Old Man Ontario: Leslie M. Frost* (Toronto: University of Toronto Press, 1990), 414–416.
3. A. K. McDougall, *John P. Robarts: His Life and Government* (Toronto: University of Toronto Press, 1986), 82; Graham, *Old Man Ontario*, 1990, 247–248, 251, esp. 412.
4. Carrière, *L'Université d'Ottawa 1848-1861*, 27.
5. An Act to amend the Laws relating to the University of Toronto, by separating its functions as a University from those assigned to it as a College, and by making better provision for the management of the property thereof and that of Upper Canada College, sec. 54; Hodgins, *Documentary History of Education in Upper Canada*, 1907, 21:36, 42, 246.
6. Shook, *Catholic Post-Secondary Education*, 142–143; the reasons for federation do not, however, appear clear on the historical record: Reford, "The Frustrations of Federation," 173; Ontario Legislative Assembly, *Sessional Papers*, no. 51.
7. An Act to amend the Acts incorporating the College of Ottawa, n.d., sec. 4.
8. Cf. Choquette, *Language and Religion*, 24–25.
9. Shook, *Catholic Post-Secondary Education*, 161.
10. An Act respecting Université d'Ottawa, 1960, sec. 4 (b).
11. "Cahier des actes de visite de 1942- (Université d'Ottawa)."
12. *Études Oblates*, vol. 23 (Montréal: Maison Provinciale, 1964), 191.
13. "Cahier des actes de visite de 1942, (Université d'Ottawa)," 244.
14. No other mention of copies being distributed exists—a mistake, given the tension LaRochelle identified with the lay faculty.
15. "Cahier des actes de visite de 1942, (Université d'Ottawa)," 212–213.
16. "Cahier des actes de visite de 1942, (Université d'Ottawa)," 206–213.
17. "Notice of Meeting" (Notice of Meeting, April 15, 1964), AC 260. C48R 14, Saint Paul University Archives.

18. "Stanislas-A. LaRochelle to Oblate Fathers" (Circular Letter, May 6, 1964), AC 260. C48R 3, Saint Paul University Archives.
19. "Agenda pour le conseil local" (Agenda, May 4, 1964), AC 260. C48R 14, Saint Paul University Archives.
20. "Agenda pour le conseil local."
21. "Cahier des actes de visite de 1942- (Université d'Ottawa)," 189–190.
22. Roger Guindon, *Coexistence Féconde : la dualité linguistique à l'Université d'Ottawa*, vol. 3 (Ottawa: Presses de l'Université d'Ottawa, 1995), 71–72.
23. "Cahier des actes de visite de 1942- (Université d'Ottawa)," 216–217.
24. "Roger Guindon to Stanislas-A. LaRochelle."
25. "Roger Guindon to Stanislas-A. LaRochelle."
26. "Roger Guindon to Stanislas-A. LaRochelle."
27. Michel Prévost, "Mgr Henri Légaré, O. M. I. (1918-2004) : un recteur visionnaire," 2006, http://www.uottawa.ca.archives/files/henri_legare.pdf.
28. "Réunion du Conseil Provincial."
29. "Réunion du Conseil Provincial."
30. "Réunion du Conseil Provincial," 2–3.
31. Bachofen, Charles Augustine, *A Commentary on the New Code of the Canon Law*, can. 2347; cf. can. 534.
32. See Oblats de Marie-Immaculée, *Constitutions 1965*, secs. 435, 528–529, 592.
33. "Réunion du Conseil Provincial."
34. "Réunion du Conseil Provincial," 5.
35. Roger Guindon, *Béatitude et Théologie Morale Chez Saint Thomas d'Aquin* (Ottawa: Édition de l'Université d'Ottawa, 1956), 9.
36. "Réunion du Conseil Provincial," 5.
37. "Allocution du R. P. Roger Guindon lors de son installation le mercredi 28 octobre 1964" (Speech, October 28, 1964), AR 1964 G96 CL 4, Saint Paul University Archives.
38. Guindon was named rector-designate at the first preliminary meeting of the Board on June 8, 1965, alongside Gérald Fauteux, who was designated president of the Board. These were confirmed on July 5, see: "First Meeting of the Board of Governors" (Minutes of Meeting, July 5, 1965), Fonds 1 Board of Governors, MCF-062, uOttawa Archives; "First Preliminary Meeting of the Board of Governors" (Minutes of Meeting, June 8, 1965), Fonds 1 Board of Governors, MCF-062, uOttawa Archives.
39. "Pepin, The Right Hon. Jean-Luc," Government, Parl Info, n.d., accessed May 28, 2015.
40. "Bélanger to Deschâtelets, May 26, 1964," 1–2.
41. "Bélanger to Deschâtelets, May 26, 1964."
42. "Bélanger to Deschâtelets, May 26, 1964."
43. "Bélanger to Deschâtelets, May 26, 1964."
44. An Act respecting the College of Ottawa, sec. 21 (1).
45. "Bélanger to Deschâtelets, May 26, 1964."
46. "André Guay to Jean-Charles Laframboise" (Letter, June 8, 1964), AG 23 .G43 R 1, Saint Paul University Archives.
47. "Act Constituting the Central Oblate House of the University of Ottawa" (Letter, June 27, 1964), NB-6600, uOttawa Archives; "Léo Deschâtelets to Jean-Charles Laframboise" (Letter, June 19, 1964), NB-6600, uOttawa Archives.
48. "Act Constituting the Central Oblate House of the University of Ottawa"; "Léo Deschâtelets to Jean-Charles Laframboise."
49. Roy, "Marcel Bélanger," 297.
50. "Marcel Bélanger to Léo Deschâtelets" (Letter, March 29, 1965), AC 260. C48R 14, Saint Paul University Archives, Bélanger to Deschâtelets, Mar. 29, 1965.

51. "Marcel Bélanger to Léo Deschâtelets."
52. Roy, "Marcel Bélanger," 314.
53. "Marcel Bélanger to Léo Deschâtelets" (Letter, April 27, 1965), AC 260. C48R 14, Saint Paul University Archives, Bélanger to Deschâtelets, Apr. 27, 1965.
54. "Réunion tenue à Montréal, le 28 Août 1964 en présence du Très Réverend Père Léo Deschâtelets, O.M.I. Supérieur Général" (Report, August 28, 1964), AC 260. C48R 14, Saint Paul University Archives.
55. "Réunion tenue à Montréal."
56. "Pizzardo to Chancellor Lemieux" (Letter, April 6, 1965), NB-10454.7, uOttawa Archives.
57. "Réunion tenue à Montréal."
58. "J.C. McRuer to Roger Guindon" (Letter, December 9, 1964), AR 1964 .G96Z 226, Saint Paul University Archives; see also "Thomas G. Feeney to Roger Guindon" (Letter, July 24, 1964), AR 1964 .G96Z 1–213, Saint Paul University Archives.
59. "Thomas G. Feeney to Roger Guindon."
60. "G. W. Boss to Roger Guindon" (Memorandum, December 10, 1964), AR 1964 .G96Z 228, Saint Paul University Archives.
61. J. J. Kelly, "Rev. J. J. Kelly to Roger Guindon" (Letter, November 20, 1964), AR 1964 .G96Z 200, Saint Paul University Archives.
62. Michel Prévost, "Décès du fondateur du Service des communications, Bill Boss," 2007, http://www.uottawa.ca.archives/files/bill_boss.pdf.
63. "G. W. Boss to Roger Guindon."
64. "G. W. Boss to Roger Guindon"; original emphasis.
65. "G. W. Boss to Roger Guindon."
66. "G. W. Boss to Roger Guindon."
67. "Robert Keyserlingk to Roger Guindon" (Letter, December 14, 1964), Box: AR 1964 .G96Z 214, Saint Paul University Archives.
68. "Robert Keyserlingk to Roger Guindon."
69. "Fernand Landry to Roger Guindon" (Letter, January 14, 1965), AR 1964 .G96Z 261, Saint Paul University Archives.
70. "Fernand Landry to Maurice Chagnon" (Letter, May 8, 1967), Fonds 7, NB-7861, File 11, uOttawa Archives.
71. "D.M. Baird to Roger Guindon" (Letter, March 19, 1965), AR 1964 .G96Z 336, Saint Paul University Archives.
72. "CAUT and NCCUC. 'Proposal to the Ford Foundation.'"
73. See "Roger Guindon to J. Percy Smith (Secretary, Study of University Government)." (Letter, January 18, 1965), Fonds 3, Box NB-68, uOttawa Archives; and "Donat Pharand (President, APUO) to Roger Guindon" (Letter, January 5, 1965), AR 1964 .G96Z 249, Saint Paul University Archives; "Paul Marcotte to Roger Guindon" (Letter, January 14, 1965), AR 1964 .G96Z 259, Saint Paul University Archives.
74. "Roger Guindon to Council of Administration" (Memorandum, January 19, 1965), Fonds 3, Box NB-68, uOttawa Archives.
75. "Roger Guindon to Paul Marcotte" (Letter, January 22, 1965), Fonds 3 Office of the Rector, Box NB-68, uOttawa Archives.
76. "APUO Report on UO Government," 53–55.
77. "APUO Report on UO Government," 53–55.
78. Sir James Duff and Robert Oliver Berdahl, *Structure administrative des universités au Canada* (Québec: Les Presses de l'Université Laval, 1966), appendix II.
79. An Act respecting Université d'Ottawa, 1960.
80. Guindon, *Coexistence Féconde : la dualité linguistique à l'Université d'Ottawa*, 3:78.
81. "Administration Provinciale O.M.I." (File Folder, n.d.), AP 11 .P24R, Saint Paul University Archives, accessed July 11, 2014.

82. "Report of a Meeting Held at the General House in Rome."
83. "Sacra Congregatio de Seminaris et Studiorum Universitatibus to Archbishop of Ottawa" (Letter, March 24, 1965), Fonds 3 Office of the Rector, Box NB-10454.2, uOttawa Archives.
84. One day before the assembly rose for summer recess.
85. "An Act respecting the University of Ottawa, Commentaires" (Memorandum, March 8, 1965), Fonds 3 Office of the Rector, Box NB-10454.1, uOttawa Archives.
86. "Marcel Bélanger to Léo Deschâtelets," April 27, 1965.
87. "Gérard Gagnon to Roger Guindon" (Memorandum, Ottawa, March 3, 1965), NB-10454.6, uOttawa Archives.
88. "Maurice Chagnon to Roger Guindon" (Letter, March 8, 1965), NB-10454.1, uOttawa Archives.
89. "Roger Guindon to Archbishop of Ottawa" (Letter, March 20, 1965), Fonds 3 Office of the Rector, Box NB-68, uOttawa Archives; confirmed by the Sacred Congregation of Seminaries and Universities: "Joseph Pizzardo to Marie-Joseph Lemieux" (Letter, Rome, March 24, 1965), NB-10454.2, uOttawa Archives.
90. Such obedience was in keeping with Pauline thinking, as stated in Colossians 3:22–24: "Servants, obey in all things your masters according to the flesh; not with eyeservice, as menpleasers; but in singleness of heart, fearing God: / And whatsoever ye do, do it heartily, as to the Lord, and not unto men; / Knowing that of the Lord ye shall receive the reward of the inheritance: for ye serve the Lord Christ."
91. Oblats de Marie-Immaculée, *Constitutions 1965*, secs. 223, 228, 231, for details on expulsion, see secs. 785–798.
92. There was only a commitment to education: see Oblats de Marie-Immaculée, sec. 133.
93. Oblats de Marie-Immaculée, *Constitutiones et regulae congregationis Missionariorum Oblatorum Sanctissimae et Immaculatae Virginis Mariae* (Romae: Oblatorum sanctissimae et Immaculatae Virginis Mariae, 1966), Constitutiones et regulae 1966.
94. "Discours de la collation des grades"; original emphasis.
95. "Discours de la collation des grades."
96. "Discours de la collation des grades."

Chapter 4: Contract with Saint Paul: Meshing the Old and New

1. Philips v. Bury, 90 English Reports at 1299; the reception of this law, along with attendant academic literature, is reviewed at length in: strömbergsson-denora, "Caught by Private Law: Public Law Implications of Visitors in Canada."
2. McCullock Finney c. Barreau (Québec), 2004 SCC 36 (n.d.).
3. Chaput v Romain, 834 SCR (SCC 1955).
4. "Collation des grades d'automne" (Speech, October 24, 1965), AR 1964 G96 DR18, Saint Paul University Archives.
5. Paul calls for such unity in Ephesians 4:1–3; again in Philippians 1:27.
6. Roger Guindon, "Le caractère permanent de l'Université d'Ottawa" (La Rotonde Article, August 16, 1965), Fonds 3 Office of the Rector, Box NB-9337.2, uOttawa Archives.
7. An Act respecting Université d'Ottawa, SO 1965, c.137 § (1965).
8. "Roger Guindon to Claude Ryan" (Letter, October 13, 1965), Fonds 3 Office of the Rector, Box NB-69, uOttawa Archives; original emphasis.
9. "Collation des grades d'automne" (Speech, 24 October 1965), AR 1964 G96 DR 18, Saint Paul University Archives.
10. This role is somewhat confirmed by the existence of the "Hospitals and Charitable Institutions Inquiries Act," RSO 1960, c. 177 § (n.d.), which mimics the

role of visitors' ability to inquire into affairs in institutions that received public financial support.

11. "Collation des grades d'automne" (Speech, 24 October 1965), AR 1964 G96 DR 18, Saint Paul University Archives.
12. "Collation des grades d'automne" (Speech, 24 October 1965), AR 1964 G96 DR 18, Saint Paul University Archives.
13. See "Report on the Government of the University of Ottawa Made by a Committee Appointed by the Board of Governors of the Association of Professors of the University of Ottawa" (Report, February 1965), 53–55, MG28 I 208 container 55, f. 10 - University Government - Documents - Ottawa, Library and Archives Canada.
14. "Collation des grades d'automne" (Speech, 24 October 1965), AR 1964 G96 DR 18, Saint Paul University Archives.
15. "Roger Guindon to Bernard B. Vedder" (Letter, December 8, 1965), Fonds 3 Office of the Rector, Box NB-68, uOttawa Archives.
16. "Antanagoge, n.," in *Oxford English Dictionary* (Online: Oxford University Press, July 2018): "A figure of speech in which an undesirable continuation is averted; spec. (a) introduction of a positive modification of, aspect to, or conclusion from an initial negative statement; (b) use of counter-accusation or recrimination to avoid answering a charge, etc."
17. "Collation des grades d'automne" (Speech, October 23, 1966), Fonds 3 Office of the Rector, Box NB-9337.3, uOttawa Archives.
18. "Collation des grades pour marquer le centenaire de la Confédération" (Speech, February 17, 1967), Fonds 3 Office of the Rector, Box NB-9337.4, uOttawa Archives; original emphasis.
19. Roger Guindon, "Bienvenue aux nouveaux membres du personnel enseignant" (Speech, Ottawa, September 6, 1967), Fonds 3, NB-9337.5, uOttawa Archives.
20. See Romans 11:17–22.
21. Romans 11:18–21.
22. "Minutes of the Conseil d'Administration" (Minutes of Meeting, June 10, 1965), Fonds 260 – NB-6600, uOttawa Archives. See also Caparros, Thériault, and Thorn, *Code of Canon Law Annotated*, can. 1292, for the requirement of authorization for large sales of property.
23. "Convention entre Université d'Ottawa [...] et [...] les Fiduciaires" (June 25, 1965), Fonds 315 University Saint Paul, NB-45052, uOttawa Archives.
24. "Federation Agreement."
25. "Federation Agreement," sec. 2.
26. "Federation Agreement," sec. 7.
27. "Federation Agreement," sec. 4.
28. "Federation Agreement," sec. 3.
29. "Federation Agreement," sec. 12. The Board of Governors' power to contract in this regard was not challenged by anyone, although it significantly modified the academic Senate's powers. While the Senate was not constituted, its power to control academic policy existed in the charter, and any modulation of that power presumably had to pass through it. The lack of formal consultation assumes the Board's power to contract in the name of the Senate, and the lack of challenge effectively creates the private law.
30. "Federation Agreement," secs. 10, 11, 24.
31. "Federation Agreement," sec. 34.
32. "Federation Agreement," secs. 5–6.
33. "Federation Agreement."
34. "Federation Agreement," secs. 13, 14.

35. "Meeting of the Governors-Designate of the University of Ottawa" (Minutes of Meeting, June 8, 1965), MCF-062, uOttawa Archives.
36. "First Preliminary Meeting of the Board of Governors"; see also "First Meeting of the Board of Governors."
37. "Procès-verbal de la réunion inaugurale du Bureau des gouverneurs de l'Université d'Ottawa" (Minutes of Meeting, July 5, 1965), MCF-062, uOttawa Archives.
38. "First Meeting of the Board of Governors."
39. "First Meeting of the Board of Governors."
40. See chapter 3 for a detailed discussion of the Church's desire for control in the new corporation, and its eventual acceptance of the corporation's civil status and the need to influence its culture rather than its formal administrative structures.
41. One witness is "Meeting at Rideau Hall with Madame Vanier and W.G. Davis" (Report, October 25, 1966), Fonds 3, Box NB-10454, File 4, uOttawa Archives.
42. "Mémoire sur la Faculté de Philosophy dans l'Université d'Ottawa re-structurée"(Report, March 19, 1965), Fonds 3, Box NB-10454, File 12, uOttawa Archives.
43. "Mémoire sur la Faculté de Philosophy dans l'Université d'Ottawa re-structurée."
44. "Mémoire sur la Faculté de Philosophy dans l'Université d'Ottawa re-structurée."
45. Vatican Council II, *The Conciliar and Post Conciliar Documents*, ed. Austin Flannery (Grand Rapids, MI: William B. Eerdmans Pub. Co., 1987), no. 55, 725–737.
46. For an in-depth examination of the similarities between Aquinas and Aristotle, see John Finnis, *Aquinas: Moral, Political, and Legal Theory* (Oxford: Oxford University Press, 1998), 187–218.
47. Vatican Council II, *The Conciliar and Post Conciliar Documents*, no. 55, 725–737. I reproduce the citations for notes 31 and 32, which are the relevant notes for this passage: 31. Cf. Paul VI's allocution to the International Thomistic Congress, Sept. 10, 1965: l'Osservatore Romano, Sept. 13–14, 1965. 32. Cf. Pius XII's allocution to teachers and students of French Institutes of Higher Catholic Education, Sept. 21, 1950: Discourses and Radio Messages, 12, 219–221; letters to the 22nd congress of Pax Romana, Aug. 12, 1952: Discourses and Radio Messages, 14, 567–569; John XXIII's allocution to the Federation of Catholic Universities, April 1, 1959: Discourses, Messages and Conversations, 1, Rome, 1960, 226–229; Paul VI's allocution to the Academic Senate of the Catholic University of Milan, April 5, 1964: Encyclicals and Discourses of Paul VI, 2, Rome, 1964, 438–443.
48. "Mémoire sur la Faculté de Philosophy dans l'Université d'Ottawa re-structurée."
49. "Mémoire sur la Faculté de Philosophy dans l'Université d'Ottawa re-structurée."
50. Indeed, Vatican II was mandated in the 1966 Oblate constitution and rules, which came into force January 1, 1967. From this point on, Oblates were required, as Oblates and not simply as Catholics, to obey the dicta of the Holy See. The constitution stipulated at articles 38 and 39 that "38 - Tous les membres de la Congrégation sont soumis au Souverain Pontife comme à leur premier Supérieur, et sont tenus de lui obéir en vertu du vœu. 39 - Ils sont soumis au pouvoir des supérieurs ecclésiastiques, selon les normes du Droit." The law was, therefore, explicit after 1967 and not simply a common prescription (Oblats de Marie-Immaculée, *Constitutiones et regulae congregationis Missionariorum Oblatorum Sanctissimae et Immaculatae Virginis Mariae*).
51. "Jacques Croteau to Jacques Gervais" (Letter, July 21, 1965), Fonds 3, Box NB-1535.3/46, uOttawa Archives.
52. "Jacques Croteau to Jacques Gervais."
53. "Jacques Croteau to Jacques Gervais."

54. "Roger Guindon to Marie-Joseph Lemieux" (Letter, December 21, 1965), NB-68, uOttawa Archives.
55. "Edgar Scully to J.-M. Quirion" (Letter, July 22, 1966), Fonds 3, Box NB-1535.3/46, uOttawa Archives.
56. "Daniel Dineley to Maurice Chagnon" (Letter, December 22, 1967), Fonds 7, NB-7861, File 8, uOttawa Archives.
57. "Edgar Scully to J.-M. Quirion."
58. "Edgar Scully to J.-M. Quirion."
59. "Edgar Scully to J.-M. Quirion."
60. "Opinion of the Council of the Faculty of Philosophy on the Legality of Article 5 of the 'Convention' and on the Question of its Possible Modification" (Report, September 8, 1966), Fonds 3, Box NB-1535.3/46, uOttawa Archives.
61. "Opinion of the Faculty of Philosophy."
62. "Opinion of the Faculty of Philosophy."
63. "Faculty of Philosophy Council" (Minutes of Meeting, December 1, 1965), Fonds 31, MCF-571, uOttawa Archives; "Faculty of Philosophy Council," October 7, 1965; "Faculty of Philosophy Council" (Minutes of Meeting, September 8, 1966), Fonds 31, MCF-571, uOttawa Archives; "Faculty of Philosophy Council" (Minutes of Meeting, September 18, 1967), Fonds 31, MCF-571, uOttawa Archives.
64. "Roger Guindon to Members of the Academic Senate" (Circular Letter, January 27, 1966), Fonds 3 Office of the Rector, Box NB-68, File: Correspondance chronologique du recteur Roger Guindon, 01-01-1966 au 30-06-1966 (1 de 3), uOttawa Archives.
65. "A.P.U.O. Les Faits et Documents" (Report, March 15, 1966), Fonds 7, NB-7861, File 16, uOttawa Archives.
66. "Roger Guindon to Richard Lebrun (President, APUO)" (Letter, March 14, 1966), AR 1964 G96 L 11, Saint Paul University Archives. A selective point, for the Board of Governors was happy to relinquish the Senate's power over academic degrees in the 1965 contract.
67. "Roger Guindon to Richard Lebrun (President, APUO)."
68. "Andrew Robinson to Arthur Wishart, Attorney General of Ontario (Encl. Correspondence)" (Letter, June 5, 1966), RG 4-2, 299.4, Archives of Ontario.
69. "Andrew Robinson to Arthur Wishart, Attorney General of Ontario (Encl. Correspondence)."
70. "Roger Guindon to Jacques Gervais, Correspondence with J.R. McCarthy Encl." (Letter, August 11, 1966), Guindon AR 1964 G96 L 9, Saint Paul University Archives (since transferred to uOttawa at NB-45052).
71. "Roger Guindon to Jacques Gervais, Correspondence with J.R. McCarthy Encl."
72. See "Meeting at Rideau Hall with Madame Vanier and W.G. Davis," 4–5.
73. "Gerald Fauteux to Hon. Dana H. Porter, cc. Leslie Frost." (Letter, July 6, 1966), Fonds 3 Office of the Rector, Box NB-10454, File 8, uOttawa Archives.
74. "Meeting at Rideau Hall with Madame Vanier and W.G. Davis," 3.
75. "Meeting at Rideau Hall with Madame Vanier and W.G. Davis," 2.
76. "Fauteux to Porter."
77. "Fauteux to Porter."
78. "Meeting at Rideau Hall with Madame Vanier and W.G. Davis," 1.
79. "Meeting at Rideau Hall with Madame Vanier and W.G. Davis."
80. "Meeting at Rideau Hall with Madame Vanier and W.G. Davis," 3.
81. "William Davis to General Allard" (Letter, February 27, 1967), Fonds 3 Office of the Rector, Box NB-10454, File 5, uOttawa Archives.
82. "Leslie Frost to General Allard" (Letter, February 28, 1967), Fonds 3 Office of the Rector, Box NB-10454, File 5, uOttawa Archives.

83. "Roger Guindon to Jacques Gervais" (Letter, March 14, 1967), Fonds 3, Box NB-10454, File 5, uOttawa Archives.
84. "Jacques Gervais to Roger Guindon" (Letter, March 22, 1967), Fonds 3, Box NB-10454, File 5, uOttawa Archives.
85. "Roger Guindon to William Davis" (Letter, March 27, 1967), Fonds 3 Office of the Rector, Box NB-10454, File 5, uOttawa Archives.
86. "Province Urged to Provide 100% of Capital Costs for Universities" (Newspaper Article, March 22, 1967), Fonds 3 Office of the Rector, Box NB-10454, File 5, uOttawa Archives.
87. "Roger Guindon to William Davis," March 27, 1967.
88. "Roger Guindon's Handwritten Notes" (Notes, March 1967), Fonds 3, Box NB-10454, File 5, uOttawa Archives; original emphasis.
89. "Roger Guindon to Jacques Gervais" (Letter, March 23, 1967), Fonds 3, Box NB-10454, File 5, uOttawa Archives.
90. "Roger Guindon to William Davis" (Letter, April 19, 1967), Fonds 3 Office of the Rector, Box NB-10454, File 5, uOttawa Archives.

Epilogue: Settling the Religious Character
1. For the technical description of that structure, see the Education Act, RSO 1990, c. E.2 § (n.d.).
2. See parts 6 and 8 of the Education Act for further details.
3. I use the phrase "home statute" advisedly, with reference to administrative law. See Dunsmuir v. New Brunswick, 1 SCR 190 (SCC 2008).
4. An Act respecting Université d'Ottawa, 1965, sec. 4 (b).
5. "Rapport du Comité sur le caractère chrétien de l'Université" (February 3, 1969), MCF-060, uOttawa Archives.
6. "Rapport du Comité sur le caractère chrétien de l'Université."
7. Senate Committee for the Study of "Christian Principles," "February 13, 1967" (Minutes of Meeting, n.d.), NB-8051.16, uOttawa Archives, accessed June 24, 2014.
8. Senate Committee for the Study of "Christian Principles," "February 27, 1967" (Minutes of Meeting, n.d.), NB-8051.16, uOttawa Archives, accessed June 24, 2014.
9. Senate Committee for the Study of "Christian Principles," "January 26, 1967" (Minutes of Meeting, n.d.), NB-8051.16, uOttawa Archives, accessed June 24, 2014; "February 13, 1967"; "February 27, 1967."
10. Senate Committee for the Study of "Christian Principles," "March 13, 1967" (Minutes of Meeting, n.d.), NB-8051.16, uOttawa Archives, accessed June 24, 2014.
11. See "Edgar Scully to J.-M. Quirion."
12. Senate Committee for the Study of "Christian Principles," "March 13, 1967."
13. Senate Committee for the Study of "Christian Principles."
14. Senate Committee for the Study of "Christian Principles."
15. "Rapport intérimaire du Comité du Sénat pour l'étude du caractère chrétien de l'Université" (Report, January 15, 1968), NB-8051.15, uOttawa Archives.
16. "Rapport intérimaire du Comité du Sénat pour l'étude du caractère chrétien de l'Université."
17. "Rapport intérimaire du Comité du Sénat pour l'étude du caractère chrétien de l'Université"; see also "November 6, 1967" (Senate Meeting, n.d.), Fonds 2 Sénat, MCF-060, uOttawa Archives, accessed June 17, 2014; and "December 4 & 11, 1967" (Senate Meeting, n.d.), Fonds 2 Sénat, MCF-060, uOttawa Archives, accessed June 17, 2014.
18. "George Ling," *Ottawa Citizen*, June 11, 2011, sec. Obituary.
19. "Présidents et présidentes de l'Association des professeurs (APUO)," uOttawa Archives, accessed June 1, 2015, http://www.archives.uottawa.ca/fra/przapuo.html.

20. See "Edward J. Monahan to J. Gordin Kaplan" (Letter, March 28, 1968), MG28 I 208 container 87 f. 13: University of Ottawa Senate Committee on the Christian Character – Correspondence (1966–1969), Library and Archives Canada.
21. Later President of Laurentian University in Sudbury, itself a non-denominational university with ties to the Catholic University of Sudbury, the Anglican Thornloe University, and the Methodist Huntington University.
22. Later a Liberal attorney general of Canada and judge of the Federal Court of Appeal.
23. Philip Girard, *Bora Laskin: Bringing Law to Life* (Toronto: University of Toronto Press, 2005), 319–322.
24. "Edward Monahan to Bora Laskin" (Letter, December 29, 1967), MG28 I 208 container 87 f. 13: University of Ottawa Senate Committee on the Christian Character – Correspondence (1966–1969), Library and Archives Canada.
25. "Bora Laskin to Edward Monahan" (Letter, January 3, 1968), MG28 I 208 container 87 f. 13: University of Ottawa Senate Committee on the Christian Character – Correspondence (1966–1969), Library and Archives Canada.
26. "January 8 & 15, 1968" (Senate Meeting, n.d.), Fonds 2 Sénat, MCF-060, uOttawa Archives, accessed June 17, 2014.
27. "January 8 & 15, 1968."
28. "January 8 & 15, 1968."
29. "Maurice Chagnon to Roger Guindon, encl. letter A. Morissette to R. Guindon" (Memorandum, February 23, 1968), NB-8051.17, uOttawa Archives.
30. "Maurice Chagnon to Roger Guindon, encl. letter A. Morissette to R. Guindon."
31. "Maurice Chagnon to Roger Guindon, encl. letter A. Morissette to R. Guindon."
32. "Dean M.R. MacGuigan to Edward J. Monahan" (Letter, March 8, 1968), MG28 I 208 container 87 f. 13: University of Ottawa Senate Committee on the Christian Character – Correspondence (1966–1969), Library and Archives Canada.
33. "Edward J. Monahan to J. Gordin Kaplan."
34. Senate Committee for the Study of "Christian Principles," "February 26, 1968" (Minutes of Meeting, n.d.), NB-8051.17, uOttawa Archives, accessed June 24, 2014.
35. Senate Committee for the Study of "Christian Principles," "March 25, 1968" (Minutes of Meeting, n.d.), NB-8051.17, uOttawa Archives, accessed June 24, 2014.
36. "Legal Opinion of Legal Opinion – Circulated to APUO Board of Directors" (Circular Memorandum, n.d.), NB-8051.17, uOttawa Archives, accessed June 24, 2014.
37. "Legal Opinion of Legal Opinion - Circulated to APUO Board of Directors."
38. "Roger Guindon to Gordin J. Kaplan" (Letter, June 11, 1968), MG28 I 208 container 86 f. 8, Library and Archives Canada, Kaplan's circular letter is appended to this correspondence in the file.
39. "Rapport du Comité sur le caractère chrétien de l'Université."
40. Education Act, sec. 0.1(2).
41. John Milton, *Of Education*, EEBO, Thomason/9:E:50[12] (London: Thomas Underhill, 1644), sig. Av.

Bibliography

Archival sources

"Academic Administration in Higher Education." Report, 1959. Fonds 197, MCF-522, uOttawa Archives.

"Act Constituting the Central Oblate House of the University of Ottawa." Letter, June 27, 1964. NB-6600, uOttawa Archives.

"Acte de visite canonique de la maison de l'Université d'Ottawa par le R.P. Charles Tatin, O.M.I., Novembre 1901." Bound Manuscript, 1901. Fonds 315 Saint Paul University, NB-45273, File 63, uOttawa Archives.

"Actes de visite de 1905 à 1941 (Université d'Ottawa)." Bound Manuscript, n.d. Fonds 315 Saint Paul University, NB-45273, File 63, uOttawa Archives. Accessed October 23, 2015.

"Address by Mr. J. R. McCarthy at Convocation in the Medical Auditorium, University of Ottawa, Saturday, November 16, 1963, at 3:00 p.m." Speech, November 16, 1963. RG 32-23, barcode B354145, "University of Ottawa," Archives of Ontario.

"Administration Provinciale O.M.I." File Folder, AP 11 .P24R, Saint Paul University Archives. Accessed July 11, 2014.

"Agenda pour le conseil local." Agenda, May 4, 1964. AC 260. C48R 14, Saint Paul University Archives.

"Allocution du R. P. Roger Guindon lors de son installation le mercredi 28 octobre 1964." Speech, October 28, 1964. AR 1964 G96 CL 4, Saint Paul University Archives.

"An Act respecting the University of Ottawa - Commentaires." Memorandum, March 8, 1965. Fonds 3 Office of the Rector, Box NB-10454.1, uOttawa Archives.

"André Guay to Jean-Charles Laframboise." Letter, June 8, 1964. AG 23 .G43 R 1, Saint Paul University Archives.

"Andrew Robinson to Arthur Wishart, Attorney General of Ontario (Encl. Correspondence)." Letter, June 5, 1966. RG 4-2, 299.4, Archives of Ontario.

"A.P.U.O. Les faits et documents." Report, March 15, 1966. Fonds 7, NB-7861, File 16, uOttawa Archives.

"Attributions, groupe d'étude sur les rapports entre l'Université d'Ottawa et le Gouvernement de l'Ontario." Order, May 30, 1963. Fonds 3 Office of the Rector, Box NB-10454.10, uOttawa Archives.

"Bora Laskin to Edward Monahan." Letter, January 3, 1968. MG28 I 208 container 87 f. 13: University of Ottawa Senate Committee on the Christian Character – Correspondence (1966–1969). Library and Archives Canada.

"Box NB-3038," n.d. Fonds 2, NB-3038, uOttawa Archives. Accessed June 17, 2014.

"Box NB-6600." Box, n.d. NB-6600, uOttawa Archives. Accessed July 17, 2014.

"Cahier des actes de visite de 1942- (Université d'Ottawa)." Bound Manuscript, 1964 1942. Fonds 315 Saint Paul University, NB-45273, File 63, uOttawa Archives.

"CAUT and NCCUC. 'Proposal to the Ford Foundation.'" Proposal, n.d. MG28 I 208 container 137, f. 12 - University Government - Early Memoranda. Library and Archives Canada. Accessed July 22, 2014.

"C.M. McDougall (Registrar, McGill) to Jean-Marie Quirion." Letter, November 22, 1962. Fonds 197, MCF-522, uOttawa Archives.

"Collation des grades d'automne." Speech, October 24, 1965. AR 1964 G96 DR18, Saint Paul University Archives.

"Collation des grades d'automne." Speech, October 23, 1966. Fonds 3 Office of the Rector, Box NB-9337.3, uOttawa Archives.

"Collation des grades pour marquer la centennaire de la Confédération." Speech, February 17, 1967. Fonds 3 Office of the Rector, Box NB-9337.4, uOttawa Archives.

Congregationis missionariorum-oblatorum sanctissimæ et immaculatæ Virginis Mariæ. *Constitutiones et regulæ*. Marseille: Episcopal Typographers, 1853.

"Constitutions et règles de la congrégation des Missionaires Oblats de la Très Sainte et Immaculée Vierge Marie." Hardback Book in Octavo. Rome, 1930. Fonds 38 Miscellaneous Documents, BB.12, uOttawa Archives.

"Convention entre Université d'Ottawa […] et […] les Fiduciaires," June 25, 1965. Fonds 315 Saint Paul University, NB-45052, uOttawa Archives.

Coupal, Annic, Jules de Sylva, Pierre Glandon, Jacques Guillotte, Anne LaFlamme, Kepline Maceaus, and Nadine Taillon. "La contribution de l'Université d'Ottawa au Patrimoine de la capitale nationale." Monograph. Ottawa, 1991. Fonds 315, FH 47 .H67R, uOttawa Archives.

"Daniel Dineley to Maurice Chagnon." Letter, December 22, 1967. Fonds 7, NB-7861, File 8, uOttawa Archives.

"Dean M.R. MacGuigan to Edward J. Monahan." Letter, March 8, 1968. MG28 I 208 container 87 f. 13: University of Ottawa Senate Committee on the Christian Character – Correspondence (1966–1969), Library and Archives Canada.

"December 4 & 11, 1967." Senate Meeting, n.d. Fonds 2 Sénat, MCF-060, uOttawa Archives.

"Discours de la collation des grades." Speech, May 30, 1965. AR 1964 G96 DR 10, Saint Paul University Archives.

"D.M. Baird to Roger Guindon." Letter, March 19, 1965. AR 1964 .G96Z 336, Saint Paul University Archives.

"Donat Pharand (President, APUO) to Roger Guindon." Letter, January 5, 1965. AR 1964 .G96Z 24, Saint Paul University Archives.

"Douglass Burns Clarke, M.A. (Vice-Principal, Sir George Williams University) to Jean-Marie Quirion." Letter, September 17, 1963. Fonds 197, MCF-522, uOttawa Archives.

"Edgar Scully to J.-M. Quirion." Letter, July 22, 1966. Fonds 3, Box NB-1535.3/46, uOttawa Archives.

"Edward J. Monahan to J. Gordin Kaplan." Letter, March 28, 1968. MG28 I 208 container 87 f. 13: University of Ottawa Senate Committee on the Christian Character – Correspondence (1966–1969), Library and Archives Canada.

"Edward Monahan to Bora Laskin." Letter, December 29, 1967. MG28 I 208 container 87 f. 13: University of Ottawa Senate Committee on the Christian Character – Correspondence (1966–1969), Library and Archives Canada.

"Entrevue avec le premier ministre de l'Ontario, l'honorable J. P. Robarts le lundi 16 décembre 1963 à 4 h 15 de l'après-midi. Le T.R. Père Recteur est accompagné du docteur J.-L. Lussier. M. Robarts est seul." Report, December 16, 1963. Fonds 3 Office of the Rector, Box NB-10454.11, uOttawa Archives.

"Faculty of Philosophy Council." Minutes of Meeting, October 7, 1965. Fonds 31, NB-5523.2, uOttawa Archives.

"Faculty of Philosophy Council." Minutes of Meeting, December 1, 1965. Fonds 31, MCF-571, uOttawa Archives.

"Faculty of Philosophy Council." Minutes of Meeting, September 8, 1966. Fonds 31, MCF-571, uOttawa Archives.

"Faculty of Philosophy Council." Minutes of Meeting, September 18, 1967. Fonds 31, MCF-571, uOttawa Archives.

"Fernand Landry to Maurice Chagnon." Letter, May 8, 1967. Fonds 7, NB-7861, File 11, uOttawa Archives.

"Fernand Landry to Roger Guindon." Letter, January 14, 1965. AR 1964 .G96Z 261, Saint Paul University Archives.

"First Meeting of the Board of Governors." Minutes of Meeting, July 5, 1965. Fonds 1 Board of Governors, MCF-062, uOttawa Archives.

"First Preliminary Meeting of the Board of Governors." Minutes of Meeting, June 8, 1965. Fonds 1 Board of Governors, MCF-062, uOttawa Archives.

"Floyd S. Chalmers to Leslie M. Frost." Letter, May 7, 1962. RG 32-23, barcode B354145, "University of Ottawa," Archives of Ontario.

"G. W. Boss to Roger Guindon." Memorandum, December 10, 1964. AR 1964 .G96Z 228, Saint Paul University Archives.

"Gérard Gagnon to Roger Guindon." Memorandum. Ottawa, March 3, 1965. NB-10454.6, uOttawa Archives.

"Gerald Fauteux to Hon. Dana H. Porter, cc. Leslie Frost." Letter, July 6, 1966. Fonds 3 Office of the Rector, Box NB-10454, File 8, uOttawa Archives.

Gosselin, Pierre H. "L'université d'Ottawa." Monograph. Ottawa, 1984. NB-1670, uOttawa Archives.

Guay, André, and Jean-Charles Laframboise, "L'Université d'Ottawa statistiques 1946-1947." Typed record, December 31, 1946. Fonds 3, Box NB-5532, File 1, uOttawa Archives.

Guindon, Roger. "Rapport annuel du recteur 1965-1966." Print Report. Ottawa, 1966. Fonds 3, Box NB-5532, File 15, uOttawa Archives.

——. "Transition 1966–1970." Print Report. Ottawa, 1970. Fonds 3, Box NB-5532, File 17, uOttawa Archives.

Guindon, Roger. "Bienvenue aux nouveaux membres du personnel enseignant." Speech. Ottawa, September 6, 1967. Fonds 3, NB-9337.5, uOttawa Archives.

"Henri Legaré to John P. Robarts." Letter, April 30, 1963. RG 32-23, barcode B354145, "University of Ottawa," Archives of Ontario.

"Henri Legaré to Leslie M. Frost." Letter, January 7, 1964. RG 32-23, barcode B354145, "University of Ottawa," Archives of Ontario.

"Henri Legaré to Leslie M. Frost." Letter, January 30, 1964. RG 32-23, barcode B354145, "University of Ottawa," Archives of Ontario.

"Henri Legaré to Leslie M. Frost." Letter, January 31, 1964. RG 32-23, barcode B354145, "University of Ottawa," Archives of Ontario.

"J. P. Robarts to Henri Legaré." Letter, August 1, 1963. RG 32-23, barcode B354145, "University of Ottawa," Archives of Ontario.

"Jacques Croteau to Jacques Gervais." Letter, July 21, 1965. Fonds 3, Box NB-1535.3/46, uOttawa Archives.

"Jacques Gervais to Roger Guindon." Letter, March 22, 1967. Fonds 3, Box NB-10454, File 5, uOttawa Archives.

"January 8 & 15, 1968." Senate Meeting, n.d. Fonds 2 Sénat, MCF-060, uOttawa Archives.

"J. C. McRuer to Roger Guindon." Letter, December 9, 1964. AR 1964 .G96Z 226, Saint Paul University Archives.

"Jean-Marie Quirion to René Lavigne." Letter, January 9, 1963. Fonds 197, MCF-522, uOttawa Archives.

Laframboise, Jean-Charles. "Rapport du T.R.P. Recteur année académique 1949-1950." Typed record. Ottawa, 1950. Fonds 3, Box NB-5532, File 7, uOttawa Archives.

"Legal Opinion of Legal Opinion – Circulated to APUO Board of Directors." Circular Memorandum, n.d. NB-8051.17, uOttawa Archives.

Legaré, Henri F. "Université d'Ottawa: rapport annuel du Recteur 1958-59." Print Report. Ottawa, 1959. Fonds 3, Box NB-5532, File 13, uOttawa Archives.

———. "Université d'Ottawa: rapport annuel du Recteur 1959-1960, 1960-1961." Print Report. Ottawa, 1961. Fonds 3, Box NB-5532, File 14, uOttawa Archives.

"Léo Deschâtelets to Jean-Charles Laframboise." Letter, June 19, 1964. NB-6600, uOttawa Archives.

"Léo Deschâtelets to Marcel Bélanger." Letter, January 28, 1963. AC 260. C48R 14, Saint Paul University Archives.

"Léo Deschâtelets to Marcel Bélanger." Letter, March 27, 1963. AC 260. C48R 14, Saint Paul University Archives.

"Les O.M.I. à l'Université d'Ottawa." Report, n.d. AC 260. C48R 14c, Saint Paul University Archives.

"Leslie Frost to General Allard." Letter, February 28, 1967. Fonds 3 Office of the Rector, Box NB-10454, File 5, uOttawa Archives.

"Leslie Frost to Henri Legaré." Letter, January 14, 1964. AC 260. C48R 13, Saint Paul University Archives.

"Leslie M. Frost to J. P. Robarts." Letter, May 29, 1963. RG 32-23, barcode B354145, "University of Ottawa," Archives of Ontario.

"Leslie M. Frost to Oakley Dalgleish." Letter, May 29, 1963. RG 32-23, barcode B354145, "University of Ottawa," Archives of Ontario.

"Lorenzo Danis to Louis Lévesque." Letter, March 5, 1964. AC 260. C48R 14, Saint Paul University Archives.

"Louis Lévesque to Lorenzo Danis." Letter, March 11, 1964. AC 260. C48R 14, Saint Paul University Archives.

"Louis-Paul Dugal to Jean-Marie Quirion." Letter, January 11, 1963. Fonds 197, MCF-522, uOttawa Archives.

"Marcel Bélanger to Léo Deschâtelets." Letter, February 10, 1963. AC 260. C48R 14, Saint Paul University Archives.

"Marcel Bélanger to Léo Deschâtelets." Letter, May 26, 1964. AC 260. C48R 14, Saint Paul University Archives.

"Marcel Bélanger to Léo Deschâtelets." Letter, March 29, 1965. AC 260. C48R 14, Saint Paul University Archives. Bélanger to Deschâtelets, Mar. 29, 1965.

"Marcel Bélanger to Léo Deschâtelets." Letter, April 27, 1965. AC 260. C48R 14, Saint Paul University Archives. Bélanger to Deschâtelets, Apr. 27, 1965.

"Maurice Chagnon to Roger Guindon." Letter, March 8, 1965. NB-10454.1, uOttawa Archives.
"Maurice Chagnon to Roger Guindon, encl. letter A. Morissette to R. Guindon." Memorandum, February 23, 1968. NB-8051.17, uOttawa Archives.
"MCF-522," Fonds 197, MCF-522, uOttawa Archives.
"Meeting at Rideau Hall with Madame Vanier and W.G. Davis." Report, October 25, 1966. Fonds 3, Box NB-10454, File 4, uOttawa Archives.
"Meeting of the Committee of University Affairs." Minutes of Meeting, December 4, 1963. Fonds 197, MCF-522, uOttawa Archives.
"Meeting of the Governors-Designate of the University of Ottawa." Minutes of Meeting, June 8, 1965. MCF-062, uOttawa Archives.
"Mémoire sur la Faculté de philosophie dans l'Université d'Ottawa re-structurée." Report, March 19, 1965. Fonds 3, Box NB-10454, File 12, uOttawa Archives.
"Minutes of the Conseil d'administration." Minutes of Meeting, June 10, 1965. Fonds 260, NB-6600, uOttawa Archives.
"Notice of Meeting." Notice of Meeting, April 15, 1964. AC 260. C48R 14, Saint Paul University Archives.
"November 6, 1967." Senate Meeting, n.d. Fonds 2 Sénat, MCF-060, uOttawa Archives.
"Rev. J. J. Kelly to Roger Guindon." Letter, November 20, 1964. AR 1964 .G96Z 200, Saint Paul University Archives.

Primary Sources

Aquinas, Thomas. *Summa Theologica*. Translated by Father Lawrence Shapcote and Daniel J. Sullivan. Vol. 1. 2 vols. Vol. 17 of *Great Books of the Western World*. Chicago: University of Chicago Press, 1992.
Blackstone, Sir William. "Chap. XVIII 'Of Corporations.'" In *Commentaries on the Laws of England*, vol. 1, 467–484. Making of Modern Law. London: J. Bell, 1813.
Hodgins, J. George. *Documentary History of Education in Upper Canada*. Vol. 8. Toronto: Warwick Bros. & Rutter, 1901.
———. *Documentary History of Education in Upper Canada*. Vol. 9. Toronto: Warwick Bros. & Rutter, 1902.
———. *Documentary History of Education in Upper Canada*. Vol. 10. Toronto: Warwick Bros. & Rutter, 1903.
———. *Documentary History of Education in Upper Canada*. Vol. 11. Toronto: Warwick Bros. & Rutter, 1904.
———. *Documentary History of Education in Upper Canada*. Vol. 14. Toronto: Warwick Bros. & Rutter, 1906.
———. *Documentary History of Education in Upper Canada*. Vol. 16. Toronto: Warwick Bros. & Rutter, 1906.

———. *Documentary History of Education in Upper Canada*. Vol. 20. Toronto: Warwick Bros. & Rutter, 1907.
———. *Documentary History of Education in Upper Canada*. Vol. 21. Toronto: Warwick Bros. & Rutter, 1907.
———. *Documentary History of Education in Upper Canada*. Vol. 17. Toronto: Warwick Bros. & Rutter, 1907.
Durham, Earl of. *Report on the Affairs of British North America*. Montréal: Morning Courier Office, 1839.
Études Oblates. Vol. 9. Montréal: Maison Provinciale, 1950.
Études Oblates. Vol. 10. Montréal: Maison Provinciale, 1951.
Études Oblates. Vol. 14. Montréal: Maison Provinciale, 1955.
Études Oblates. Vol. 16. Montréal: Maison Provinciale, 1957.
Études Oblates. Vol. 17. Montréal: Maison Provinciale, 1958.
Études Oblates. Vol. 23. Montréal: Maison Provinciale, 1964.
Fell, John. *The privileges of the University of Oxford, in point of visitation*. EEBO, Thomason / E.411[1]. London: Richard Royston, 1647.
"George Ling." *Ottawa Citizen*. June 11, 2011, sec. Obituary.
Guigues, Joseph Eugène Bruno. *Mandements et circulaires de Mgr Joseph Eugène Guigues, 1er évêque d'Ottawa*. Early Canadiana Online 94445. Ottawa, 1878.
Guindon, Roger. *Béatitude et Théologie Morale Chez Saint Thomas d'Aquin*. Ottawa: Édition de l'Université d'Ottawa, 1956.
Guindon, Roger. *Coexistence Féconde : la dualité linguistique à l'Université d'Ottawa*. Vols. 3–4. Ottawa: Presses de l'Université d'Ottawa, 1995.
———. "Le caractère permanent de l'Université d'Ottawa." La Rotonde Article, August 16, 1965. Fonds 3 Office of the Rector, Box NB-9337.2, uOttawa Archives.
———. "Re. Oblates and University Government." Report, August 31, 1963. Fonds 3 Office of the Rector, Box NB-10454.11, uOttawa Archives.
———. "Tableau comparatif des dépenses d'opération des années fiscales terminées le 30 juin," n.d. NB-10454.16, uOttawa Archives.
Hobbes, Thomas. *Leviathan*. EEBO, Wing / H2246. London: Andrew Crooke, 1651.
———. *Leviathan: The English and Latin Texts (ii)*. Edited by Noel Malcolm. Vol. 5. Oxford: Clarendon Press, 2012.
Honorat, Jean-Baptiste, ed. *Un ancien manuscrit des saintes règles*. Ottawa: Éditions des études oblates, 1943.
Mazenod, Eugène de. *Lettres aux correspondants d'Amérique: 1841-1850*. Écrits oblats, I. Rome: Postulation générale O.M.I., 1977.
———. *Lettres aux correspondants d'Amérique: 1851-1860*. Écrits oblats, II. Rome: Postulation générale O.M.I., 1977.
Milton, John. *Of Education*. EEBO, Thomason / 9:E:50[12]. London: Thomas Underhill, 1644.

National Education Office. "Présence catholique dans l'enseignement supérieur au Canada: Rapport d'une commission d'enquête sur quarante universités et collèges catholiques." Windsor: Université de Windsor, 1971.
Ontario Legislative Assembly. "Official Report – Daily Edition, April 30, 1964." In *Legislature of Ontario Debates*. Second Session of the Twenty Seventh Legislature. Toronto: The Queen's Printer, 1964.
———. *Sessional Papers*. Vol. XVII, part VI. Toronto, 1885.
Simard, Georges. *Les États chrétiens et l'Église*. Ottawa: Éditions de l'Université d'Ottawa, 1942.
———. *Les universités catholiques*. Ottawa: Éditions de l'Université d'Ottawa, 1939.
Unknown author. "Convention Guiges-de Mazenod." *Études Oblates* 15 (1956): 360–364.

Secondary Sources
Aex, Jeffrey von. *Varieties of Ultramontanism*. Washington, DC: Catholic University of America Press, 1998.
Anderson, R. D. *European Universities from the Enlightenment to 1914*. Oxford: Oxford University Press, 2004.
"Antanagoge, n." In *Oxford English Dictionary*. Online: Oxford University Press, July 2018.
Axelrod, Paul. "Business Aid to Canadian Universities—1957–1965." *Interchange* 11 (1980): 25–38.
———. "Businessmen and the Building of Canadian Universities: A Case Study," *Canadian Historical Review*, 63, no. 2 (1982): 202–222.
———. *Scholars and Dollars: Politics, Economics and the Universities of Ontario, 1945-1980*. Toronto: University of Toronto Press, 1982.
Ball, Stephen J. "Performativity, Commodification and Commitment: An I-Spy Guide to the Neoliberal University." *British Journal of Educational Studies* 60 (2012): 17–28.
Barry, John C. "Law in the Post-Conciliar Church." *Studia Canonica* 5, no. 2 (1971): 259–278.
Bebbington, David. "The Secularization of British Universities since the Mid-Nineteenth Century." In *The Secularization of the Academy*, edited by George M. Marsden and Bradley J. Longfield, 259–277. Oxford: Oxford University Press, 1992.
Berg, Maggie, and Barbara K. Seeber. *The Slow Professor*. Toronto: University of Toronto Press, 2016.
Berger, Benjamin. "Faith in Sovereignty: Religion and Secularism in the Politics of Canadian Federalism." *Istituzioni del federalismo* 4 (2014): 939–961.
Bock, Michel. "La théologie au service du bon-ententisme à l'Université d'Ottawa : le père oblat Georges Simard (1878-1956), ou comment un

groulxiste devient loyaliste." *Cahiers Charlevoix: Études franco-ontariennes* 11 (2016): 213–260.

Bourdieu, Pierre. *Homo Academicus*. Translated by Peter Collier. Stanford: Stanford University Press, 1988.

Carrière, Gaston. "Guigues, Joseph-Bruno." In *Dictionary of Canadian Biography*. Vol. 10. Toronto: University of Toronto / Université de Laval, 1972.

———. *L'Université d'Ottawa 1848-1861*. Ottawa: Éditions de l'Université d'Ottawa, 1960.

Cassidy, Thomas Michael. "The Provincial Superior within the Missionary Oblates of Mary Immaculate as an Ordinary." Saint Paul University, 1993.

"Catholic, adj. and n." In *Oxford English Dictionary*. Oxford: Oxford University Press, 2018.

Choquette, Robert. *Language and Religion: A History of English-French Conflict in Ontario*. Ottawa: University of Ottawa Press, 1975.

Clark, Howard C. *Growth and Governance of Canadian Universities: An Insider's View*. Vancouver: UBC Press, 2003.

Cook, Ramsay. *The Regenerators: Social Criticism in Late Victorian English Canada*. Toronto: University of Toronto Press, 2016.

Corbeil, Pierre. "Dunkin, Christopher, Lawyer, Politician, and Judge." In *Dictionary of Canadian Biography*. Vol. 11. University of Toronto/ Université de Laval, 2003.

Deleuze, Gilles. *Difference and Repetition*. Edited by Paul Patton. New York: Columbia University Press, 1994.

Duffy, Eamon. *Saints & Sinners: A History of the Popes*. New Haven: Yale University Press, 2006.

"Eleemosynary, adj. and n." In *Oxford English Dictionary*. Oxford: Oxford University Press, July 2018.

Fay, Terence J. "The Jesuits and the Catholic University of Canada at Kingston." *CCHA Historical Studies* 58 (1991): 57–77.

———. *A History of Canadian Catholics: Gallicanism, Romanism, and Canadianism*. Montréal and Kingston: McGill-Queen's University Press, 2002.

Finnis, John. *Aquinas: Moral, Political, and Legal Theory*. Oxford: Oxford University Press, 1998.

Gattinger, Monica, and Diane St. Pierre. "The 'Neoliberal Turn' in Provincial Cultural Policy and Administration in Québec and Ontario: The Emergence of 'Quasi-Neoliberal' Approaches." *Canadian Journal of Communication* 35 (2010): 279–302.

Girard, Philip. *Bora Laskin: Bringing Law to Life*. Toronto: University of Toronto Press, 2005.

Giroux, Henry. "Neoliberalism, Corporate Culture, and the Promise of Higher Education: The University as a Democratic Public Sphere." *Harvard Educational Review* 72 (December 2002): 425–464.

Graham, Roger. *Old Man Ontario: Leslie M. Frost*. Ontario Historical Studies Series. Toronto: University of Toronto Press for the Ontario Historical Studies Series, 1990.

——. *Old Man Ontario: Leslie M. Frost*. Toronto: University of Toronto Press, 1990.

Grant, John Webster. *A Profusion of Spires: Religion in Nineteenth-Century Ontario*. Toronto: University of Toronto Press, 1988.

Hennesey, James. "The Papacy and the Universities." *Records of the American Catholic Historical Society of Philadelphia* 103 (1991): 1–11.

Hurtubise, Pierre, Mark McGowan, and Pierre Savard, eds. *Planté près du cours des eaux: le diocèse d'Ottawa 1847-1997*. Ottawa: Novalis, 1998.

Lamirande, Émilien. "Dandurand, Damase." In *Dictionary of Canadian Biography*. Vol. 15. Online: University of Toronto / Université de Laval, 2005.

Levasseur, Donat. "Chapitre 11 – Le gouvernement général – 1947-1985." In *Histoire des Missionnaires Oblats de Marie Immaculée: Essai de synthèse (1898-1985)*, 2:283–306. Montréal: Maison Provinciale, 1985.

Macdougall, H. A. "Ethnicity and the Liberal Arts in Catholic Education." *CCHA Historical Studies* 49 (1982): 53–71.

Mahoney, Kathleen A. *Catholic Higher Education in Protestant America: The Jesuits and Harvard in the Age of the University*. Baltimore: Johns Hopkins University Press, 2003.

Marshall, David B. *Secularizing the Faith: Canadian Protestant Clergy and the Crisis of Belief, 1940–1950*. Toronto: University of Toronto Press, 1992.

McCarthy, Martha. *From the Great River to the Ends of the Earth: Oblate Missions to the Dene, 1847–1921*. Edmonton: University of Alberta Press, 1995.

McDougall, A. K. *John P. Robarts: His Life and Government*. Toronto: University of Toronto Press, 1986.

McGowan, Mark. "Rendering Unto Caesar: Catholics, the State, and the Idea of a Christian Canada." *Canadian Society of Church History: Historical Papers*, 2011, 65–85.

McGowan, Mark G. "Rethinking Catholic-Protestant Relations in Canada: The Episcopal Reports of 1900–1901." *CCHA Historical Studies* 59 (1992): 11–32.

McKillop, A. B. *Matters of Mind: The University in Ontario, 1791-1951*. Toronto: University of Toronto Press, 1994.

McLeod, Hugh. *The Religious Crisis of the 1960s*. Oxford: Oxford University Press, 2007.

McNally, Vincent J. *The Lord's Distant Vineyard: A History of the Oblates and the Catholic Community in British Columbia*. Edmonton: University of Alberta Press, 2000.

Miedma, Gary R. *For Canada's Sake: Public Religion, Centennial Celebrations, the Re-Making of Canada in the 1960s*. Montréal: McGill-Queen's University Press, 2005.

Monahan, Edward J. *Collective Autonomy: A History of the Council of Ontario Universities 1962-2000*. Waterloo: Wilfrid Laurier University Press, 2004.

Murphy, John K. "The Governance of Church Institutions and Protection of Catholic Identity with Particular Reference to Ontario, Canada" (PhD diss.), Pontifical Lateran University, 1995.

Neatby, H. Blair, and Donald C. McEown. *Creating Carleton: The Shaping of a University*. Montréal: McGill-Queen's University Press, 2002.

Noll, Mark A. *A History of Christianity in the United States and Canada*. Grand Rapids, MI: Eerdmans Pub. Co., 1992.

Parl Info. "Pepin, The Right Hon. Jean-Luc." Government. Accessed May 28, 2015.

Perin, Roberto. *Rome in Canada: The Vatican and Canadian Affairs in the Late Victorian Age*. Toronto: University of Toronto Press, 1990.

Picarda, Hubert. *The Law and Practice Relating to Charities*. London: Butterworths, 1999, uOttawa Archives.

"Présidents et présidentes de l'Association des professeurs (APUO)." University Website. Accessed June 1, 2015. http://www.archives.uottawa.ca/fra/przapuo.html.

Prévost, Michel. "Décès du fondateur du Service des communications, Bill Boss," 2007. http://www.uottawa.ca.archives/files/bill_boss.pdf.

———. "Histoire de la gouvernance à l'Université d'Ottawa depuis 1848," 2012.

———. *L'Université d'Ottawa Depuis 1848*. Ottawa: Université d'Ottawa, 2008.

———. "Mgr Henri Légaré, O. M. I. (1918-2004) : un recteur visionnaire," 2006. http://www.uottawa.ca.archives/files/henri_legare.pdf.

Reford, Alexander. "The Frustrations of Federation." *CCHA Historical Studies* 61 (1995): 171–194.

Risk, Richard, and Robert C. Vipond. "Rights Talk in Canada in the Late Nineteenth Century: The Good Sense and Right Feeling of the People." *Law and History Review* 14 (1996): 1–32.

Roy, Philippe J. "Marcel Bélanger: itinéraire d'un expert canadien à Vatican II." In *Vatican II. Expériences canadiennes. Canadian Experiences*, edited by Michael Attridge, Gilles Routhier, and E. Catherine, 294–321. Ottawa: Presses de l'Université d'Ottawa, 2011.

Ruëgg, Walter, ed. *Universities in the Nineteenth and Early Twentieth Centuries*. Vol. 3 of *A History of the University in Europe*. Cambridge: Cambridge University Press, 2004.

———. ed. *Universities since 1945*. Vol. 4 of *A History of the University in Europe*. Cambridge: Cambridge University Press, 2011.

Shook, Laurence K. *Catholic Post-Secondary Education in English-Speaking Canada: A History*. Toronto: University of Toronto press, 1971.

———. *Catholic Post-Secondary Education in English-Speaking Canada, a History*. Toronto: University of Toronto press, 1971.

Stewart, Edward Emslie. "The Role of the Provincial Government in the Development of the Universities of Ontario 1791–1964" (PhD diss.), University of Toronto, 1970.
Tourigny, Irénée. *Le Père Léo Deschâtelets, O. M. I. (1899-1974): Supérieur Général des Missionaires Oblates de Marie Immaculée (1947-1972).* Web. Ottawa: O. M. I. Communications, 1975.
Whalley, Peregrine W. F., and Gillian R. Evans. "The University Visitor – An Unwanted Legacy of Empire or a Model of University Governance for the Future." *Macarthur Law Review* 2 (1998): 109–126.

Judicial Decisions
A.P.U.O. v. University of Ottawa, 1975 CarswellOnt 739 (OLRB 1975).
Archer v. Society of Sacred Heart of Jesus, 9 OLR 474 (ONCA 1905).
C. (R.) v. McDougall, 2008 CarswellBC 2041.
Canadian Federation of Students v. Ontario, 2019 ONSC 6658.
Chaput v Romain, [1955] SCR 834.
Dunnet v. Forneri, 1877 CarswellOnt 66.
Dunsmuir v. New Brunswick, 1 SCR 190 (SCC 2008).
Forestell v. University of New Brunswick, 1988 CarswellNB 138.
Forestell v. University of New Brunswick, 1987 CarswellNB 177.
Hart v. Roman Catholic Episcopal Corporation of the Diocese of Kingston, 2011 ONCA 728.
Maurice v. Durham (Bishop of), 32 English Reports 947 (1805).
McCullock Finney c. Barreau (Québec), 2004 SCC 36.
Mckinney v. University of Guelph, 3 SCR 229 (1990).
McLean v Canada, 2019 FC 1074.
Pearlman v. University of Saskatchewan (College of Medicine), 2006 CanLII 105.
Philips v. Bury, 90 English Reports 1294 (1694).
Powlett v. University of Alberta, 1934 CarswellAlta 25 (Alberta Supreme Court, Appellate Division 1934).
Pridgen v. University of Calgary, 2012 CanLII 139.
R v Taylor, 2013 NLCA 42.
Re Polten and Governing Council of the University of Toronto et al., 59 (3d) DLR 197 (ON SC [Div. Crt] 1975).
Re Vanek and Governors of the University of Alberta, 57 D.L.R. (3d) 595 (AB CA 1975).
Re. Wilson, 18 NSR 180 (1885).
Trinity Western University v. Nova Scotia Barristers' Society, 2015 NSSC 25.
UAlberta Pro-Life v Governors of the University of Alberta, 2020 ABCA 1.
Wong v. University of Toronto, 1990 CanLII 8102.

Legislation

Act respecting educational institutions at the university level, CQLR c. E-14.1.
An Act respecting Assumption College, SO 1953 c. 111.
An Act respecting the charter of the University of Montréal, SQ 14 Geo. VI, 1950, c. 142.
An Act respecting the College of Ottawa, SO 23 Geo. V, c. 106 (1933).
An Act respecting the University of Regiopolis, SO 21 Geo. V, c 137 (1931).
An Act respecting the University of Saskatchewan, R.S.S. 1978, Cap. U-6.
An Act respecting the University of Waterloo, SO 1963, c. 193.
An Act respecting the University of Western Ontario, SO 1967 c. 137.
An Act respecting Université d'Ottawa, SO 1959 c. 138.
An Act respecting Université d'Ottawa, S.O. 1960-61, c. 138.
An Act respecting Université d'Ottawa, SO 1965, c.137.
An Act to amend the Act incorporating Bishop's College, S. Prov. Can. 16 Vict. c. 60 (1852).
An Act to amend the Acts incorporating the College of Ottawa, SO 1885, c. 91.
An Act to amend the Acts incorporating the College of Ottawa, SO 1891, c. 104.
An Act to amend the Acts incorporating "The College of Ottawa," and to grant certain privileges to the said college, S Prov-Can. 29-30 Vict., c. 135 (1866).
An Act to amend the Acts respecting the College of Regiopolis, and to erect the same into an University, S Prov-Can 29-30 Vict., c. 133 (1866).
An Act to amend the Charter of the university established at Toronto and to provide for the more satisfactory government of the said university, and other purposes connected with the same, etcetra, S. Prov. Can. 12 Vict, c. 82 (1849).
An Act to amend the Laws relating to the University of Toronto, by separating its functions as a University from those assigned to it as a College, and by making better provision for the management of the property thereof and that of Upper Canada College, S Prov Can 16 Vict. c. 89 (1853).
An Act to change the name of the College of Bytown, and to amend the Act incorporating the same, S Prov Can 24 Vict., c.108 (1861).
An Act to incorporate les Révérends Pères Oblats de l'Immaculée Conception de Marie, in the Province of Canada, S. Prov. Can. 12 Vict. c. 143 (1849).
An Act to incorporate the College of Bytown, Canada, S Prov-Can Can. 12 Vict., c 107 (1849).
An Act to incorporate the University of Windsor, SO 1962-63 c. 194.
An Act to repeal so much of the Act of Parliament of Great Britain passed in the Thirty-first year of the Reign of King George the Third, and Chaptered Thirty-one, as relates to Rectories, and the presentation of Incumbents to the same, and for other purposes connected with such Rectories, 1851 S Prov Can (14-15 Vict.), c 175.

An Acte to redress the Misemployment of Landes Goodes and Stockes of Money heretofore given to charitable uses, 43 Eliz. 1, c. 4 (1601).
Bachofen, Charles Augustine. *A Commentary on the New Code of the Canon Law*. Vol. 6, St. Louis: B. Herder Book Co., 1918.
Caparros, Ernest, Michel Thériault, and Jean Thorn, eds. *Code of Canon Law Annotated*. 2nd ed. Montréal: Wilson & Lafleur Ltd., 2004.
Constitution Act, 1867, 30 & 31 Vict., c. 3 (UK).
Constitution Act, 1982, being Schedule B to the *Canada Act 1982* (UK), 1982, c. 11.
Council on Higher Education Act, SNL 2006, c C-37.001.
Education Act, RSO 1990, c. E.2.
Faculté de Théologie. *La Constitution apostolique "Deus Scientiarum Dominus": Traduction française et notes*. Montréal: Université de Montréal, 1960.
Freedom of Worship Act, CQLR c L-2.
Hospitals and Charitable Institutions Inquiries Act, RSO 1960, c. 177.
Leo XIII. "Papal Brief of February 5, 1889."
Oblats de Marie-Immaculée. *Constitutiones et regulae congregationis Missionariorum Oblatorum Sanctissimae et Immaculatae Virginis Mariae*. Romae: Oblatorum sanctissimae et Immaculatae Virginis Mariae, 1966. Constitutiones et regulae 1966.
———. *Constitutions et règles de la congrégation des Missionnaires Oblats de la Très Sainte et Immaculée Vierge Marie*. Rome: Maison générale O.M.I, 1965.
Parliament of the Province of Canada. An Act to incorporate "Bishop's College" in the Diocese of Quebec, 5 & 6 Vict. c 49 (1843).
Pius XI. Deus scientiarum dominus, constitutio apostolica, Acta Apostolicae Sedis vol. XXIII, no. 7 (1931).
Pius XII. *Munificentissimus Deus*, A.A.S. XXXXII (1950).
Pope Leo XIII. *Epipstola encyclica Sanctissimi Domini Nostri Leonis Papae XIII ad Ordina- rios phoederatarum civitatum Canadensium quoad puerorum scholas*, Acta Sanctae Sedis, XXX: 356–362 (1897).
Religious Corporations Act, CQLR c C-71.
Religious Freedom Act, RSO 1990, c R. 22.
Royal Charter of the University of Bishop's College, 16 Vict. (1853).
Sapienti Consilio, 41 A.S.S. 462–490 (1908).
Statute of Westminster, (UK), 22 & 23 Geo V, c. 4 (1931).
The Royal Charter of McGill University, 16 Vict. (1852).
The Trent University Act, 1962-63, SO 1962-63, c 192.
The University Act, 1906, SO 1906, c 55.
University Act, RSPEI 1988, c U-4.
University Act, 1901, SO 1901, c 41.
University of New Brunswick Act, S.N.B. 1984, c 40.
Vatican Council II. *The Conciliar and Post Conciliar Documents*. Edited by Austin Flannery. Grand Rapids, MI: William B. Eerdmans Pub. Co., 1987.

Policy Documents

"2014–2017 Strategic Mandate Agreement: University of Ottawa." Strategic Mandate Agreements. Government of Ontario, February 22, 2017.

"Accountability Framework Standards Manual and Guidelines." Government. British Columbia, 2016.

Brian Gallant. Mandate Letter. "To Hon. Roger Melanson." Mandate Letter, September 5, 2017.

Duff, Sir James, and Robert Oliver Berdahl. *Structure administrative des universités au Canada*. Québec: Les Presses de l'Université Laval, 1966.

Province of Nova Scotia, and Nova Scotia Universities. "Excellence Through Partnership." Memorandum of Understanding. Council of Nova Scotia University Presidents, December 20, 2011.

Truth and Reconciliation Commission of Canada. "What We Have Learned: Principles of Truth and Reconciliation." Final Report. Ottawa, 2015.

Regional Studies

Series editor: Michel Prévost

The *Regional Studies* series touches on all aspects of the greater Ottawa-Gatineau region, which includes Eastern Ontario and the Outaouais. The series is particularly interested in the history of the Federal Capital from both sides of the river, including the history of the individuals who contributed to its development and the history of its key institutions. It also focuses on the architectural heritage of this symbolic region of the country.

Previous titles in the *Regional Studies* collection

Michelle Guitard, *Le Quartier du Musée. Histoire et architecture*, 2018.

Andrew Waldron and Peter Coffman., *Explorer la capitale. Guide architectural de la région d'Ottawa-Gatineau*, 2017.

Forthcoming

Alastair Sweeny, *Thomas Mackay: The Laird of Rideau Hall and the Founding of Ottawa*, 2021.

For a complete list of the University of Ottawa Press titles, see:
www.press.uOttawa.ca

www.ingramcontent.com/pod-product-compliance
Lightning Source LLC
Chambersburg PA
CBHW070746020526
44116CB00032B/1993